CARDIFF
CAERDYDD

ECONOMIC CONTROVERSIES

Innovative and thought-provoking, the Economic Controversies series strips back the often impenetrable facade of economic jargon to present bold new ways of looking at pressing issues, while explaining the hidden mechanics behind them. Concise and accessible, the books bring a fresh, unorthodox approach to a variety of controversial subjects.

Also available in the Economic Controversies series:

Yanis Varoufakis, *The Global Minotaur: America, Europe and the Future of the World Economy*

Robert R. Locke and J.-C. Spender, *Confronting Managerialism: How the Business Elite and Their Schools Threw Our Lives Out of Balance*

Lorenzo Fioramonti, *Gross Domestic Problem: The Politics Behind the World's Most Powerful Number*

D1630793

ABOUT THE AUTHOR

HEIKKI PATOMÄKI is Professor of World Politics at the University of Helsinki, Finland. Previously he has also worked as a Professor of World Politics and Economy at Nottingham Trent University, UK, and RMIT University, Melbourne, Australia. In 2012 he was a Visiting Professor at the Ritsumeikan University in Kyoto, Japan. Patomäki's research interests include philosophy and methodology of social sciences, peace research, futures studies, economic theory, global political economy, and global political theory. His most recent book is *The Political Economy of Global Security. War, Future Crises and Changes in Global Governance* (Routledge, 2008). He is currently working on two new books, *Unprincipled Economics* (with Jamie Morgan) and *Global Futures.* Patomäki is a founding member of Network Institute for Global Democratization (NIGD) and has also been an activist in the international ATTAC movement from its inception, and is currently chairing ATTAC Finland.

THE GREAT EUROZONE DISASTER

From Crisis to Global New Deal

HEIKKI PATOMÄKI

Translated by James O'Connor

Zed Books

LONDON | NEW YORK

The Great Eurozone Disaster: From Crisis to Global New Deal
was first published in English in 2013 by Zed Books Ltd,
7 Cynthia Street, London N1 9JF, UK and
Room 400, 175 Fifth Avenue, New York, NY 10010, USA

Originally published in Finnish in 2012 under the title *Eurokriisin
anatomia. Mitä globalisaation jälkeen?* by Into kustannus

www.zedbooks.co.uk

Copyright © Heikki Patomäki, 2012
English language translation © James O'Connor, 2013

The right of Heikki Patomäki to be identified as the author
of this work has been asserted by him in accordance with
the Copyright, Designs and Patents Act, 1988

FSC
www.fsc.org
MIX
Paper from
responsible sources
FSC® C013604

Designed and typeset in Monotype Bulmer
by illuminati, Grosmont
Index by John Barker
Cover design: www.roguefour.co.uk
Printed and bound by CPI Group
(UK) Ltd, Croydon CR0 4YY

Distributed in the USA exclusively by Palgrave Macmillan, a division
of St Martin's Press, LLC, 175 Fifth Avenue, New York, NY 10010, USA

A catalogue record for this book is available from the British Library
Library of Congress Cataloging in Publication Data available

ISBN 978 1 78032 479 1 hb
ISBN 978 1 78032 478 4 pb

Contents

Preface

The European Community aimed from the start to contribute to global economic liberalization. By the time of the arrival of the euro, this project had achieved a single market within the EU and continued to foster globalization outside it.

But this kind of globalization comes at a cost. As Dani Rodrik argues in *The Globalization Paradox*,[1] global markets, sovereign states and democracy can't coexist. One option is to constrain democracy to earn 'market confidence' and attract trade and capital inflows. This has been the main response of the EU leaders to the euro crisis, itself a second phase in the global financial crisis that began in 2007–08. The second option is to limit globalization – possibly also European economic integration – in the hope of building democratic legitimacy at home. As I discuss in Chapter 5 of this book, the European Commission has proposed measures that amount to tiny steps in this direction (while, of course, leaving market freedoms intact within the Union).

The third option is to globalize democracy, or at least Europeanize it, at the cost of national sovereignty. This has not been considered by the current EU leaders, and is deemed impossible by Rodrik: 'Real federalism on a global scale is at best a century away.' The development of the EU, including persistent discontent about its democratic deficit, highlights the inherent difficulties of this project. But Rodrik acknowledges the attractions of democratic global governance: 'When I ask my students to pick one of the options, this one wins hands-down. If we can simultaneously reap the benefits of globalization and democracy, who cares that national politicians will be out of a job?'[2]

I argue in this book that there are several economic problems (which also arise within Rodrik's 'smart' or limited globalization framework) that can only be tackled with global Keynesian mechanisms and institutions. To be legitimate, these mechanisms and institutions must be democratic. At the same time, it is possible to design global governance so as to limit also economic globalization and strengthen state autonomy in certain ways. The EU itself may be in the process of becoming a federal state – that is, one state among others.

My point is that mere nostalgia for the Bretton Woods–GATT regime that lasted until the 1970s and 1980s is without merit. The dialectics of world history continue to move on. There were real reasons why the original Bretton Woods system broke down. Had John Maynard Keynes's more ambitious plans been realized in the 1940s, the post-war system would probably have lasted longer. And yet by the 1990s, or early 2000s at the latest, it would have eroded.

A feasible twenty-first-century system of global governance should be more abstract and generalizable as well as more changeable and open to revision than Keynes's 1940s' vision. Throughout the book I emphasize the need for global Keynesianism to be not only democratic but also environmentally responsible. No universal consensus is needed for its realization. A coalition of the willing can establish any new system of global governance.

I am grateful to several people for their contribution to this book. Originally it was supposed to be a short report in Finnish for a non-specialized domestic readership, co-authored with Jussi Ahokas, Lauri Holappa and Ville-Pekka Sorsa. For practical reasons the text evolved into a single-authored monograph. Its origin explains why it was written in Finnish.

The first edition was published by Into Publishers in Helsinki in February 2012. Mika Rönkkö's role was crucial in allowing the speedy and professional finalization of the text. In addition, several people read and commented on the manuscript or parts of it, including Jussi Ahokas, Tuomas Forsberg, Lauri Holappa, Pekka Sauramo, Katarina Sehm-Patomäki, Ville-Pekka Sorsa and Teivo Teivainen. James O'Connor translated the text into English, in close cooperation with me, and also proposed a number of small improvements. I am also grateful to Zed Books, and to Ken Barlow in particular, for so swiftly processing the proposal for this book.

This book is dedicated to all those for whom 'the Earth is our home'.

Heikki Patomäki
Helsinki, August 2012

1

Introduction

When the European Economic and Monetary Union (EMU) was being established in the mid-1990s, many economists were sceptical of its prospects. 'The European states are behaving as if they are preparing for collective suicide', Milton Friedman said at the time.[1] Considering the ideas behind the EMU, this succinct judgement was not short on irony.

The European Central Bank (ECB) was built on the monetarist principles propounded by Friedman and like-minded neoclassical economists.[2] Insulated from democratic politics, the ECB has as its foremost task the promotion of price stability, even if this must be done at the expense of other economic policy goals. Why did Friedman decide that an economic project resting on principles he himself espoused would be doomed? For Friedman, the range and extent of differences between European countries was too great for monetary union to work. If labour did not move freely in accordance with price signals and market developments, differences in unemployment and inflation levels between European countries would widen. Fluctuations in trade cycles would not keep pace. And if one member country fell into recession, EMU membership would mean it was no longer free to choose many of its own policy instruments for correcting the situation, such as devaluation or changing the central bank interest rate.

This book is not based on Friedman-style economic theory. In Chapter 4 in particular I criticize the so-called optimal currency area theory on which Friedman's dim view of the EMU was based. The onset of the euro crisis was a wide-reaching simultaneous shock that hit suddenly; it was not merely a question of business cycles falling out of sync. As a result of the global financial crises of 2008 and 2009, many of the debts of the highly overdrawn private sector were transferred to states. The EMU's criteria for economic convergence, the deficit and debt ceilings stipulated in the Maastricht Treaty, cause problems during recessionary periods. To make things worse, the European Union (EU) failed, and still fails, to muster the collective political will to create an effective common fiscal policy. All in all, from its inception the EMU has been a fragile mechanism involving self-contradictions. Its failure, however, is mainly due to reasons other than those suggested by Friedman and many other US economists in the 1990s.

The common currency project is somewhat deceptive: things are not always what they seem or what they are claimed to be. It has been intertwined with global developments in a way that is not always apparent from its rationalizations. Plans for a common European currency were first proposed in the 1920s, but when they finally came to fruition it was also in response to the instability of global financial markets. The international economic system inaugurated at Bretton Woods in New Hampshire in 1944 endured until the early 1970s. Two important steps in its dismantlement were the delinking of the value of the US dollar from the price of gold, and the move towards deregulation of financial markets.

In the face of the Bretton Woods decline and the ensuing instability, European countries began working on plans for stabilizing currency exchange rates. The first attempt in this direction, the so-called 'snake in the tunnel' policy of the 1970s, was unsuccessful. The next, more vigorous attempt was the establishment in 1979 of the European Monetary System (EMS), the idea of which was to promote economic stability by keeping the exchange rates of European currencies as closely linked as possible to the value of the US dollar. The EMS nonetheless fell victim to speculation and currency collapses in the early 1990s, which partly provided the incentive for establishing a single currency, the euro. The establishment of the EMU removed the inter-European currency exchange rates, and gave the world a new common currency to compete with the dollar.

But the establishment of the EMU didn't calm global financial turbulence. On the contrary, at the same time as the EMU countries' national currencies were being linked to the new common currency, in May 1998, the world was still reeling from the effects of the Asian financial crisis. The crisis eventually spread to Russia, Brazil, and even Wall Street, the nerve centre of global financing activity. In autumn 1998 the United States' central bank, the Federal Exchange Commission, brought the crisis to heel by bailing out the ailing Long-Term Capital Management hedge fund. The LTCM's spiralling losses were threatening to cause a domino effect on Wall Street, which would have almost inevitably created global crisis.

New booms and busts occurred during the late 1990s. The IT boom reached its peak in March 2000, and its subsequent bust created a minor recession in many countries. Employment rates consequently declined, both in the United States and elsewhere. In tandem with these economic difficulties, the financial crises of the developing countries continued unabated. The most dramatic case was Argentina, which became partly insolvent in early 2002, although the country's government managed to hold firm and eventually, after years of complicated bargaining, succeeded in having its debts restructured.

FIGURE 1.1   William Hogarth's *South Sea Scheme* (1721)

From 2003 until 2007, global financial markets expanded at an unprecedented pace. But bubbles are intrinsically fickle, and cycles of booms and busts are by no means a recent phenomenon. Already in the 1720s, the British Empire experienced the infamous South Sea Company scandal. Sir Isaac Newton bought a notable amount of shares in the company when prices were at their peak, and after the bust is said to have repented: 'I can calculate the motions of the heavenly bodies, but not the madness of men.'[3] In William Hogarth's scathing commentary on the affair (Figure 1.1), a crowd jostle for a place on the Wheel of Fortune, which is topped by a goat, as a winged demon with a scythe throws Fortune's dismembered remains to the crowd. In the foreground Honesty is depicted being broken on the wheel of Self-Interest, and, at the foot of a monument commemorating the South Sea Company, Honour is flogged by Villainy.

The most recent global financial bubble began to show signs of rupture in autumn 2007. The mounting difficulties of the secondary mortgage market began to affect banks' and investors' balances, and the collapse came within months. The repayment difficulties then spread incrementally throughout the whole system, and prices began to plummet. The outcome was a world-scale financing crisis and recession much more severe than the crises of the late 1990s and early 2000s. According to economist Jack Rasmus, the finance crisis rapidly developed into 'an epic recession', more acute and longer-lasting than a typical slump.[4] The epic recession could last for years, but may prove to be even more enduring. Signs that the recession was indeed developing into a great depression have become gradually more evident in late 2011 and 2012, and even the Asian centres of economic growth may be seriously affected by it.

Behind every financial crisis is the growth of debt and speculative capital. Billionaire investor and activist George Soros has written of the 'superbubble', which he argues had been in the making for decades.[5] The manifold increases in finance values are intimately connected with increased debt. As I will show in Chapter 3, the greatest increases in debt have been among privately owned companies, and above all among financial investors. Householders' debts and nation-states' debts form only moderate shares of the total amount of debt. The debt problem is real, but it is not only, and not even primarily, a crisis of *public* debt.

In the United States, for example, the total amount of debt relative to gross domestic product (GDP) is at the time of writing greater than in any year since 1929. The 2008–09 crisis has not led to any major reduction in debt. The general outcome of the various packages of economic rescue and resuscitation policies that were implemented to handle the crisis has been the shifting of debt from the private to the public sector. The continuing public debt crises of the United States and Europe constitute

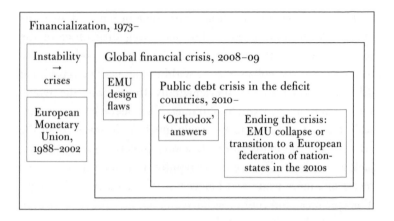

FIGURE 1.2   The euro crisis and global economic processes

the second phase of the epic recession. It has been during this phase that the underlying weaknesses of the EMU system have become most evident. The same problem that the EMU was intended to provide protection against, the instability of global financial markets, is now threatening to derail the European common currency. Figure 1.2 shows the main ways the euro crisis is connected to wider global trends.

Financialization is the name given to the processes by which finance markets, finance institutions and the elites involved in financing gain increasing hold over both private economic processes and public economic policymaking. Financialization has been the cause of recurrent instability and many crises, and these provided much of the incentive for European monetary union. Processes of financialization began in the 1960s, but global finance really re-emerged and took centre stage in the world economy in the 1970s and 1980s. (The first golden age of 'high finance' occurred before the First World War; the financial boom of the 1920s came to a halt with the stock market crash of 1929 and the Great Depression of the ensuing decade).[6]

In the summer of 1988, the president of the European Commission Jacques Delors was given the task of leading a committee of central bankers in drawing up plans for European fiscal
and monetary union and a timetable for transfer to a common
currency. The criteria for convergence and other central principles were confirmed with the Maastricht Treaty of 1992. The
EMU was established incrementally throughout that decade.
The euro began life as an accounting currency at the start of
1999, and came into actual physical use on 1 January 2002.
The global finance crisis began some five years later, and with
its onset the EMU's shortcomings quickly came to the surface.
By 2010, the question of the public debt crisis in the eurozone
member states with budgetary deficits topped the agenda at
EU summits. The crisis has become a turning point for the
European Union: either the EMU collapses or major steps are
taken towards a European federation.

These are not mutually exclusive possibilities. *Crisis*, in its
most general sense, connotes a turning point in a process – in the
life of some being, say, or in the fortunes of a society – and the
change can even be so momentous as to alter the very nature of
the being or society in question. In the case of the EU, crisis and
partial fragmentation could be the catalyst for a transition to a
social-democratic European federation. Very often in discussions
of crisis, what is at issue is not prediction but the etymologically
related practice of *critique*, which focuses on the causes of the
crisis.[7] Although these will almost invariably be disputed, the
crisis itself will often function as a clear indicator that previously influential theories have been faulty. Crisis also means the
opportunity to learn, as in the Chinese saying that every crisis
is both a threat and an opportunity. As will become clear in the
course of this book, crises are inherently occasions for power
struggles: the same crisis can provide the pretext for realizing a
myriad different possibilities.

In political debates and in the media there has been a tendency to treat the 2010–11 debt crisis of sovereign nation-states as separate and distinct from the financial crisis of 2008–09. The blame for the more recent of these two crises is put on the affected states themselves, for borrowing beyond their means. Another characteristic of the dominant interpretation is that both the 2008–09 crisis and the later crisis are at least partly composed of distinct stages, each of which has its own separate guilty parties. Behind the first credit crisis – so the story goes – were indebted households that should have known better than to get themselves deeper into debt by taking out loans, and on the other hand reckless lenders who peddled mortgages to people they knew to be without adequate incomes. As the crisis worsened into a global recession during 2008 and the following year, easy culprits were in plentiful supply. Should not investors have been able to act more responsibly? Were the laws and regulations infringed, or not enforced? Would it not have been possible to save Lehman Brothers? This list could be extended almost infinitely.

However, credible moralizing has its limits. As the 2008–09 crisis progressed, there was a noticeably greater readiness in various quarters to admit that the global finance system itself has blind spots and structural flaws that could be tackled with better regulation and planning.[8] But because the systemic and comprehensive nature of the crisis was not understood in its entirety as it was unfolding, many of the proposed corrections – both at EU and at global level – have been too superficial.

In light of this, the central aim of this book is to provide a deeper, more holistic analysis of the causes of the European debt crisis. A proper understanding of the ultimate reasons for the crisis requires a grasp of both the global financial system and the operating mechanisms of the European Monetary Union. The EMU has become intimately intertwined with the development of the global political economy, but the whole does not by itself determine the nature of its component parts.

The early chapters focus on the history and causes of the euro crisis. Chapter 2 explains the shortcomings of mainstream economic discourse, and in doing so also provides an introduction to Keynesian economic theory. The motto of this discussion is simply that the whole is more than the sum of its parts. In Chapter 3 I look more closely at the roots of the 2008–09 crisis and its emergence. The crisis was foreseeable, because the mechanisms that gave rise to it were well known. Nevertheless, many journalists, researchers and financial market operatives remained oblivious to it. In this chapter I explain why.

Chapter 4 turns to look more closely at the European debt crisis itself and the contradictions of the EMU. The main aim of the chapter is to show how the functioning of the global financial system, the 2008–09 crisis and the 2010–11 euro crisis are closely connected to each other. As important as it is to appreciate this, it is equally important to understand the internal contradictions of the EMU. Why is monetary union without political union bound to fail? Why are deficits and surpluses both problematic from the point of view of European political economy as a whole?

From Chapter 5 onwards the book is directed towards the future, and I present a range of different, successively broader perspectives. First I examine the official proposals for reform of the EU, which are familiar from hastily convened summits. European heads of state and heads of EU institutions have reacted to the crisis by creating emergency aid packages and stabilization mechanisms in cooperation with the International Monetary Fund (IMF). EU and IMF leaders have driven through cuts to public spending and deflationary economic policies in the crisis-hit countries. The criterion for admission of emergency funding is acceptance by the crisis-hit countries of the same austerity measures that have for decades been imposed on heavily indebted developing countries under the name of 'structural adjustment'. As I show in Chapter 7, these measures have rarely been successful.

From the perspective of economic theory the official strategies have been partly successful, but they have also made some things worse. Interest rates may have come down, but at the cost of a downturn that most severely hits those who are already economically vulnerable. Neither do the proposals include sufficient re-regulation of the finance markets; nor do they do much to tackle the root causes of financialization or the disparities of the global economy. What is more, the existing proposals do not promote efficient overall demand in Europe, to say nothing of the rest of the world economy. The officially sanctioned steps towards a federation of European states are merely technocratic, and serve only to worsen the EU's democratic deficit. As such, they may lead to an even greater legitimation crisis and broader nationalistic counter-reactions within the member states.

In Chapter 6 I first present a number of prognoses based on economic and legitimation theories. These will be of use both in assessing explanations of the past and articulating a range of possible and likely futures. What kind of system will emerge from the present crisis and (likely) partial disintegration of the current European Union? According to the first scenario I discuss, the EU project will continue and deepen. This may work for a while, but its longer-term prospects are poor. Partial disintegration will call into question and politicize the basic founding principles of the EU. The attendant problems of legitimation may eventually force the core EU states to form a federation that espouses the ideals of democracy and common welfare, instead of competitiveness and budgetary discipline. According to the second scenario, the EU will develop into a social-democratic federation of states, and possibly a Great Power. But the more Eurocentric and short-sighted the federation's own self-perception, the more prone it will be to adopt the contradictions of the global political economy. In the third scenario, rather than focusing on Eurocentric solutions and policies, a cosmopolitan EU pursues democratic and social objectives on a worldwide scale.

In Chapter 7 some historical lessons for the future are appraised. The twentieth century offers many enlightening examples of how debt crises have been handled in international politics. Even though their precise details are, of course, unlikely to be repeated, there is much to be learned from historically significant choices and their consequences. In this respect, consideration of Germany's twentieth-century economic history is especially fruitful. The actions of Germany and other surplus countries during the 2012–11 economic crisis recall the treatment meted out to Germany by the victors of the Great War from 1919 to 1932. In 1953, by contrast, German debt negotiations were carried out on a sustainable basis, which greatly facilitated the West German 'economic miracle' and democratization. The contrasting choices that were made in 1919 and 1953 were decisive for their vastly different outcomes. They provide useful hints as to what sorts of policies work and what to avoid.

Germany's historical experiences are not the only source of learning available. The debt crises of many countries in the global South are now in their fourth decade. Their debt burdens triggered a worldwide campaign with the key aim of creating an international debt arbitration mechanism. A shared, permanent and universally equitable mechanism of this sort is still lacking, although minor steps towards controlled debt rearrangements have been taken. In Chapter 7 I suggest that the lack of such a mechanism was one reason for the euro crisis. Because the Third World debt cancellation movement failed to bring about institutional change, the new target for structural readjustment is now Europe. Given this and the long-term process of financialization, I argue, a mere debt arbitration mechanism is no longer enough.

What is also needed is a new institutional framework to regulate the whole dynamic of debt.

Chapter 8 brings the book to a close with an argument for a global-Keynesian New Deal. Based on the arguments presented in the book, it is clear that an adequate solution to the euro crisis requires comprehensive reform of the institutions of global political economy. What is needed are mechanisms of global governance that can contribute to controlling the supply of money in the world economy, as well as balance surpluses and deficits, and mechanisms to govern the rate, composition and distribution of growth on a planetary scale. Although enabling states to develop autonomous economic policies is an important and laudable ethical-political goal, the proposals for new institutional arrangements outlined in this book point in another direction, towards the development of global democracy. Reconciling these two distinct but compatible aims results in a vision for democratic global Keynesianism.

2

The economic theory of debt crises

Metaphors, frames and stories form the basis of how we think. Metaphors are indispensable to all abstract thought, but can also be misleading.[1] For instance, in everyday thinking about the euro crisis, as well as in economic theory and particularly in so-called microeconomic theory, states are generally understood as operating within the same constraints as households. Households and small businesses must adjust their outlay (including debt repayments) in accordance to the level of income they are able to generate through their own labour power and sales. At times of trouble, they must reduce their expenditure to match their incomes. Similarly, public discussions routinely make reference to the feelings, intentions, desires, hopes and needs of associations, firms and states. Through metaphorical thinking, the state can also become a person.[2] If a state is a person and can be held liable for its actions, it must be possible to moralize its conduct.[3] Instead of critical examination and causal explanations, it is thus common simply to settle for a narrative about character flaws, as part of which blame is usually assigned. For instance, it is quick and convenient to decide that Greece, Italy, Spain and Portugal have been living beyond their means and must now pay back their debts.

'Time is money', 'the state is a household' and 'the state is a person' have long since attained the status of everyday metaphors, and consciously or otherwise they affect how we think. Mainstream economic theory also rests on metaphors.[4] Concepts interweave to create a field of speech and thought that organizes and restricts the lines of argumentation that are possible. With these metaphors and frames in place, it is thus all too easy to create simplistic narratives, for instance about the Greek, Portuguese or Spanish debt crises, especially if those narratives fit comfortably with established cultural prejudices and stereotypes.

One of the most astonishing features of Western culture is the instrumentalization of time as a resource. The 'time is money' metaphor is a special instance of this general pattern, following as it does many of the established practices of capitalist market economy.[5] Salaries are usually paid according to the amount of time worked, for instance. When the dominant metaphors are taken as given, it is easy to make quick, unreflective decisions about causes and effects. Time being money, when someone is short of the latter then the most convenient conclusion to draw is that he or she has not worked enough, or hard enough. Is it not clear that although the temptation to laze in the sun under an orange tree is understandably great, nobody can live on debt alone for very long? Contrary to this stereotype, the Greeks, for example, work more hours in the week and annually than most other nations in Europe.[6] And during the first five years of the euro, from 2002 to 2007, Greece managed to keep its public debt more or less at pre-euro levels.[7]

With adequate economic theory, it is easy to understand why these metaphors can be misleading. Households form only a small part of the overall economy. Size does matter, however, whether one is considering businesses or states. Large-scale industrial production is often more efficient than small-scale, and megacorporations are able to manipulate their environment – including consumers' preferences – for their own maximum benefit. Nor is their creditworthiness as precarious as that of smaller companies and households, although short-term income fluctuations often do occur.

What is more, in the member countries of the Organisation for Economic Co-operation and Development (OECD) roughly half of all economic flows pass through state and municipal channels. Their expenditure affects the sales and incomes of many other actors and sectors of the economy. It matters greatly to overall economic development how states act. In addition, those states with their own currency issue money and can print more, at virtually no cost. Their funding positions are entirely different to those of households. But if one does accept the analogy between the two, then it follows that states, like households, are obliged to balance their expenditure to coincide with the income of any given budgetary period.

The consequent assumption is that each country must take care not only to balance its own budget, but also to ensure that its volume of imports do not exceed its exports, otherwise debt will be the result. And if capital and export income are insufficient, the best option is to cut consumption, especially public consumption. Export surpluses should be lauded, in accordance with the general wisdom of saving for a rainy day. And yet, in reality, the overall sum total of states' surpluses and deficits is always precisely nil. One's surplus is another's deficit, and vice versa, and it is impossible for them all to run surpluses simultaneously.

The formulaic and often fallacy-prone nature of everyday thinking is ripe for exploitation, most obviously in political rhetoric and propaganda. Despite its sometimes running counter to some common intuitions, adequate economic theory is not especially difficult to understand. By considering a few simple fallacies, one can easily explain how the whole of political economy is more than the sum of its parts. In principle, it is enough to understand *the fallacy of composition* and the concept of *effective aggregate demand*. I will discuss these below, and at the end of the chapter also briefly discuss monetary theory. In the capitalist market economy the value of commodities is measured in money, but the actual nature of money is rarely given much thought. This makes it difficult to properly understand debt, debt crises and the possibilities of public funding. Some consideration of monetary theory also sheds further light on why the state–household analogy is a poor guide to political economy.

Necessary metaphors and misleading rhetoric

Metaphors and frames are not arbitrary but are based on everyday human experiences. Metaphors work because they help in making sense of things that are distant, abstract and unfamiliar in terms of things that are already familiar and of which we have prior, direct experience. The dominant truths about money and debt really do correspond to the everyday experiences of many people: indebted households cannot get by for very long, and one has to work to make a living. Effort is required to get work done. With the help of machines and external sources of energy human labour can become more efficient.

The problem with everyday truths and the metaphors to which they give rise is that they do not always help in making sense of the broader picture. There are limits, in other words, to the applicability of common-sense reasoning, and these limits are easily exploited in public debate by incessant repetition of the same ideas. Moralizing talk about individual countries and their debt burdens has an effect on public attitudes, and favours particular groups and their own interests. Above all, it makes it harder to see the situation at hand in its broader context and from others' point of view. Joseph Goebbels was one of those who realized that although propaganda must have popular appeal, it need not be rationally grounded, or even approximately true. It is enough to ply different sections of the public with various appealing images, phrases and narratives.[8]

Moralizing about the indebted eurozone countries also privileges a specific political agenda. What is in question with the demands made on the individual indebted countries is not 'adjustment' to technical requirements, but moral and political choices. If the basic premiss is that the affected countries are themselves responsible for their own debt problems, and if the right way to restore the economic balance is to cut public spending and sell off publicly owned assets to pay off the debt, the goal becomes privatization and the dismantlement of the welfare state, achieved through reductions to public services, salaries, pensions, and to redistribution of wealth in favour of the well-off. At the same time as crisis packages are implemented to restore profitability to the banking sector, and bonuses given to investors and upper management, they punish the most vulnerable citizens of the indebted countries. Typically, the crisis packages that have been put in place also include tax breaks for privately owned firms, and employer-friendly reforms to labour laws. This weakening of the status of the trade unions, in turn, has a tendency to lead to further pay cuts for employees. The crisis packages, then, correspond logically to a particular sort of political programme. It is less clear, but true, that economic policies of this sort also tend to be self-defeating.

Economic paradoxes

The conditions in which actions are taken form a whole in which the various parts are dependent on each other. The whole cannot be fragmented into distinct and abstract constituent elements; it is more than the sum of its parts. Economist Steve Keen has compared the logic of neoclassical microeconomic theory to the

FIGURE 2.1   An illustration of the whole–part fallacy

effort to prove that the Earth is flat: if a sufficiently small segment of the Earth's surface is selected, it is for all practical intents and purposes flat, and the same holds true for any other, similarly de-limited sample. Once these micros-analyses are then aggregated, the conclusion can only be that the world is indeed flat.[9]

Already in antiquity there existed philosophers, mathematicians and physicists who could demonstrate that the Earth is a sphere and orbits the Sun. The argument did not sit well with the reigning everyday beliefs and experiences of the general populace, however. If a more critical approach were to have been taken by the philosophers, however, they might well have asked: why do ships disappear below the horizon when they travel far out to sea?

Analogously, the breakthrough of Keynesian economic theory stands out as one of the scientific revolutions of its time.[10] Economic theory since Keynes contains many apparent paradoxes, which are only so because they clash with certain everyday intuitions.[11] There is nothing illogical as such about these economic paradoxes; nor is there anything particularly complex about how they work. The simultaneous action of several factors can bring about self-defeating results, and, like the flat-Earth conclusion, what seems to hold true in part of a situation, or for a single agent, may well not be true for the larger whole. Mainstream economists routinely speak of micro- and macroeconomic theories, but this distinction itself exhibits the compositional (or whole–part) fallacy.[12]

The compositional fallacy occurs when it is assumed that what is possible for a single given actor at a given time is possible for all of them simultaneously. For instance, if there are 30,000 jobs on offer in a country, and 300,000 unemployed, all of them could get jobs, but obviously only 10 per cent of them at most could do so at the same time. The problem of unemployment affects the whole of a country, not only individuals.[13] This is a simple illustration of the fallacy. Understanding more complex economic paradoxes requires understanding the concept of effective aggregate demand.[14] Demand is based on the readiness of agents to pay for goods and services, and on their actually making good on this willingness. Whether the agents have money to do so, however, depends on a complex of conditions. Money is essentially a form of credit, rather than being something of intrinsic value, and its degree of liquidity can vary (think about a fixed time deposit in a bank). In a sense, money binds the present to the future and vice versa.

Savings and investments are commitments in time, and they are planned ahead. Wages are also usually planned in advance, and agreed privately or collectively. Prices, in turn, are typically based on unit costs, which remain fixed for the short term, and are usually fairly stable and dependent on prices set by other companies and on the profit goals on the basis of which the

investments were originally made. Demand depends on the fulfilment of previous expectations (on the actually realized incomes
and profits), and on expectations about the future, which are by
nature never capable of being met entirely. The future is open
and uncertain, although anticipatable.

Due to technical developments and real fixed investments,
production capacity tends to grow continuously. But there is
no automatic guarantee that a company can sell its products
as planned, or that the overall demand for goods and services
will coordinate neatly with production capacity. Insufficient
demand leads to unused production capacity, including unemployed people. Increases and decreases in demand can be self-
reinforcing, as can be economic developments in general.[15] For
this reason, under certain conditions demand and production
can even collapse.

The compositional fallacy and the concept of effective aggregate demand make it easier to understand more complicated
economic fallacies, one of the best known being the paradox of
thrift.[16] Thrift is usually considered a virtue, both in moral thinking and in classical economic theory. Living thriftily entails a
simple and undemanding life, avoiding waste and creating savings
for investment. But if every individual and every firm acted in the
same way, aggregate demand would dwindle, harming incomes
and profits. Gluts and unemployment result, and whatever savings
have accumulated may soon become depleted. From the point
of view of the whole, then, austerity and thrift are by no means
unquestionably virtuous, and do not necessarily contribute to
savings and investment. Indeed, the central claim of Keynesian
theory is that investments create savings, rather than the other
way about.[17]

Also contradictory is the urge to reduce firms' costs. It is
convenient to assume that cutting wages will increase profits and
perhaps make it possible to hire more staff, which would improve

employment levels. But if many employers follow this strategy at the same time, the overall consumption levels of wage earners will plummet rapidly, with a consequently drastic reduction in demand. As Joan Robinson – one of the very few noted female economists – has shown, the central paradox of capitalism is that '[e]ach employer individually gains from a low real wage in terms of his product, but all suffer from the limited market for commodities which a low real-wage rate entails.'[18] The result, unsurprisingly, is increased unemployment.

Efforts to reduce state and household debts can also be self-defeating.[19] It is generally held that companies can reduce their level of debt whenever they wish, but this is not always true, especially not during downturns. If a large enough number of companies more or less simultaneously cut back on investments in order to rein in their expenses and pay off debts, the sudden dip in overall production levels will quickly be seen on the balance sheets of even more companies. And when income dries up, debts are even harder to pay off. Eventually, many companies may then be left with no other option than to take on debt in order to meet their daily expenses. This strategy of paying of debts, in sum, tends to have the effect of landing companies in even greater debt. The same dynamic can play out with consumers' efforts to pay off debts and accumulate savings. Paul Krugman, a Nobel laureate in economics, argued in 2009, during the first phase of global financial crisis, that this was the reason why increasingly many American households were getting into serious debt.[20]

Economic paradoxes, in general, arise when the aggregate effect of many individual actions of a similar kind have an effect that is more or less the exact opposite of what was intended. Even a single actor can sometimes be large enough for the effects of its actions to produce an economic paradox. A state's spending arrangements have a particularly decisive effect on the overall economy. If a state is heavily indebted and has difficulty repaying (partly because interest rates are set beyond its own control), it can attempt to save on public spending and increase taxation levels. This sort of solution reduces aggregate demand, however. As the economy slides into recession, the state's tax revenue decreases at the same time as spending on unemployment payments and other recession-related outlay increases.

The significance of the compositional fallacy can also be seen at the global economic level. A single large or middle-sized state may take global market demand for granted. But if sufficiently many states simultaneously attempt to cut their public spending levels in order to pay off debt, aggregate global demand will inevitably wane. Similarly, if several countries simultaneously try to improve their competitiveness by taking measures to keep wages low – that is, through internal devaluation – each of these countries' levels of exports to each other will be likely to deteriorate. And as export levels drop, the economies of the countries inevitably suffer and public spending may in fact increase, also in proportion to income.[21] According to many estimates, the major problem of the global economy has been precisely that the neoliberal global regime of accumulation is unable to establish reasonable levels of demand and productivity growth due to systemic lacks and contradictions.[22]

On money

A distinction is commonly made between the real economy and finance. This division is based on the idea that the latter, comprising exchange of money, stocks and bonds and their derivatives, is not 'real'. The distinction forms part of many well-established economic theories. Particularly in neoclassical economics textbook models, one of the basic premises is that money is merely a so-called *numéraire good*; that is, that it forms an arbitrarily chosen basic standard to facilitate the comparison of the exchange rates of different goods. By and large, the same assumption is also made in classical Marxian economic theory.[23] The economy is essentially a production and exchange economy, and money has no real significant role in how market capitalism functions.

This negligence often comes close to the assumption that financial markets function in more or less the same way as markets in goods or services. Buyers and sellers meet in the market and agree on a price that is acceptable to both parties. If there are many buyers and sellers, and if they are all at liberty to trade with each other, prices will be determined impersonally. All parties will continue trading for as long as each derives some benefit from it. Demand and supply exist in balance, and if the whole is only the sum of its parts, then it would follow that satisfactory deals for each trader should add up to the maximum benefit for society as a whole. Although instances of overshooting cannot be ruled out, in general, so the mainstream assumption goes, financial markets are stable.[24]

The *numéraire good* idea also supports the analogy between households and the public economy. The state can consume only that part of the produced utility and services that it can collect in the form of tax revenue. Money circulates throughout the economy steadily, and thus the amount of money is connected only to price levels and to the total amount of transactions. If the state increases the amount of money in the economy by more than the rate of growth of the national product, the result will be inflation, the decline in money value.[25] The principal function of the European Central Bank, for example, is defined on the basis of this part of orthodox economic doctrine: the ECB aims to ensure that inflation remains low and that the supply of money is increased by only so much as is strictly required for growth of the gross national product.

Keynesian economic theory also marked a revolution in monetary theory.[26] In capitalist market economy, all plans and decisions are assigned a monetary value, essentially connected to the uncertain future. The idea is to sell products for more money than the products' cost (fixed real investments and debt repayments are marked down as expenses). In principle there is no limit to the supply of money. Paper and electronic money can be created at almost no cost. Commercial banks also create money in granting credit, and in fact this is the largest single source of money in capitalist economies. The total amount of money depends on the dominant institutional arrangements and agreements, and on the mechanisms for money creation that they make possible. Demand for the various forms of money, however, is subject to fluctuation and is influenced by a wide variety of factors, not least by future expectations and by the amount of income transactions and financial transactions. No matter its format, all money can be understood as a relation of debt.[27] Money is debt in relation to the commodities and services that can be purchased with it in the future. The form of money depends on the specific nature of that debt relation and on what kinds of temporal commitments it is based, on how liquid or fixed the form of money is.[28]

This type of monetary theory has far-reaching consequences for grasping the mechanisms of the financial markets, and also for understanding the funding of the public economy. For one thing, money can constitute simply a promise or commitment to generate more money in the future. Monetary agreements can be used for the same purposes as money, which is not the case with many other fungible goods such as cars. Money and finance are real – not just paper economy separate from the real economy – in the sense that they have causal effects on everything that happens in the economy. The precise mechanisms depend on institutional arrangements. The problem, though, is that money and bond markets easily create an environment in which they become laws unto themselves, with money debts being created at an ever-accelerating pace in the hope of large speculative profits.

As long as the processes of financial multiplication and mounting debt are allowed to continue, profits on speculation can be so attractive as to sideline many other economic activities, in particular productive investments. From the perspective of banks and various financial investors, the best situation would be one in which inflation of prices and of wages does not occur, whereas the value of financial assets rises quickly and there is thus rapid inflation in the financial sector. Part of the price increase in assets can be converted into private consumption of wealthy investors; in this case, the speculative monetary economy and economic inequality become mutually sustaining.[29]

Optimism tends increasingly to take hold as the prices of assets continue to rise. Debt can be used to create a leveraging effect for investments: even small predicted changes in asset prices or interest or exchange rates can generate large profits if one's own investment capital can be increased many times over through debt. On the other hand, leveraging reinforces these changes while introducing more money into the system. The more indebted market operators are relative to their income levels, the more precarious their finance base becomes. A developing finance system thus becomes increasingly chaotic over time, and even relatively small payment problems can escalate into systemic crises. The multiplication of finance values and increases in the amount of debt, therefore, can cause capitalist market economies to oscillate more and become unstable and crisis-prone.[30]

The question of the relation between money supply and debt is also more complicated than traditional orthodox theory allows.[31] The money created by central banks is only part of the total amount of money. To a large degree, the total sum is created by the market actors' own actions – that is, through the banking system in response to the demand for money (credit). On the other hand, if the business cycle is such that there is redundant production capacity and high unemployment, central banks have

a number of means at their disposal to increase overall monetarized demand, such as public investments, consumption or redistributive measures. Increasing the amount of money can stimulate
production, although depending on the circumstances this may
also contribute to inflation. Inflation becomes self-reinforcing,
however, only when public confidence in the value of money
and in the authorities issuing it is lost, and concern about loss of
savings and value of money starts to spread. In such a situation,
the desire to hold on to money or grant credit (including bonds
and various financial assets, which are a form of credit) depletes
so much that a sharp downward spiral sets in.

The main point is, though, that in the context of legitimate
institutions, and especially in recessionary periods, money can be
created in order to increase effective aggregate demand through
public spending. For this reason, the financing of public spending
is not dependent only on tax revenue and other forms of income.
States have more freedom of action than households could ever
possibly have. This applies, of course, only to those states that
have their own central bank. On the other hand, it is also true
that states that fail to implement or enforce a sustainable taxation regime, or cannot cover expenses by income generated by
returns on fixed public investments, cannot print money willy-
nilly without causing severe inflation. But, irrespective of the finer
details, the main point still stands: the analogy between the state
and the household is seriously misleading.

Conclusions

The metaphors and models of everyday reasoning are the basis
of all abstract thinking, but situations arise in which they can
be treacherous. Their formulaic and at times fallacious nature
makes them vulnerable to manipulation. This can be seen in the
establishment and justification of the crisis packages developed

by the European Union and the International Monetary Fund. The common sense appears to confirm that these packages are a reasonable response to the crisis, although they tend to aggravate the situation through reducing efficient demand. What also goes frequently unnoticed is that these projects further particular, controversial political agendas. Those in favour of reducing public spending, privatization, market liberalization and the interests of employers get what they want.

Economic paradoxes show why everyday thinking and economic policies based on orthodox neoclassical economic theory can both become contradictory. The paradoxes stem from the fact that the cumulative effect of many individual actions can be self-defeating. The number of actors needed to bring this about is not necessarily high: even a single very large company or any big state could on account of its size end up creating the same effect. The ways in which states spend or save money are major sources of such paradoxical effects.

Moreover, states and their central banks can, and do, create money; households, obviously, do not and cannot. Given the right conditions, states also have the power to use themselves the money they create to stimulate effective aggregate demand without increasing the inflation rate. It is precisely for this reason that the unfounded state-as-household metaphor has practical significance: it precludes the possibility of economic policy that would be rational from the point of view of the economy as a whole, especially at times of recession and depression.

3

The predictability of
global financial turmoil

The EU is deeply interwoven with global economic processes. The European Community aimed from the start to contribute to global economic liberalization, including free movements and operations of financial capital. The introduction of the euro was also a response to the increasing financial instability that tended to undermine European monetary arrangements from the early 1970s through to the early 1990s. The euro crisis, which is threatening the existence of the single European currency, is a second phase in the global economic recession that started in 2008–09. It is important to understand the sources and root causes of this turmoil and the ensuing epic recession.

The financial crisis of 2008–09 affected the everyday lives of a great many people around the world. Jobs were lost, the values of houses and investments collapsed, and in the early stages food and energy prices rose sharply (before moderating somewhat as the crisis proceeded). Financial collapse affected people regardless of location or income level. Even those who were left more or less unscathed by the crisis became keenly aware of its ferocity through the media. This was big-time drama. The question was: how to make sense of what was happening?

Although the effects of the crisis quickly became common knowledge, its causes have not been so easily perceptible. Many explanations of the crash have been attempted, at varying levels of sophistication. Some commentators have been unable to find any rational explanation for it, and present the crisis as something that struck an uncertain and chaotic world out of the blue. Such 'explanations' are accepted because of the widespread assumption that the world is in essence unpredictable. Even swans can be black, although for centuries this was unthinkable.[1] Usually, abstract uncertainty alone is insufficient as a form of explanation. One alternative is to search for culprits, and indeed many attempted explanations of the crisis are based on one or other form of finger-pointing. In the popular media, a great many villains abound: greedy creditors or short-sighted loan-takers, including those poor people acquiring mortgages without incomes. The finger of blame has also been directed at bankers and investors, and at political decision-makers.

The crisis was undoubtedly partly the result of thoughtlessness and irresponsibility. It was soon noticed that blame was not enough, however. The Group of 20, the heads of the world's twenty largest economies, met in September of 2009 to approve an institutional interpretation of the crisis. According to this analysis, mistakes had been made in the deregulation of finance markets and the main result of this was a large increase in the amount of high-risk speculation. A case of moral hazard then arises when banks and investors act on the convenient assumption that states and international organizations will shoulder the lion's share of the risks.[2] High-risk speculation and moral hazard were taken as plausible explanations of the crisis. So, in addition to increasing the amount and rigour of regulation, the G20 leaders and others began to demand that investors pay their share of the cost of tackling the crisis, for instance by paying banking or financial transaction taxes.[3] The reaction of the G20 leaders was an encouraging example of collective learning, but it was also too little too late and not systematically implemented. Moreover, the primary concern of the G20 remained the goal of getting 'free market' operations back to normal.[4]

The 2008–09 crisis prompted many journalists and economists to return to the economic theories of Hyman Minsky (1919–1996).[5] Minsky was a Keynesian economist who mainly made his career in studying the dynamics of financial markets. The central question that guided much of his research was, could the Great Depression of the 1930s happen again? I concur with these journalists and economists that the suddenly popular Minskyian theory can, with suitable amendments, offer much help in explaining the crisis. Increasing amounts of private debt, taken largely for speculative purposes, makes the financial system fragile and, eventually, liable to collapse.

Understanding the structural factors behind the crisis demands a deeper analysis of political economy than has so far been offered, however. The finance crisis resulted from the disparities of the global economy, one of which is the Chinese surplus relative to the United States' massive deficit. This and other asymmetries cannot be explained without reference to the rise in inequality, and to the transformations of common sense under the circumstances of free-market capitalism. The rapid growth in inequality within many countries, for its part, is the result of both changes in power relations that favour the transnationally mobile capital, and the ideals of the free market, which have been hegemonic in the mainstream (and especially commercial) media, among the political class, and also partly within academia. The more firmly established global economic liberalism becomes through institutional changes, the more it becomes a self-reinforcing process that, among other things, tends to create the conditions for economic crisis, epic recessions and even great depressions.

If we can properly understand the processes that combined to create the 2008–09 economic collapse and the equally dramatic follow-on effects of early 2010 onwards, we will be in a better position to avoid similar disasters in future. In the previous chapter I noted that everyday schemes of thought are often poorly applicable to understanding the actions of broader social systems, even though they may work well on the smaller scale for which they evolved. Things are often not all that they appear to be on first sight, and this is true also for the fast-moving events and episodes in the world economy. They look different when viewed from the perspective of many actors simultaneously and of broader social processes. In this chapter I will first summarize the short history of the global financial crisis, and then turn to the deeper background processes that created the conditions for the worldwide epic recession.

What really happened?

The financial crisis was as much a surprise for the specialists as it was for laypeople. For instance, in October 2007 International Monetary Fund economists were still predicting that the global economy would continue to grow at the rate of approximately 5 per cent annually over the coming years.[6] Central bankers and politicians gave assurances that the levels of debt in their countries were sustainable and that there was no bubble. Everything was supposed to have been in order, despite the gripes of dissenters.[7] The basis of optimistic expectations derived from a very short-sighted view of history. The mathematical and statistical models used handled quantitative data from only a few years back, and no use was made of the historical knowledge gained from previous bubbles and crises. The 1997 Asian crisis and the 2000–2003 Internet bubble were not treated as they should have been, as bellwethers of a larger crisis, but as isolated anomalies.

FIGURE 3.1   In the early phases of every bubble, optimism runs high and those involved are typically convinced that their luck will hold.

In late 2007 and early 2008, the term 'subprime' appeared more and more frequently in the news. A franker term would be 'second-rate'. Suddenly it became clear that the US mortgage market was saturated with junk bonds. Many households were granted subprime mortgages, despite having no means of repaying them. Mortgage brokers worked hard in bringing banks and non-creditworthy lenders together and maximizing the amount of mortgages because of the large incentives on offer. The banks for their part seemed to believe that the economy would continue to grow and that housing prices would rise accordingly. This, after all, would guarantee that even the poorest lenders would not default on their mortgages, since due debts could be paid off with new debt. The risks, spread throughout the system, seemed to be under control.

The view seemed to be widespread among bankers that granting mortgages had become a risk-free affair. In reality, the housing bubble in the United States had first started to develop in 1997–98, around the same time as the banks had started to turn on a large scale to mortgage and other forms of securitization. The essence of speculation is that short-term changes in prices are anticipated, and decisions to buy or sell are then quickly made and carried out on the basis of these anticipations. Speculators know that actual prices depend on other investors' expectations. Securitization – the practice of converting assets, and especially loans, into securities – took speculation to a whole new level, however. The basic idea now became to sell on loans as part of broader packages of various sorts of loans. These loan packages could then be resecuritized to form new, ever more complex securities. Various credit insurance packets were developed and taken out to cover the loans, for both primary and secondary assets.[8] The risks appear to be dispersed on the market – at least if one accepts the assumption that in so far as the markets worked rationally enough, whatever risks that arose would show in the prices of assets and their insurances. Freed from regulation, speculative markets were assumed to be capable in this way of predicting the future.[9]

Securitization created strong incentives to maximize the amount of mortgages and other debts, irrespective of the ability or other-wise of the debtors to repay them. Because the loans could later be repackaged and resold on the market – with each phase of this securitization process generating handsome profits for some – the priority became maximizing the amount of mortgage debt. When the information technology (IT) crash of 2000–2003 occurred, many wealthy investors switched to the housing market, and soon the annual rate of housing price increases rose from 10 to 20 per cent. This phenomenon did not affect only the United States; real-estate prices soared to unrealistic highs in parts of Europe

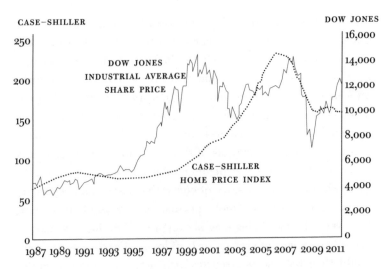

CASE–SHILLER

DOW JONES

FIGURE 3.2   The development of housing and stock prices
in the USA, 1987–2011[10]

also, above all in Spain and the Republic of Ireland. The further
the process went, the clearer it became that the value of secondary
loans was a bubble that was soon fit to burst. And when that time
came, the loans would exceed the prices properties could get on
the market. Although housing prices in the USA had begun to
drop in 2006, the upward trend in securitization continued into
the following year, and banks and investors worldwide joined in
the speculation.

From 2007, housing demand began to peter out, and new
debtors were increasingly hard to find. The unprecedentedly high
prices started to deter buyers, and investors gradually became
more circumspect. Soon there was a glut on the housing market,
and prices began to fall. The granting of new mortgages and
renewal of existing mortgages was based on the continuing appreciation of housing prices. But when appreciation turned to
depreciation in 2006 (see Figure 3.2), many households were no

longer able to meet the regular mortgage repayments. Nor was time on their side, since for many the initial two-year low-interest phase had just expired. Households were now in a squeeze, but because of their great number the industrialist John Paul Getty's aphorism rang true: 'If you owe the bank 100 dollars, that's your problem. If you owe the bank 100 million, that's the bank's problem.'

It was not only households that were in debt. Investors had also used 'debt leverage' on financial markets. The amount of mortgage debt had risen to an unprecedented high, but the total debt of financiers was over two and a half times greater, at almost $20 trillion (for comparison: the US gross national product for 2011 was 15.04 trillion).[11] The five largest US investment banks alone were over $4 trillion in debt. When it became clear that a large part of the loans in circulation and the bonds based on them had already become worthless, or were well on their way to becoming so, finance markets were overtaken by panic. Traders rushed to sell before prices collapsed, so as to be able to cope with their own debts, thus further reinforcing the collapse. The first to get into deep trouble were those who had used mostly borrowed capital to speculate.

Banks noticed that their strategy of shunting the risks forward had not succeeded. The value of securitized debt packages and their brokers plunged dramatically. Banks urgently needed more cash in order to staunch the now-negative cash flow and to be able to cope with the sudden loss of capital. Mutual trust between banks collapsed, and money markets between them froze. This was the start of a liquidity crisis. There was nothing left but to call in the lender of last resort: the United States' central bank, the Federal Reserve, began plugging the liquidity deficits of individual banks with extremely large sums of money, part of which was used to bail out European banks as well. Despite these efforts, many, especially smaller, banks went bankrupt since their capital had dried up after the write-down and their subsequent expulsion from the banks' shared money market system. The US government rescued one of the largest single issuers of credit derivatives, the insurance company AIG, and the country's largest bank, the Bank of America. The principle of 'too big to [be allowed to] fail' was not followed in all cases, though, and the Lehman Brothers investment bank was allowed to go under. It had been one of the five largest investment banks, and thus became one of the largest bankruptcies in US history. This was September 2008, and the panic on bond markets was threatening to get completely out of hand.

The crisis became global. Investors knew that there was no longer any such thing as risk-free investments. And because investors all over the world had bought securities that were based on junk bonds, the losses were far from being confined to the United States. The problem was no longer limited to secondary loans or variable-interest mortgages. Figure 3.2 also shows how the Dow Jones stock index developed after the 2000–2003 IT bubble burst. From late 2003 on, stock exchanges had expanded in pace with the development of the housing bubble, until a sharp fall-off began in October 2007 and accelerated in late 2008. Securitization and the development of new, exotic financing mechanisms were by no means restricted to the housing market, of course. Complex packages were also built on the basis of consumer debt, and these very often had the appearance of the notorious Ponzi schemes. In such schemes, debt and new shares are used to pay returns on previous investments in the company, which creates the illusion of a stably profitable enterprise – until the newest and broadest level at the base of the pyramid ceases to hold together, and the whole shoddy edifice collapses.

The financial crisis spread throughout the world, with global economic prognoses weakening most markedly in the USA and Europe. Banks practically stopped granting loans and focused instead on ensuring their own financial standing. In a money-based economy, this moratorium on lending was catastrophic. It meant, among other things, that loans became difficult to renew, and that productive companies could no longer get enough funding for investments, or could not get it at reasonable prices. On the other hand, the drop in aggregate demand reduced many companies' motivation to make new investments. Among the general public, real income levels began to drop. Many also lost their homes and jobs, and uncertainty created a pervasive air of caution. There was little interest in taking out new loans, and many people went to great lengths to rid themselves of existing loans. Consumer credit became increasingly difficult to get, and aggregate demand continued to fall. Unemployment levels took an upward turn, and over the course of 2009 the overall total of world trade decreased by almost one-tenth on the previous year. Slumps on a similar scale had not been seen since the 1930s and the war years of the following decade.

The crisis also spread to developing economies, many of which suffered currency crises when investors became wary of holding on to any but the largest and most stable currencies. In Cambodia, for example, the 10 per cent annual growth rate that had continued for several years came to a total halt in 2009. In all, hundreds of millions of people around the world were plunged into severe relative poverty, and many into absolute poverty. The speculative economy had shown its true force.

How could this happen?

The chain of events that unfolded could have been otherwise. When the US housing bubble was growing, the US government and Congress investigated the loan practices that had given rise to it. They refused to take any action, however, due to their principled opposition to regulation. The Federal Reserve kept interest rates at a historical low, although the Fed leaders were well aware of the rises in housing and share prices and of the mounting levels of debt in the system. Many operators resorted to outright fraud: the leadership of Lehman Brothers, for example, doctored its accounts to keep its growing financial difficulties hidden, and continued expanding its programme of reckless speculation until the very end. Nor were the charges of bankers' and investors' greed without foundation. The general public in many parts of the world seemed to be particularly aggrieved by the fact that the top-level management of many financial firms continued to receive massive bonuses even in the middle of the crisis. An investigative committee was set up in 2009 to determine the extent to which the bonus system contributed to triggering the crisis.[12]

Deregulation, lackadaisical monitoring and a perverse bonus culture exacerbated the growth of the bubble, and its eventual rupture. The United States and Britain spearheaded the dismantlement of the financial regulation system, starting already in the 1970s. The defining project of Ronald Reagan's and Margaret Thatcher's terms in office (1981–89 and 1979–90 respectively), market deregulation, and particularly of financial markets, was made into a global project. Under President Bill Clinton, the USA in 1999 abolished the Glass–Steagall Act, which had been in place since 1933 and above all maintained a separation between investment banks that can engage in speculation and the rest of the banking system. This move created further space for cosy connections between speculators and financiers. It is also clear that technological developments had a contributing role in the occurrence of the 2008–09 crisis. Within the scope of time differences, interconnected computer systems enabled coordinated and simultaneous actions across the globe. This was a major benefit to efforts to evade bookkeeping and other regulations, just as much as it was to synchronization of developments across financial markets.[13]

From a historical perspective, of course, there is nothing new about scams, poor regulation and the development of closer ties between different finance systems. Charles Kindleberger, for one, has argued on the basis of a broad historical survey that dishonesty and fraud have been prominent features of all the finance market crises of modern capitalism, at least since the Netherlands' tulip crisis of 1637: 'Commercial and financial crises are intimately bound up with transactions that overstep the confines of law and morality, shadowy though those confines be. The propensities to swindle and be swindled run parallel to the propensity to speculate during a boom.'[14]

In addition, financial crises have had a tendency to spread from one centre to another. A case in point is the Vienna Stock Exchange crash of 1873, which quickly spread to other European financial centres. By the early 1900s, it was already possible to trade in stocks between New York and London by telephone. The USA was not yet the world's financial hub by this time, however, and the 1907 New York crash remained a domestic one (and prompted the establishment of the Federal Reserve). During the Great War and soon afterwards, the global economic significance of the United States grew, so that the 1929 New York Stock Exchange crash spread panic and economic calamity throughout the world.

The same sort of enabling and contributing factors regularly come together in financial crises. The propensity to swindle and be swindled is only one of the characteristics that are enhanced by the proliferation of speculative activity. Some financial crises spread far and wide even before the invention of the telephone, so it is clear that technology in itself is not a sufficient explanation for their occurrence. This raises the question of the extent to which the enabling and contributing causes that have already been identified are not enough to explain fully the 2008–09 global crisis. A wider and deeper perspective is needed. It must be asked where all the funds for speculation and debt actually came from. How does the propensity to speculate emerge and develop? Why do different actors get into debt, and what consequences does this have? On the other hand, why is it that high rates of financial inflation cannot continue indefinitely? How do financial bubbles and the ensuing panic and crisis spread from economy to economy? Why do widespread unemployment and poverty tend invariably to follow banking crises and stock market crashes? Such questions bring one closer to the fundamental causes of financial crises.

On extravagant saving and accumulation of debt

The American economist Ben Bernanke, who is now head of the Federal Reserve, suggested in 2005 that there is a far too great total amount of savings in the world economy in relation to meaningful real investment opportunities. Bernanke's criticisms were aimed at the burgeoning economies of Asia, and particularly at China, which saves excessively and consumes too little. One indicator of this is that China's exports of goods and services far outstrip its level of imports. On the other hand, China invests a large amount of its surplus in US dollar securities, especially US Treasury Bills, which creates massive cash flows into US financial markets. These funds can then be lent further, including for mortgages and speculative purposes.

But many economists responded to Bernanke that the largest savings were held by private companies, primarily in the United States, Japan, Germany and Britain. In the USA, the largest profit-making firms saved significant proportions of their profits or distributed them in bonuses and shares rather than reinvest them.[15] It seems strange that financial-sector companies could simultaneously be responsible for the vast bulk of overall debt and also be the largest savers. This is a simple matter of bookkeeping, however, since savings are defined as whatever profits are not invested in fixed capital, the latter usually meaning buildings, goods, equipment and the like, in general anything with a long lifespan.

The speed of circulation is crucial, and financial market investments are characteristically short-term. Debt is taken out to create leverage and thereby to increase the profitability of these investments. Existing investments can be used as collateral for new debt. And as long as financial values increase, more money can be created by taking on new debt. So, rather than invest in fixed capital, profits are lent at interest to new investors, or else distributed to upper-level management and owners. Bonuses and dividends are usually so large that managers and owners could not possibly consume all their income. Therefore they invest the majority of the surplus where it will produce the largest profits in the shortest possible time. When the profits reaped on speculative financial markets are larger than those achievable elsewhere, this money stays on the financial markets, which can multiply financial values and the total amount of debt many times over.

The context to this state of affairs is the struggle over the appropriate distribution of wealth and over the socially created opportunities for consumption. The increased propensity of firms to save has many causes, including wrangles over income distribution between capital and labour. During the past thirty to forty years, the interests of capital have increasingly won out over the interests of labour. According to an OECD report published in 2007, this trend, supported by cutting taxation levels on capital gains and low non-financial inflation, explains a significant part of the increased ability of firms to save.[16] On the other hand, the gradual transition towards an economy dominated by financial speculation is a powerful disincentive to investment in fixed capital.[17] Of the investments they do make, many companies prefer to buy existing production facilities rather than build anything new; in this way long-term commitments can be avoided. Many means are available for turning the increasing proportion of overall production accounted for by capital into savings.

The trade imbalances of the USA and China are largely due to the growing levels of inequality in both countries. Since the late 1970s, increased labour productivity in the United States has mainly benefited only the higher income levels. The proportion of the national product composed of capital has risen markedly, and the proportion of the total accounted for by labour has dropped from 60 to below 50 per cent (the lush salaries of top-level management are included in this 50 per cent). The average hourly pay of regular employees peaked around 1973, and since then wage levels have generally stagnated or even dropped. The modest increase in average household income can be explained above all by the fact that people generally have a longer working week now than they did before; more women are also working, and holidays tend to be shorter. By contrast, in three decades the incomes of the wealthiest fifth have risen by around 80 per cent, and those of the wealthiest 1 per cent have more than doubled over the same period. The most dramatic increases have been among the ultra-rich top 0.01 per cent. This minority now accounts for more than 6 per cent of GDP in the United States, which is more even than in 1929, and far more than in 1973, when the same elite accounted for 0.9 per cent of the country's GDP.

The same trend applies to ownership. At the beginning of the 2000s the USA's richest 1 per cent owned 40 per cent of the country's wealth. Their income and assets were so high that any further amassment of wealth seemed practically impossible; this plight, naturally, was a godsend for investment consultants and portfolio managers. The consumption of the majority of the population, by contrast, was and continues to be on an increasingly fragile basis, and consumption levels have been commonly sustained by easily obtainable debt. While the elite saves and

ploughs its money into speculation, among regular households
in the United States the overall level of debt has long been rising,
and savings are virtually non-existent.[18]

In China, increasing economic inequality has caused notable
underconsumption on the domestic market and overinvestment,
particularly in the export sector. Labour productivity in the
country has grown by a massive 20 per cent a year, but only a
fraction of this has translated into higher wages. The share of
Chinese GDP accounted for by labour income had dropped from
57 per cent in 1978 to 37 per cent by 2005. Although the level
of investments in China is very high, with a large share being
directed at successful parts of the export sector, it has not been
enough to absorb the amounts of savings in the economy. The
result has been a massive current account surplus and continually
mounting Central Bank reserves, the bulk of the latter in the
form of US-dollar-nominated assets, with far smaller amounts
in euros and other currencies. Ironically, underconsumption and
excessive saving in a country like China, where the majority of the
population are still relatively or very poor, has partly contributed
to the United States being able to take on still more debt in order
to continue overconsuming. This lopsided state of affairs also
provides one source for speculative funds.[19]

The speculative economy
and the changing nature of debt

Financialization is a process in which financial markets, financial institutions and financial elites gain an increasing hold over
economic process and economic policy decisions. In Minsky's
view, the capitalist market economy has an inherent tendency to
develop in the direction of financialization. When the industrial
economy grows and the owner and managers of private capital
consolidate and strengthen their position in society, it becomes

easier to believe that the good times will continue indefinitely. In line with this disposition, further deregulation of the financial system is demanded to facilitate ever-greater profits.[20] The attractiveness of these new opportunities for profit create a positive feedback chain, and lead to further, increasingly strident calls for deregulation. States can also turn quick profits generated in financial markets within their territory into a competitive advantage, and so the turn to a speculative economy becomes all the more comprehensive.

It is crucial to consider the extent to which these expansionist propensities may indeed be a deep hallmark of capitalist market economy, and the extent to which they are due to particular historical choices and conditions. Is enduring institutional learning possible?

Global finance made its way back to the foreground of the global economy in the 1960s and 1970s. Somewhat higher inflation rates at the time facilitated argumentation for changes in economic policy, but inflation was often invoked as a rationalization for policy changes rather than as the foremost reason for them. The real causes of the changes lie deeper.[21] Particular causes for the wave of financialization that took place at the end of the last century can be found in the efforts of the USA and Britain to use financial mechanisms to solve their economic problems and strengthen their own position.[22] Another and more fundamental part of the explanation can be found in the contradictions between the state and the global economy, which intensified in the second half of the 1900s. Levels of state taxation and regulation continued to increase simultaneously with often-revolutionary developments in transport and communications. A state's powers to impose taxes and regulations tend to be restricted to a limited territorial area, whereas in the liberalized world economy companies, financial institutions and individuals are free to transfer their activities and assets elsewhere. The structural power of

TABLE 3.1   The mutually reinforcing effects of financialization

Income distribution	Corporate behaviour	Economic policy
New income distribution benefits capital and wealthy households, increases cashflow to financial markets, which provide credit for speculation	Financier and investor dominance changes corporate behaviour, the main aim being: • cutting short-term costs, especially wages, to maximize short-term profits As a result, long-term fixed investments tend to decrease	Capital's stronger position changes states' economic policies: • competitiveness and low inflation become primary policy goals • EU principles also reflect financialization interests

transnational capital relative to the state supported the process of financialization, and financialization in turn has contributed to increasing structural dependency of states on transnational capital.[23] Once the movement in this direction started, small and apparently inconsequential choices began to mount up and reinforce each other.[24] And so the pace of financial deregulation picked up during the 1980s and 1990s, and became worldwide in scope.

Financialization takes three routes (Table 3.1). First, changes to the practices and structures of financing transform how loans and other debts are taken on. Financialization and inequality are mutually reinforcing processes. Income redistribution in favour of capital and well-off households directs flows onto the financial markets, where new debts are then created and loans granted, including for speculative purposes. Second, the dominant position of financial networks impels important changes in the behaviour of corporations. Their overriding task becomes the generation of quicker profits and appreciation in the value of their stocks. Short-term expenses, above all wages, are reduced by all means possible to maximize short-term profits. At the same time, the interest of firms in long-term fixed investments and innovations requiring time-consuming and broad-based research and development generally tends to decrease. Third, the strengthened structural position of especially financial capital comes to be increasingly reflected in the economic policies of states. Through these hegemonic struggles, states adopt as their primary economic goals the maintenance of low inflation rates and competitiveness, rather than aiming, for instance, at full employment. Capital-influenced economic policies also typically involve increasing the 'flexibility' of the labour market, the 'liberalization' of speculative activity, the creation of new funds, and the privatization and outsourcing of previously public services.[25]

Generally speaking, structures and practices are reformed in the interests of maximizing short-term profits. This includes such tactics as the placement of pensions into funds, which are then used to invest in various assets. In this way additional liquidity is created for use in the speculative economy. Insurance companies also get involved in business activities that contribute to the investment funds. The greater the amount and variety of things that are insured privately, the greater the amount of money capital that will be made available for investment. As these practices have gained ground, the goals of monetary and finance policy have changed over time. The low-inflation-pursuing competitive state, intent on making itself as attractive as possible to highly mobile transnational interests, is a characteristically late-twentieth-century invention. Throughout the world, the mainstream media now routinely report on how 'markets react' to economic policy decisions, or even to policy proposals.[26]

From the 1960s and 1970s, these trends have been strengthened by the increasingly rapid development of offshore financial centres.[27] Many are in the Caribbean and similarly exotic locations, but they are also plentiful throughout Europe and North America. The vast majority – an estimated US$10 trillion worth

– of the world's funds are placed in or run through these centres, which operate under the names of various banks and funds. Among other things, the centres make it possible to avoid financial regulations, to create financial instruments that are prohibited in many countries, and to evade taxes, transfer profits and conceal incriminating or otherwise sensitive information. Regulation in companies' home countries may be rigorous and taxation levels relatively high, but if activities and profits can be diverted to tax havens with minimal regulations and taxes the most mobile capital and largest profits will remain largely unscathed. One outcome of this is that the tax burden is increasingly left to mid- and low-income earners. This makes their consumption practices more fragile, which tends to deplete further overall consumption levels. The institution of state sovereignty protects offshore centres: due to the widely accepted principle of non-interference, governments have so far been seldom willing to take them to task.

Financialization practices have been longest in development in the United States, although other parts of the world are not far behind. When the composition of debt in the USA for the last quarter-century is examined, it is clear that the accumulation of debt in the private sector has been particularly drastic (see Figure 3.3). The pace of indebtedness has been particularly fast in the financial sector, where total debt in 2009 had risen to 120 per cent compared to below 30 per cent in 1986. Over the same period, household debt rose from 52 per cent to 98 per cent, and corporate debt from 60 to 80 per cent of gross domestic product. Debt increases the inherent riskiness of investing and financing, and even small fluctuations in profit levels or adjustments to interest rates and debt conditions can make debt management extremely difficult, if not impossible.

As a further example, the Finnish case can shed light on the general relation between increasing debt and financial crises. Finland experienced a severe recession in the early 1990s after

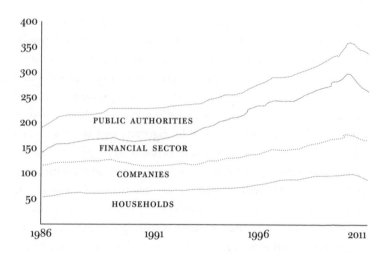

FIGURE 3.3   Debt levels in the US economy, 1986–2011 (debt/%GDP)

a deep crisis in the country's banking sector. When the banks could no longer provide loans, businesses were unable to continue funding their operations and the result was a wave of bankruptcies. Figure 3.4 shows that the amount of debt in Finland had grown at a significantly faster pace than the country's GDP throughout the preceding decade, and financial sector debt had grown fastest of all. The development of Finland's debt structure during the 1980s, then, was similar to that of the United States in the 1990s and 2000s. The difference is that the total amount of debt in the USA is 3.5 times its annual national product, whereas during the 1990s' Finnish recession the total debt was just twice, and at the very worst point 2.5 times, the annual national product. Another difference, and one that stood in Finland's favour in the 1990s, is that recession is easier to beat if the world economy as a whole is growing, since this provides the possibility of job creation and

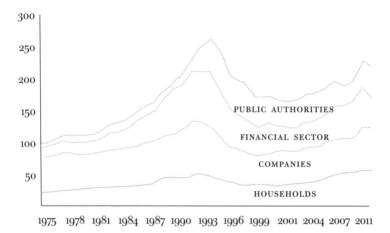

FIGURE 3.4   Debt levels in Finland, 1975–2010 (debt/%GDP)[28]

recovery through export trade. The global recession is obviously far more serious in this regard, since it is not restricted to any particular country or region.

Two interpretations of late modern capitalism and its weaknesses

A sufficient level of effective aggregate demand is an essential requirement for adequate real investments and economic growth. In the USA and elsewhere in the OECD region before the 2008–09 crisis, demand was maintained largely through debt. This includes households also, which were thus in a very vulnerable position. In trying to explain the accumulation of debt and the growth of the financial bubble in the early 2000s, one must also explain why households have been willing to get into debt rather than adjust their consumption habits to the available disposable income. In the USA, in particular, employees have been willing to exchange their free time, holidays and some of their pension years for working time in order to maintain or improve their standards of living, in conditions in which hourly pay has remained stagnant or even dropped and jobs are increasingly insecure and temporary.

From a sociological standpoint, these economic developments can be explained in at least two ways. These explanations are not mutually exclusive in every respect, but there are certain tensions between them, partly because they each refer to different ethico-political ways of responding to the fragility of consumption. In addition, both explanations start from the premiss that declining salary levels are a consequence of growing inequality (work productivity has continued to improve, although not anymore at a particularly fast rate). Easily obtainable loans and the home price bubble easily explain some of the household debt burden, but how can one explain people's drive to consume more in situations where it is clearly not the sensible option?

The first explanation refers to some general human tendencies. People have a marked preference for holding on to their current standards of living, but what also matters is their status. There is thus a very widespread tendency to want to adopt the consumption habits of those who are better off. According to the second explanation, people's needs and desires are extensively shaped by the mechanisms of capitalist market economy: advertising and marketing create distinctions between different commodities and brands, thus encouraging a particular form of identity-formation, and also condition consumers to want even more. I will elaborate on both explanations now.

The first explanation is based on research by the Norwegian-American sociologist and economist Thorstein Veblen (1857–1929).[29] Just as in a 'primitive' society in which people scar and paint their skin and adorn themselves with feathers or animal hides, so too in capitalist economies people endeavour to impress each other. Consumption is used as a means both of obtaining status and of advertising one's status to others. Veblen's contention was that attention-seeking, occasionally bordering on exhibition-ism, is the fundamental purpose of consumption. The immediate benefits of any given act of consumption are secondary to its display value, especially when basic needs have already been met. Progress towards a consumption-centred lifestyle may also be connected to secularization. When religions (or secular ideologies with similar functions such as Marxism) no longer provide life with meaning or purpose, the 'philosophy of futility' may come into effect. Consuming may assuage the feeling of emptiness, and at least brings with it the purpose of making an impression on others.[30] Those who manage to make the biggest impression become objects of admiration and envy; and, naturally, those who are most capable of keeping up appearances are the wealthiest and the most culturally refined and sophisticated.

From a Veblen-inspired perspective, many things can in princi-ple be easily explained. For instance, it partly shows why average, basically well-off Americans or Europeans find it hard to accept being left behind when others' incomes rise, and when their own incomes fall, especially when the incomes of the very wealthiest rise all the time, as do the opportunities for status-driven con-sumption. Often the most important symbol of affluence is a home of one's own. But it is crucial to the attainment and maintenance of status that distinctions are made in all areas of life, such as in modifications of the body, dress, eating, exercise and physical activity, and travel. Public forums also require careful attention to detail: what events one attends, how one is visible in the media, the restaurants and cafés one frequents, type of car, and so on.

Veblen's theory also suggests why the desire of elites to get even richer may be limitless. When one reaches the top, one's status can be paraded through fame, acceptance by peers, or by donating to philanthropic and other charitable causes to attract attention and praise. It is also possible to use one's wealth to wield influence, for instance through politics and the mass media: Rupert Murdoch and Silvio Berlusconi are two of the most prominent and notorious examples. Moreover, the ranking list of highest net worth value of individuals is relational: one's rise is another's decline. Currently there are an estimated 38 million US dollar millionaires in the world, of which a small fraction are classified as ultra-rich (having at least $30 million in investible income). There are rather more than a thousand billionaires – fewer than there are government ministers. Ministers are rotated, whereas the billionaires tend to stay put.

What Veblen's theory can't explain, however, is how societies can become more democratic over time, as most societies did in the Bretton Woods era, until the 1970s and 1980s. Neither does it shed much light on why savings levels fluctuate so dramatically. For example, why do relatively low-earning Chinese save a large proportion of their incomes, whereas their much wealthier American counterparts have negative savings – that is, debt? Why so much is spent on advertising and marketing is also unaccounted for by Veblen's theory, which was developed in an era when these institutions were in their infancy. They soon developed rapidly, however, first and foremost in the USA, and brand and product distinction have long since become a central explanation of how companies grow, monopolize and form transnational conglomerates or mega-corporations. (In some cases price differences between otherwise equivalent goods are the key competitive factor, but in most others quality and product differentiation are much more decisive.[31])

In the USA alone, over $300 billion is spent annually on advertising in the media, and massive amounts are also spent on other marketing of goods and services. Already in the 1960s economist

John Kenneth Galbraith argued that large firms systematically mould people's values and consumer choices; naturally they do so within the bounds of pre-existing cultures, but they also do much to shape those cultures.[32] Consumerism entails that people begin to focus, even obsessively so, on material consumption, perhaps in the belief that this is the primary source of hope and happiness. Or at least they do so as a way to kill time in the midst of emptiness, for lack of anything better to do.

Comparisons with ancient tribes help to highlight how individuals' efforts to maximize their own status display certain universal features that are not reducible to any single social system or culture. It can therefore be credibly argued that human societies still have many 'primitive' hallmarks. As was also suggested by Veblen – himself a proponent and contributor to evolutionary economic theory – certain historical institutions and conditions can, however, either weaken or strengthen these features. In this light, it may be that the development of continually greater social and economic inequalities will lead to a return to the rule of ceremonial elitism that was characteristic of earlier, hierarchical societies.[33]

The financialization and increasing inequality of the last few decades have contributed to making social relations more primitive, in the sense Veblen used that term. This interpretation should, however, be supplemented with Galbraith's insight, and in doing so we arrive at the realization that consumerism is partly the outcome of modern marketing, which unceasingly transforms cultures in a consumer-dominated direction. Inequality, for its part, has supported the progress towards a 'neo-primitive' world in which there are no longer any constraints or limits to the economic elite's fulfilment of its own desires, regardless of the social and economic effects this pursuit may have. The ideology that is orthodox neoclassical economic theory contributes to this process, by filling in the gaps and papering over the incongruences between belief, wishful thinking and reality.

On the fast circulation of money
and its consequences

In explaining the global financial crisis of 2008–09 and the early 2010s, one must strive to get beyond a superficial level. Individual events and specific agents do of course have their own roles, but it is crucial to look beyond them in order to uncover the real causes of the crisis. The chosen timescale must also be sufficiently broad: what can seem surprising or anomalous on a five- or ten-year scale can reveal itself to be anything but surprising when placed in a broader historical context.

Like David Ricardo and other classical economists, Karl Marx believed that money is merely a measure of underlying value. Real value, on the classical view, was determined by labour input, by the number of hours needed to create the product or service. Although in this Marx was sorely mistaken, he did succeed in capturing something essential about how money circulates in the capitalist market system.[34] He summarized the profit motive in a formula: M–C–M′, the transformation of money (M) into commodities (C) – that is, capital in the form of goods – and of commodities back again into money. Money is first invested in productive capital and in labour (more specifically, working time), the latter bought on the labour market. The production process thus creates more money, M′, when the output is sold on the commodity market. Several things can be included in the equation, for instance labour costs and debt maintenance costs; all these are deducted from M′. In the final analysis and after accounting for inflation, the amount by which M′ exceeds M is the net profit of the business activity or financial year. The overriding objective, clearly, is to maximize this difference.

Banking makes it possible to make money out of money. The process can thus become purely financial: M–M′. The speculative money economy can multiply and significant profits can be made even in a single day, and a year in this ever-accelerating system is a very long time indeed. The easier it is, or looks, to make a quick fortune, the less attractive other forms of economic activity begin to appear.[35] Financial inflation can be strengthened by a variety of processes. The inflation of financial values is characteristically supported by accumulation of savings and creation of funds not invested in long-term productive purposes. Growing inequality, the channelling of pensions and insurances into funds, the effects of financialization on corporate structure and behaviour, and current account surpluses all create liquidity, and thus contribute to the further appreciation of financial values.

In spite of all this, the profit margins on rapid financial investments are small. They can be increased by taking on more debt to create leverage, and to increase the total number of investments. When the amount of investments is sufficiently massive, even modest profit margins on each investment can in a short time create large profits relative to the amount of capital on which the investments are based. Debt can also be used to expand possession of assets, in the hope of increasing revenues. As long as the financial values continue to increase, there will be a corresponding increase in the amount of possibilities for borrowing, since existing investments can be used as surety on new loans. Financialization also affects the everyday lives of ordinary people and households, since the finance bubbles and debt accumulation are closely connected to other parts of the economy, including the housing market, and influence the way people live.

Conclusions

All bubbles eventually burst, including financial ones. These incessantly expanding, interconnected systems that are built on debt tend to become more chaotic over time. As the economic activity of the elites comes more and more to revolve around debt and speculation, due to its promise of fast opportunities to maximize wealth and status, many parts of the financial system become gradually more fragile. Home prices may already be so high that those outside the elite are finding it impossible to take on any more debt, even at the lowest available rates. There is so much consumer debt that lenders are beginning to impose more stringent conditions, and serious difficulties with repayments are becoming more common. At the critical point investors, for their part, are in such deep debt that even small reductions or interruptions to their cash flow can wreak havoc.

It will at some stage be realized that credit has been granted also to individuals and corporations that have never had the capacity, even in theory, to repay it, even if the bubble had remained intact and growing. It will also, sooner or later, be revealed that many have been swindled by elaborate pyramid schemes, which follow always the same simple logic: rapid profit is an illusion that can be maintained as long as a growing number of new investors can be found who are willing to buy into it. At the final stage of the development of the bubble the quality of debt deteriorates further. Ponzi-finance is taken to cover only the most immediate costs of previous debt and for no other purpose.

What exactly triggers the eventual collapse is of no major significance. What is more important is how long the processes of financialization and debt accumulation have been in development, and what kind of interdependency has developed between different market sectors and the financial centres. The bursting of the IT bubble in 2000–2003 affected only a limited part of the financial markets, and led to relatively limited recession. The superbubble that lay concealed behind that smaller bubble and that fed into it continued to grow, until 2007, and burst the following year. This was the beginning of epic recession, which has since morphed into the debt crisis of states with which Europe in particular is now saddled.

4

Contradictions at
the heart of the EMU

The effects of the global financial crisis became evident in Europe throughout the course of 2008. Iceland, Hungary and Ukraine were forced to resort to IMF emergency loans, and many European banks received support. In November 2008, the president of the European Commission, José Manuel Barroso, sought to seize the initiative with a European economic recovery plan, which he said could transform a crisis into an opportunity.[1] Despite these and other emergency measures, Europe's economy sank into deep recession, and the GDP of the eurozone dropped by over 4 per cent in 2009.

The global economic crisis triggered automatic stability mechanisms in the EU countries. Most of them also resorted to deliberate increases in national expenses to stimulate the economy. These expenses were paid off with new public debt, which was also used to shore up the rapidly depleting reserves of banks and investors. The second phase of the crisis and epic recession began in spring 2010, when the credit ratings agency Standard & Poor's demoted Greece's credit rating to the junk bond category. At the same time, interest rates on the country's two-year loans rose to an unprecedented 15 per cent. Perhaps an even greater worry was caused by the Greek government's revelation that previous governments had forged public-sector financial analyses and under-reported deficits. And Greece was not alone. Several other eurozone countries such as Ireland and Portugal were suddenly facing difficulties in renewing their loans with reasonable interest rates.

Greece and Ireland were in some senses at opposite extremes. Although economic growth in both countries had been brisk before the crisis, Greece was already indebted to start with, and through the crisis its debt levels rose rapidly from 115 to 143 per cent of GDP. By contrast, Ireland's debt crisis resulted solely from the global financial crisis. The country's housing bubble burst, and the banking system collapsed. The proportion of public debt relative to GDP rose from a very reasonable 24.8 per cent to over 96 per cent, and the country's central bank has estimated that this will grow to 118 per cent by 2013.[2] Debt crises soon developed in other EU countries also, including Portugal, Spain and Belgium, and these were aggravated by debt speculation on financial markets. In May 2010, Britain's Conservative Party-led government opted to tackle the country's budget deficit by introducing the largest ever programme of cutbacks and austerity measures in the country's history, even though the country's debt levels were lower than those of many eurozone countries. The debt crisis later spread to Italy, and in January 2012 Standard & Poor's dropped the credit ratings levels of nine eurozone countries, France included. In spring and summer 2012, not only many European countries such as Spain but also a number of major European banks saw further deterioration of their credit rating.

The rescue packages devised for Greece and other crisis-hit countries by the EU and the International Monetary Fund – following the model imposed earlier on many developing countries – oblige the recipient governments to impose public spending cuts in order to stem further deficit increases. But this tends to depress the economy. The tax reductions to private firms that the packages also typically include increase the state burden even more, by reducing tax revenue. The packages also impose retrenchment on public services and distribution policies, wage and pension cuts, and impel restrictions to labour laws under the euphemism of 'flexibility' – typically also implying wage cuts, thereby lessening citizens' purchasing power and even further reducing overall effective demand.

Austerity programmes exacerbate recession, and can even make it chronic. As the economy recedes the state's intake of tax revenue dwindles, and public expenses grow due to increased demand for unemployment payments and other relief measures. Thus here also efforts to save easily become self-defeating: Greece's goal of limiting its deficit to 7.4 per cent in 2011, for example, came to nothing because of the worsening recession. Many news reports around this time noticed the effects of deepening recession on the country's savings objectives.[3] The problem is not just Greece's, and there is no solution in sight. Despite the rescue packages, the fears of insolvency surrounding some euro countries have continued to mount. Even eurozone leaders have estimated that Greece, at least, may be forced to leave the common currency. The question is whether it or any other individual euro country can be insulated from the rest of the eurozone financial system, or whether any departure from the eurozone could trigger a chain reaction.[4] The worst fears have been allayed somewhat by the aid packages, stability mechanisms and the promise of a permanent stability mechanism on a hastened schedule that came into effect in 2012 (it had earlier been planned for 2013), mainly through their effects on interest rates and expectations (see Chapter 5). The crisis persists, however.

The plight of the euro came as little surprise to those who had originally been critical of the plan to give Europe a common currency without a common economic policy. The European Monetary Union took two crucial economic policy instruments, interest rate policy and devaluation, out of the hands of states, without putting anything in their place. The central argument of this chapter is that some of the most prominent critics were wrong in their basic assumptions. The theory of an optimal currency area is inadequate for explaining the EMU's difficulties. These have been due not so much to differences in timing of business cycles in different euro countries as to the problems and asymmetries in the formation of aggregate demand, which have been caused by the prevailing institutional arrangements and the dynamics of financial market speculation. The 2008–09 crisis brought all these inadequacies of the EMU to light and at the same time contributed to worsening them.

An optimal currency area?

The Delors Committee report published in 1989 recommended the establishment of a Europe-wide economic union. National currencies would be replaced by a common currency, in the hope of thereby doing away with the risks and costs brought about by unstable exchange rates.[5] In relation to the rest of the world, the European Union is the world's largest trading bloc. The majority of EU countries' trade is done with other EU members, however, and figures range from Britain's 58 per cent to the Czech Republic's 85 per cent (2007 figures).[6] Currency exchange within the newly founded eurozone ceased on 31 December 1998, eliminating currency speculation and exchange-related risks. Internal trade became simple. Moreover, the euro emerged as the world's second most important currency, after the US dollar. Predicting its fluctuations in value on world markets is easier than predicting the fluctuations of a host of different currencies. Independently of the other effects of the euro, trade has at least become more

FIGURE 4.1   Robert Mundell, pioneer of optimal currency area theory, has trenchantly supported the euro project; in 2000 he predicted that by 2010 fifty states would have joined the eurozone.[7]

straightforward, although this has not benefited all sectors and actors in the same way. Parts of the export sector, for instance, can be negatively affected by high exchange rates for the euro.

The common currency can be seen primarily as a political project,[8] but its foundations and justification are grounded in economic arguments also. Through economic and fiscal union the EU has aimed for stability and predictability, but is the European currency zone sustainable? This was vigorously debated before and during the creation of the EMU, and it is still often examined from the perspective of the theory of optimal currency area. Evaluations of the optimality of the eurozone have changed significantly over time, of course. Optimal currency area theory, pioneered by Robert Mundell, has also been used by EMU opponents. How credible is it as a basis for judging the feasibility and sustainability of European monetary union?

Mundell first outlined his theory in the early 1960s.[9] Some
three decades later it was widely debated whether the European
Union could form a functioning unified currency area. Monetary
policy would be handled by an independent central bank insulated from politics and political decision-making processes of
the EU.[10] Adjustment to both internal differences and external
changes would primarily have to be achieved through market
mechanisms, since no common economic policy was planned
for the eurozone. The central premiss of Mundell's theory is that
it is the autonomous mechanisms of private capitalist markets,
and not a central state's regional, financial or social policies,
that determine the ideal size of currency areas. According to the
theory, a given geographic area can form a functioning currency
zone only if capital, labour and goods can and will circulate
sufficiently freely within the system in accordance with market
signals (high factor mobility prevails), and if the production
structures within the zone are homogenous enough for business
cycles to occur more or less simultaneously within the system,
and with the same intensity.

The problem, according to the theory, is that demand for
commodities and services fluctuates, with each country or region
having its own production structure, and thus the business cycles
of different countries or regions come into synchronization only
intermittently, if at all. Difficulties arise if people do not change
their place of residence in search of work as employment rates
change in different parts of a currency area, and if capital does
not relocate in response to changes in demand and productivity.
Markets' automatic price stabilization mechanisms only work if
prices and production factors are highly flexible and mobile within
a currency area. If this is not the case, then unemployment levels
may rise in one part of an area while inflation rises in another;
or one part of the currency area may go into recession, while
another experiences a boom. Contradicting Mundell's optimistic

views about the prospects of a single European currency, several economists criticized the project on the grounds that Europe as a whole does not constitute an optimal currency area.[11]

The different structures of production and asymmetry of business cycles were also contentious issues in political debates on the prospect of European monetary union. If the Finnish forestry industry, for instance, experienced a drop in business because of decreased international demand, EMU would bar the Finnish state from increasing competitiveness in the sector through devaluing its currency. Moreover, if the losses in this important sector began to adversely affect the rest of the Finnish economy, the government would be unable to tackle it by adjusting interest rates (unless business cycles happened to synchronize closely with some other parts of Europe, in which case the European Central Bank might possibly act accordingly). In this way, the critics anticipated that with the EMU the autonomy of a country's economic policy would become confined to the domain of fiscal policy, itself limited by the convergence criteria of the EMU.

On the other hand, it was widely expected that the fiscal policies of the member states would over the long term converge, in line with the requirements of the Maastricht Treaty, and that this would create a framework for unification, also through the rational expectations of market actors. The optimal European currency area, in other words, was supposed to come about through adjustments to and convergence with free-market requirements.[12] Countries intent on EMU membership were required to achieve low inflation rates, low public spending deficits and low levels of debt, and convergence of their long-term interest rates with those of German state-issued bonds.[13] A stable and market-friendly framework was meant to guarantee convergence of economic situations.

When the euro crisis deepened during 2010, many critics became convinced that their suspicions about the EMU's international contradictions had finally been proved correct.[14] It really looked to be the case that excessively disparate economies had been cobbled together in a single currency zone, since the member states had clearly divided into two camps: the 'irresponsible economies', which were deep in debt and the solvency of which was beginning to be questioned on bond markets, and the 'responsible economies', which kept their deficits in control and their bond interest rates in reasonably good shape.

However, asymmetrical shocks and non-synchronous business cycles did not trigger the debt crisis; rather, the crisis resulted from the financial shock that simultaneously affected all the euro-economies. The 2008–09 crisis and the consequent credit slump simultaneously hit practically all the economic sectors of the eurozone and all EU countries. Bailout and stimulus packages were needed throughout the Union. The limits on annual public-sector deficits that were set out in the EU's Stability and Growth Pact in 1997 were exceeded in just about every member state. Fiscal policy restraints came into effect only after the debt crisis was already well under way, once states began to return to the obligations they had undertaken under the Maastricht Treaty. They had striven to demonstrate their solvency to credit rating agencies and investors in the financial markets by imposing spending cuts and tax increases.

The developments in Europe proceeded in tandem with the worsening of the debt crisis in the United States. At the heart of the US situation, however, was the current account, especially trade deficit; this was not the case with the EU, since imports and exports between the eurozone and the rest of the world remained more or less in balance. From 2002 to 2004 the EU imported more goods and services than it exported, whereas 2005 to 2007 were deficit years. Trade between the eurozone and the rest of the world showed a surplus between 2002 to 2005, and a slight deficit from 2006 to 2007.

The causes of running into debt
in the crisis countries

The complex knot of the European debt problem can only be undone by carefully retracing the twists and turns that created it. Everyday metaphors and chains of reasoning are not enough to understand the causes of the euro crisis; nor can the theory of optimal currency area help in this regard. The immediate problem is that debt levels in EMU countries have risen. The 2008–09 crisis led to rapid and in some cases dramatic increases in levels of public debt. But in the deficit countries, in particular, longer-term developments have also played a major role. Uncovering the real reasons for the eurozone crisis requires a detailed examination of trade balances and their development, and of financial institutions and mechanisms not only within states and the EU but in the entire world economy.

The global economy is a closed trade system; each and every imported item or service for one country is at the same time an export for another. Within a closed system, it is obviously impossible for all parties to increase their exports and reduce imports simultaneously; and from this it follows that not all parties can have balance-of-trade or balance-of-payments surpluses at the same time. In addition, the basic equation of national bookkeeping entails that, in a deficit country, either the public or the private sector must be in debt (or spending its savings). The development of a country's import and export system has a crucial effect on whatever economic policies are implemented. Low inflation, or even deflation, in terms of wages and prices stimulates export trade, since it improves price competitiveness. But this sort of economic policy also depresses the economy. Expansionist economic policies, by contrast, increase demand and can improve growth, but can easily leave the country with a deficit relative to the rest of the world. This basic connection between trade balances and debt is important in understanding the development of European political economy.

But even though not all states can have balance-of-trade surpluses at the same time, this does not deter them from trying. And when they do, the problem becomes effective aggregate demand. Deficits can help to maintain adequate levels of overall demand, whereas trade surpluses suppress it. The problem is that deficit implies increased levels of debt of the deficit countries, but at the same time the simultaneous push by all states for trade surpluses diminishes the conditions for common growth. The EU struggles with this problem both internally and globally. It is the internal struggle that is especially problematic, since currently and overall there is no significant trade imbalance between the EU and the rest of the world. The internal imbalances, by contrast, have long been mounting.

As Figure 4.2 shows, economic policy in the Netherlands, Austria, Germany and Finland in particular are based on strong export trade and the resulting trade surpluses. Germany is by far the most important: its balance-of-trade surplus has been in the order of 100–200 billion euros annually, which is more than the annual GDP of many small EU countries. Most of this surplus results from trade within the EU.

The downside has been other eurozone countries' deficits. For their own part, the deficit countries of southern Europe have maintained northern European states' surpluses. Because of the common currency, the indebted states are prevented from coping with this imbalance through adjusting exchange rates – that is, through devaluation. But if all eurozone member states were to pursue 'responsible' economic policies all at once, the outcome would be recessionary economic policies throughout the whole of Europe. This sort of myopic and fallacious action within an interconnected EU will inevitably reduce economic growth. This kind of policy, if consistently and rigorously followed, can lead

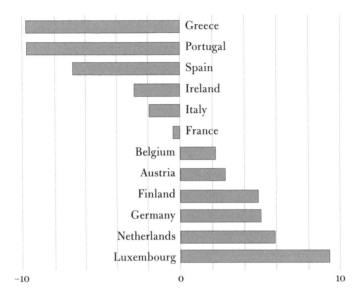

FIGURE 4.2 Average annual current account deficits and surpluses in twelve EMU countries, 2002–09 (%)[15]

to a long-drawn-out epic recession and may even result in a great depression. Demand from outside the EU might relieve matters somewhat, but would not solve the internal problems. Moreover, if the EU were to have a significant and stable balance-of-trade surplus relative to the rest of the world, the problem just described would repeat itself at a global economic level.

The global financial crisis forced the public sector to resort to rescue and resuscitation packages. Both automatic resuscitation and newer, discretionary finance and expenditure packages were paid for with debt. This rapidly increased the public debt levels in Ireland and Spain, for example, and their debt structure began to resemble those of Greece, Italy and Portugal. The financial crisis and its aftermath revealed that the major problem of the European Monetary Union was not, after all, in the currency zone's heterogeneous production structures but in its lack of mechanisms and institutions that could ensure adequate levels of efficient demand in the European political economy as a whole. Practically no attention was paid to the demand side when the EMU system was created. Economic union was embarked upon on the hegemony of supply-side economic theories and recommendations, such as the freedom of movement of capital, the goal of low inflation, lower taxes, and the establishment of an independent central bank.

Various mechanisms are available for balancing import and export trade. Mundell's optimal currency area theory takes for granted the existence of certain previously developed production structures, and conveniently assumes also that adjustments will occur 'naturally' via market mechanisms.[16] Depending on fiscal policy, the result of spontaneous changes in demand is either heightened unemployment in one part of the currency zone and inflation in another part, or increased inflation and unemployment levels in both. If the owners and movers of capital are very sensitive to price signals, and if labour also responds to unemployment and better pay opportunities by readily relocating itself, adjustments to the relative changes in demand will take place through automatic market mechanisms. Mundell's theory focuses attention on rapid and relative changes in market demand for goods and services, and overlooks political, public-sector and state mechanisms.

The eurozone's problem has not been sector-specific changes in demand, but rather persistent trade imbalances and their cumulative effects. One way of guarding against such imbalances would be through coordinated economic policies within the whole eurozone. If each euro country were to have increased wage levels according to the commonly agreed principle 'inflation goal (2 per cent) + the increase in labour productivity', the countries' relative levels of price competitiveness would have remained stable. However, since the creation of the euro only one country,

France, has consistently followed this principle. In Germany, trade unions have long been subjected to intense pressure to prevent them from demanding increases to wage levels, which have consequently remained practically stagnant since the euro came into use. By contrast, Greece, Portugal, Spain and Italy have increased nominal wage levels more than was necessary to keep in line with inflation and increased labour productivity. Although the annual increase to the salary gap between eurozone countries is generally fairly modest, over a number of years it accumulates and becomes quite significant.[17]

Also, the pay gap could have been further reduced even after the damage caused by the euro crisis had already occurred. Wage reductions in the crisis countries would worsen their deflationary spiral. Economist Pekka Sauramo has summarized the problem succinctly: 'If salaries in the crisis countries cannot be lowered sufficiently, their competitiveness can be improved by increasing salaries in the important exporting countries. Of these countries, the most important by far is Germany.'[18] Best of all, wage increases in Germany would increase effective aggregate demand in the whole EMU area. Another way of achieving trade balances would be redistribution mechanisms within the EU, which could be carried out as part of a common fiscal policy or through the European Central Bank. The only significant income transfer systems within the EU at the moment are concerned with agricultural and regional policies, and neither of these is large enough to have much effect on the EMU's macroeconomic developments. Institutional mechanisms for balancing surpluses and deficits, or common area policies, business cycle policies and social policies, could replace the present market-based system and make the single currency more viable.

A common fiscal policy and a de facto federal system could also mean that the eurozone countries would no longer engage in foreign trade with each other. Within a federal system, budget deficits within individual states are possible for many reasons, but they cannot result from their foreign trade imbalances. Many things hinge upon institutional arrangements.

Theories of money and problems of public finance in the EMU system

If we go one step deeper in analysing the eurozone crisis we come to the theory of money. The theory of optimal currency areas is based on the historical assumption that money developed spontaneously out of the needs and interests of traders – and in particular out of their interest in reducing their transaction costs – and that a functioning monetary system must still be based on the same needs and interests. Judged in light of the available anthropological, archaeological and other historical evidence, this theory of money is mistaken.[19] Money did not develop spontaneously from traders' needs to reduce the costs of their transactions, but was instead created by religious-political centres. As early towns developed, so did various divisions of labour, taxation and stores of taxed goods. These stores required the development of writing and simple mathematical operations to administer and maintain them. In this way, the development of abstract value became possible. Through the use and adaptation of metaphors that formed the basis for both mathematics and abstract value, conceptions of justice, law and then money developed.[20]

There are exceptions to every historical trend and there is little certainty about the early history of money, because it developed alongside the development of writing. No historical documents exist from this formative period in the history of money. However, from the available archaeological and other evidence it would generally seem that early state formations first developed numbers, which were used for bookkeeping. Writing later developed, which made it possible to distinguish the set norms and conventions from 'the voice of the gods'. Laws were written on stone tablets for all to see. Law prevailed when, for instance, one person's physical sufferings were compensated with another's goods or prized possessions. In this way an abstract value developed that paved the way for the development of money as a measure of value. For a long while, taxes came to be paid in standard measures of grain, for example. The first coins were minted only around 700–600 BCE, in the eastern kingdoms of the Mediterranean region (present-day Greece and Turkey), where the first alphabets emerged at the same time.

Coins were originally used more for displays of power, religious meaning and other values, and for financing public expenses, especially war, than for private commerce. Over the subsequent course of history, the metamorphoses of religious-political centres and related broader societal changes have regularly meant far-reaching monetary reforms. Through money-based taxation systems, the use of money gradually spread to become increasingly the dominant means of conducting trade. The religious-political authorities encouraged or forced taxpayers to earn money through selling goods and services in the markets.

China was the first empire to use paper money, in the course of a proto-industrial and proto-capitalist revolution of sorts in the eleventh century CE. Over the intervening centuries, Chinese dynasties carried out more or less successful experiments with 'fiat money', meaning money established by decree.[21] Paper money was adopted in Europe only later, as part of the development of the capitalist market economy. States issued papers that could be exchanged for specified quantities of precious metals, and banks created promissory notes in order to facilitate international trade and payment transactions. As means of payment became increasingly abstracted from concrete debt relations, paper money instruments began to be developed for speculative purposes, often with catastrophic consequences.[22]

Almost without exception, all sovereign states over the past three centuries have had their own currencies, irrespective of how disjointed their territories may have been with regard to forces of production and markets. During the nineteenth century and the first part of the twentieth century, the European great powers formed large, even intercontinental, empires, for which money provided a unified basis for taxation. Much of the value of money derives from the fact that it can be used for paying taxes in a set territorial area. This is especially true in the case of fiat money, which in the past took paper formats and now takes electronic formats. Trust in money and in the stability of its value was, and is, dependent on state policies. This trust can be lost, for instance, if a country resorts to inflation as a substitute for collecting tax revenue. On the other hand, through implementing active regional, financial and social policies a state can improve the conditions for a functioning and unified economy. Money, in short, is a political institution.[23]

The EMU is a neoliberal experiment in which, for the first time in history, a monetary union has been created without a state or political community.[24] The EMU has no right to levy taxes or to decide on finance policies or other common centralized decision-making structures. The citizens of the member states are also euro-citizens, but citizenship and its attendant rights and responsibilities are primarily determined within the states themselves. Equally, democratic institutions and wage negotiations, for example, remain national, although many conditions are set and many things decided at EU level.

If a state's accumulated debts are primarily in its own currency, in normal conditions it is largely free to set its own interest rates. If the state can also credibly pay off part of its budget deficit with loans from its central bank, the growth of public debt is not necessarily problematic, at least not when there is insufficient demand. Under what conditions is indebtedness unsustainable?[25]

This is a complicated equation, the solution of which depends not only on the nature of the debt and prevailing institutional arrangements but also on several other considerations, including average growth rates, the level of unemployment of productive capacities in the state in question, and the state's position in the global economic division of labour. The balance-of-trade deficit can be funded in foreign currencies, but because there may be idle currency reserves, or the country could receive investments or other sources of capital, neither would this necessarily lead to indebtedness in other currencies unless the question is one of long-term trade deficits.

A country's having its own central banks does not, of course, guarantee that unsustainable external debts will not develop. The history of the preceding two centuries offers plenty of instances of sovereign debt crises.[26] However, if a country is free to exert at least some control over its own interest rates and currency exchange rates, serious debt problems are less likely to develop, at least within central parts of the global economy (the development of terms of trade favours technologically dynamic economic centres and the production of goods and services with high value-added content). Matters are worse in less developed areas and in recession-hit central areas, where balance-of-trade deficits can easily become chronic. These observations, however, are dependent on the specifics of the prevailing institutional mechanisms, for example on whether prevailing mechanisms exist for managing trade surpluses and deficits on a global scale.

The EMU took away the power of its member states to borrow directly from the central bank. This and some other public spending privileges were prohibited by the Maastricht Treaty.[27] In this way, the eurozone states went from being issuers of currency to mere users of it, which reduced their possibilities of implementing expansive finance policies. In countries that have retained their own currencies, such as the United States, Britain, Japan and

Sweden, the state is at least in principle able to use central bank funding when necessary to give itself more leeway in economically difficult times. Whether a country actually avails itself of this opportunity will depend on the dominant economic theory and ideology, and on the country's previously established institutional arrangements.

Circular reasoning and self-fulfilling prophecies

The key idea of the EMU is to discipline public finances through market mechanisms and to control the supply of money so as to keep inflation as low as possible. If public-sector budgets are not in balance, the state or municipality must take on debt from the private sector, thereby making itself vulnerable to interest rate increases. Even though eurozone countries are still free to borrow on the domestic market, they have no control over interest rates, which are determined in the financial markets. Transnational commercial banks set their own margins for the loans, based on their profit goals and on their assessment of the risk involved in granting the loan. Because the European Central Bank is unwilling to intervene in market developments, for example by recommending specific interest rates for certain eurozone countries, market logic determines the price levels on the bond market.

In his *General Theory*, Keynes makes a distinction between entrepreneurship and speculation.[28] Entrepreneurship is based on estimation of the whole lifespan of the prospective investment. Speculation, by contrast, is above all a question of trying to predict market psychology or market prognoses. Keynes compares speculation to a newspaper beauty contest, in which the aim is not to compare and rank the beauty of the contestants as such but rather to forecast what features the average observer will find beautiful. There are different levels in this sort of competition: at the second level guesses are made as to what the first-level players will decide, and the third-level players guess what the second-level players will decide, and so on. This description fits well also the activities of speculative finance – with the proviso that here the situation is of course more complicated, in that there are very many competitions going on all at once, each with a great many players and levels.

Despite their convoluted nature, the difference stages of the finance game can be reduced to a fairly schematic chain, which tends to generate self-fulfilling predictions. During the euro crisis, the speculation chain usually went as follows:[29]

- Investment banks, for example Goldman Sachs or Deutsche Bank, and various hedge funds buy up credit default swaps – derivatives that function as guarantees against credit risk – in case Spain, Ireland, Greece, Portugal or some other country becomes insolvent. These swaps can be bought even if the investors who buy them have no bonds issued by the countries in question.
- Increased demand for credit default swaps is interpreted as a sign that the economic situation in the country in question is deteriorating.
- Credit rating agencies, such as Moody's or Standard & Poor's, react to the increased demand for bad credit swaps and reduce the creditworthiness rating of the country in question.
- The credit rating agencies' intervention raises the price of the credit default swaps, which makes it possible for speculators to make short-term profits, which increases the demand for swaps still further.
- Banks with bonds issued by a crisis-hit country become alarmed and begin to sell off the bonds. In some cases they are legally obliged to sell bonds if their value drops below a certain level, since retaining them would increase risk of loss to the banks.

- If the crisis countries' bond prices drop significantly in value, it becomes profitable to 'sell them short' – meaning that speculators first borrow the assets from some party and sell them at the going market price. Once the price drops, speculators buy the same assets back and then 'return' them to the lender. Short-selling increases the tendency of assets to depreciate.
- The outcome of all the foregoing stages is that the crisis country finds itself in a situation in which it can renew its loans only by agreeing to exorbitant interest rates, as high as 20 or 30 per cent or even much more (interest rates can climb up to hundreds of per cent). This dramatically worsens its debt situation.

Global financial markets have been instrumental in causing the euro crisis, first through the 2008–09 financial crisis and, second, by transforming the worst-hit countries' potential insolvency problems into an acute debt crisis. Figure 4.2 outlines the self-reinforcing circle of expectations of financial market actors and other decision-makers who follow the efficient market hypothesis. Assuming, for example, that Greece's national debt is around 300 billion euros (which is close to the actual figure), an annual interest rate of 1 per cent would amount to 3 billion euros a year, which can be serviced without undue difficulty. However, interest rates can rise also due to speculative mechanisms, as outlined in Figure 4.3. If Greece were eventually forced to pay interest rates of 25 per cent on all its loans, the annual interest burden would become 75 billion euros – roughly 25 billion more than the country's total budget for 2011. This is clearly way beyond what is even theoretically possible.

Although only part of the loan would eventually become this expensive, repayment costs could easily exceed the state's ability to pay. In small eurozone economies, government budget negotiations can become strained over multi-million-euro sums;

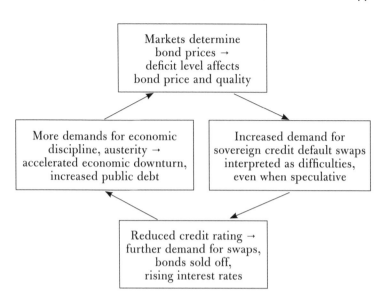

FIGURE 4.3 The public debt interest cycle

tens of billions of euros in additional interest payments would be unsustainable for practically any small or medium-sized country. As such, setting of interest rates is the crucial issue.

All in all, financial market mechanisms can worsen debt problems, and even trigger a debt crisis by themselves. In this way, the global financial system also has structural power over states. The expectations of financial investors determine the conditions by which states must abide in order to keep interest rates low and their credit ratings high. These expectations are themselves shaped by the views of private credit rating agencies, most prominently Moody's, Standard & Poor's and the Fitch Group, as to what constitutes acceptable economic policies and how problems should be handled.[30] If the situation worsens, the International Monetary Fund steps in, along with the heads of state of the

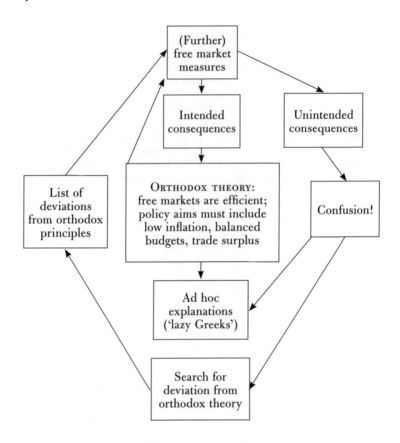

FIGURE 4.4   The circular reasoning of orthodox economic
liberalism[31]

largest industrial countries and the European Commission. In
recent decades, these interpretations have formed the basis of
different variations on the orthodox liberal economic theme.
The idealized model of perfect competitiveness works always
and everywhere as the standard against which reality and the
success and failure of political recommendations and initiatives
are measured.

The doctrine of efficient free markets and sound money comprises a circular chain of reasoning that is used to impose discipline on states and their policymaking. First, orthodox neoclassical economic theory decrees how economic success is possible. States' subservience to these requirements brings unintended consequences, however, which leads to surprise and confusion that time and again manages to appear genuine. To deal with the ensuing puzzle, makeshift explanations are concocted and convenient scapegoats found. Ad hoc explanations make it possible to continue with the same basic framing of problems. The logic of the circular system is such that its main goal becomes sustaining the orthodoxy as it is, rather than revising it, or even replacing it, in light of the unintended consequences of its implementation.[32] There follows a new round of implementing the theory, new problems and crises, renewed confusion, and so on. The circle continues until a crisis or catastrophe develops that is sufficiently momentous to finally motivate collective learning, the first step of which is realization of the counterproductive nature of the economic orthodoxy.

Conclusions

The difficulties facing the European Monetary Union have been primarily caused by the asymmetries in the formation of overall demand in the European political economy as a whole, and also by the institutional arrangements and restrictions that were put in place by the Maastricht Treaty. Global financial markets have intensified these difficulties by first causing the 2008–09 financial crisis, and then by dramatically increasing the costs of debt of the worst-hit countries.

As the difficulties in the early 2010s and the debt crisis continued to spread, the central bank and debt constraints of the Maastricht Treaty have in fact started to be relaxed – which suggests that the Treaty was not built on sustainable foundations in the first place. Under Article 122, the EU member states are prohibited from distributing responsibility for debt among themselves, and Article 123 prohibits the ECB from directly purchasing government bonds and other budget-supporting debt instruments from member states. These stipulations have now been interpreted and stretched so as to make the financial stability mechanisms (see Chapter 5) compatible with Article 122 of the Maastricht Treaty. At the same time, the ECB began buying relatively large amounts of crisis-hit member states' bonds on the market. By the end of 2011 the Bank had already spent around 200 billion euros in this way, and in the process sustained losses of over 30 billion euros.[33] Even if direct ECB funding is not taken into account here (and as much as 40 per cent of the purchases seem to have directly supported eurozone finance ministries), this spending is still clearly contrary to Article 123 of the Maastricht Treaty.

Many commentators believe that the situation had deteriorated to the point that the only hope was for the ECB to issue more money. According to economist Marshall Auerback, however, the ECB leadership is reminiscent of army generals who declare that they are unwilling to resort to armed force, even when all options have run out; some of the generals even become conscientious objectors. This may be morally justified in the context of war, but similar hesitation in the case of a central bank comes necessarily at the expense of a potentially crippling loss of credibility.[34] And yet, how could the ECB be credible? Central banking funding was prohibited already in 1992, by the Maastricht Treaty.

Although the euro crisis is the result of EMU contradictions and inadequacies, the development of European integration – including the EMU as one of its central institutions – has not proceeded solely as a result of its internal dynamics. The EMU was originally proposed also as a measure against the instability of financial markets, especially in foreign exchange. The project of European integration was also intended to consolidate and improve the EU's standing in the global economy; a functioning unified economic community and common market system would increase efficiency and economic growth.

The efforts to increase Europe's well-being and power have been undertaken within a Western and global system of governance, which since the collapse of the original Bretton Woods system (1944–1973) have been founded on transnational economic liberalism. Also the EMU design drew heavily on the ideas of monetarism, supply-side economics and new classical macroeconomics, which came into vogue in the 1970s and 1980s. Although things can be done otherwise within the European Union and new EU institutions can be devised, they are somewhat unlikely to be realized and take real effect, and even less likely to be fully sustainable, without comprehensive global reforms.

5

The trouble with the
EU's official reform proposals

Throughout 2011 and the first half of 2012 the euro crisis deepened further. What could be done about the immediate problems that the 2008–09 financial crash and its aftermath have brought to light? The range of available options is limited: the European Union has no significant taxation, no fiscal policy, budget or regional policy. What may prove fateful for the common currency project is the assumption that no common European fiscal policy is needed, that the markets will balance themselves.

European heads of state and EU institutions have reacted to the crisis by creating emergency aid packages in conjunction with the International Monetary Fund. The leaders of the two organizations have urged cuts in public spending and deflationary economic policies on the crisis countries. The aid packages belong to the same belt-tightening regime that has for decades been thrust on developing countries under the name of 'structural adjustment'. Its results have rarely been good, as I discuss in Chapter 7.

A transition was soon made from the hastily arranged rescue packages to temporary financial stabilization mechanisms, the European Financial Stability Facility (EFSF) and the European

Financial Stabilization Mechanism (EFSM). A permanent version, the European Stability Mechanism (ESM), was planned to come into operation from the beginning of 2013, but due to the continued worsening of the crisis it is coming into use already in 2012 (following constitutional disputes in Germany, which were resolved in September 2012). All these arrangements, in so far as they do or will work as planned, function by reducing the debt service costs of the crisis states.

The required savings led, however, to reduction in effective demand and slower growth (see the discussion of economic theory in Chapter 2). As growth weakens and becomes negative, unemployment levels rise and tax revenue falls. This harms the state's budget situation, and can force it to take on additional debt to cope. When a sufficient number of EU states decide to cut public spending at the same time, it has a marked negative impact on the level of effective aggregate demand within the whole of the EU. Because the EU is a major part of the global economy, its economic situation has also global effects. But even a worsening of the crisis does not seem to be enough to convince eurozone and EU leaders that austerity measures have a tendency to be self-defeating – not to speak of their impact on social and democratic objectives.

Throughout 2011, further steps were taken towards tighter austerity measures and budgetary discipline in the eurozone countries. The package of six legislative initiatives – the so-called six-pack – towards this end came into force in December 2011. The Treaty on Stability, Coordination and Governance in the Economic and Monetary Union (the Fiscal Compact in short), signed by twenty-five European Union member states on 2 March 2012, is so far the most far-reaching proposal for solving the euro crisis by increasing the level of budgetary discipline within the eurozone. The Compact gives rise to legal norms which override EU member states' own constitutions, and which cannot be changed by democratic means. The main guiding assumption of the Fiscal Compact is that increased fiscal discipline will reassure banks and financial markets that the situation is under control, and that lenders and investors can expect stable conditions in the future.

In contrast to this orthodox focus on fiscal discipline for the member states, the EU bodies have realized that the 2008–09 financial crisis significantly increased the amount of public debt. According to figures released by the European Commission in September 2011, during the crisis and immediately afterwards the EU member states made commitments to support the financial sector to the tune of 4.6 trillion euros – 39 per cent of the region's combined gross domestic product.[1] Because of the global financial crisis, a significant proportion of private debt was in effect transformed into public debt. Awareness of this has shaped the EU agenda somewhat. New regulation and taxation of financial activities have become higher priorities on the EU's official agenda. Particular urgency has been attached to the implementation of a financial transaction tax, and to prohibiting short-selling and sovereign default credit swaps.

EU leaders have pushed the financial transaction tax onto the agenda of the Group of 20; a number of countries calling for new sources for financing development have for many years advocated financial transaction taxes and other global taxes. At the G20 summit in Cannes in November 2011, however, several countries joined with the United States in opposing the idea.[2] This leaves the Commission's September 2011 proposed new EU directive as the most momentous initiative currently on the table.[3] The Commission maintains that such a tax is necessary both from an economic perspective and in the interests of fairness. In practice, it would also be a move towards fiscal federalism: the Commission aims for a Europe-wide tax that would generate revenue for the Union's common budget.

Faltering though they may be, both the ESM and the financial transaction tax are steps towards a federation of European states, albeit in different ways. The proposed common European bond system would be another step in the same direction: the member states would thereby abandon their individual and separate identities on global financial markets. Under this system, the eurozone states' interest rates for loans would be bound together, making their economic fates ever more deeply interconnected. The member states with budget surpluses (which still receive cheap loans) have opposed the plan, often vehemently, but if the crisis persists and especially if it worsens they may come to see no alternative to it. In the view of the Commission, a eurobond system, strict budgetary discipline, and transfer of budgetary powers to EU bodies would be prerequisites for the eurobond system.

The European Stability Mechanism

The European Financial Stability Facility was created in December 2010. The eurozone countries gave a total of 440 billion euros in loan guarantees to the fund, to which the IMF and various other leverage mechanisms were later added. The goal has been to expand the capacity of the crisis fund to as much as 1 trillion euros.[4] The EFSF is intended as only a temporary arrangement, to be replaced (or complemented) by the more permanent ESM. A problem for both arrangements, however, is Article 125 of the Lisbon Agreement, which prohibits sharing the debt burden. The Commission considers the EFSF to be merely a lending arrangement, but the ESM goes further.

In December 2010 the European Council agreed on a simple two-line addition to the wording of the EU Constitution that could be passed without referenda in any of the member countries.

> The Member States whose currency is the euro may establish
> a stability mechanism to be activated if [doing so becomes]
> indispensable to safeguard[ing] the stability of the euro area as
> a whole. The granting of any required financial assistance under
> the mechanism will be made subject to strict conditionality.[5]

The strict conditions mentioned in the amendment to the Constitution follow the standard neoliberal structural adjustment formula. The stability mechanism itself must be established by international legal treaty, and will come into effect when the countries that have the ratified it have paid at least 90 per cent of the total capital required. Because of the 90 per cent minimum, non-cooperation of a small eurozone member such as Finland or Austria would not by itself be able to prevent the establishment of the mechanism.

Amending international treaties is even more difficult than making constitutional amendments. With the aid of international contractual arrangements, certain substantial rules, norms and principles can be set in place more or less permanently. Once implemented they are hard to modify, even when they begin to operate in ways that defeat their own original purpose or become harmful or undesirable for some other reason. Political scientist Stephen Gill has labelled this aspect of the European Union and global governance 'neoconstitutionalism' and 'disciplinary neoliberal constitutionalism'.[6]

According to the original plan, the base capital of the European Stability mechanism is 80 billion euros, and is intended to create a loan capacity of around half a trillion euros.[7] Half of the capital will be paid in the initial start-up stage of the ESM, with the remainder to be paid in instalments within the subsequent three-year period. If Europe's debt situation deteriorates even further, the ESM can have serious effects also on the economies of the relatively buoyant eurozone economies. According to Article 9 of the 2012 version of the ESM Treaty, 'the Board of Governors may call in authorised unpaid capital at any time and set an appropriate period of time for its payment by the ESM Members'. Moreover, by simple majority decision it may also call in authorized unpaid capital to restore its balances. If the power of the ESM to ask for more funds from the member states is taken into use quickly, and if the loans taken by the member states to respond to these calls raise the country's interest rates or lead to a lower credit rating, a member country with relatively low levels of debt may also be drawn into financial dire straits of its own.

For Europe as a whole, a united effort to spend hundreds of billions or even several trillion euros on debt payments and bank bailouts is a project that could by itself prolong and worsen the crisis. The more these resources actually have to be used, the worse also the financial situation of the guarantor states will become. This may be seen in their credit ratings, for one thing. If the ESM lending capacity is increased, implying further capital payments by the member states, the likely result is further extensive austerity measures and cutbacks throughout Europe. The ESM is forcing Europe onto the path of deflationary economic policies, which will lead to bleaker prospects for economic growth. This will hardly help in finding a solution to the financial crisis.

But, imposing as the amounts of money contained in the temporary mechanisms and the ESM are, and despite the huge burden placed on the countries financing them, the overall sums are still only a fraction of the crisis countries' total debt. For example, the public debt in Italy alone is in the region of 2 trillion (2,000 billion) euros. In addition, a consensual decision-making mechanism, with the largest decisions being made jointly among eurozone finance ministers, and tough conditions for sustainability could mean that the ESM would not in fact be able to prevent member states from becoming insolvent. It might not be able to prevent this even if the amounts required could actually be covered by the mechanism's funds.

So the ESM is not an alternative to debt arbitration, or to the ad hoc processes of debt restructuring that are resorted to in the absence of an institutionalized debt arbitration mechanism. The stability mechanism may, however, defer the inevitable for so long that the eventual costs of insolvency and debt restructuring become greater for all parties than they would have been if renegotiations about the fair amount and quality of debt had been begun immediately. The outcome of the self-inflicted economic crisis may be at least partial fragmentation of the euro system, with one or several countries returning to national currencies.

The ESM and IMF coordinate their responses. The voting rules of the ESM are more in line with the IMF practice of one dollar, one vote than with the relatively more democratic procedures of the EU's own institutions.[8] The qualified majority decisions of the ESM can be used to authorize the European Commission to negotiate with the recipient countries on a structural adjustment programme, and to choose the leadership of the ESM itself. Otherwise put, the IMF and the Commission set up and implement the programmes of austerity and privatization that are prescribed for the crisis countries. Within the limits of the ESM's powers to set interest rates, its leadership can decide by simple majority whether or not to pay the outstanding portions of payments to recipient states.

The private sector participates in accordance with IMF practices. The affected countries have no option but to agree to contractual arrangements that will keep bankers and investors committed to the financing arrangements. So banks and funds are in practice given the power to determine the economic and social policy of the crisis countries. Moreover, the current plan will give the EU's permanent stability mechanism, the IMF and the European Commission budgetary control over and above the member states. In spite of this, the ESM draft agreement leaves the mechanism free of all possible legal responsibility, not to mention political responsibility:

> The ESM, its property, funding and assets, wherever located and by whomsoever held, shall enjoy immunity from every form of judicial process except to the extent that the ESM expressly waives its immunity for the purpose of any proceedings or by the terms of any contract, including the documentation of the funding instruments ... The property, funding and assets of the ESM shall, wherever located and by whomsoever held, be immune from search, requisition, confiscation, expropriation or any other form of seizure, taking or foreclosure by executive, judicial, administrative or legislative action.[9]

It is even separately specified that all those individuals who are centrally connected to the ESM are exempt from all possible legal responsibility concerning their activities relating to the mechanism.[10] There is no precise mention of political responsibility or answerability in the treaty. Given this state of affairs, the ESM can only further deepen Europe's democratic deficit.

Regulating financial markets: the financial transaction tax

The European Commission released its proposals for a financial transaction tax on 28 September 2011.[11] According to the Commission, the present proposal is a first step:

- to ensure that financial institutions make a fair contribution in covering the costs of the recent crisis and to ensure a level playing field with other sectors from a taxation point of view;
- to create appropriate disincentives for transactions that do not enhance the efficiency of financial markets, thereby complementing regulatory measures aimed at avoiding future crises.

As a by-product the tax could enhance the powers of the Commission over the member states in so far as the revenues go to the EU budget. The proposal was to implement the FTT in the EU as a whole. However, as the UK and some other EU members have continued to reject the FTT, the eurozone or a part of it is taking the lead as an area of enhanced cooperation. This is a procedure whereby at last nine member states can agree on something similar to an intra-European coalition of the willing, as it has been demonstrated for the Schengen Agreement on migration. In June 2012, it was agreed that since the proposal for a financial transaction tax will not be adopted by the Council within a reasonable period, several Member States will launch a request for enhanced cooperation in this area. The proposal was approved by the Council in January 2013.[12]

The tax base would be broad, but excludes spot trade on currencies and issuing of bonds and shares. For these reasons, the tax envisioned by the Commission is not the famous currency transaction tax proposed by James Tobin; nor does it include it.[13] But the Commission's tax would apply to currency derivatives markets. The ESM's proposed tax rate on shares and bonds is 0.1 per cent, and 0.01 per cent on derivatives. The estimates on tax revenue are very tentative, since the likely effects of the tax on trade are unknown. According to the Commission the tax will produce at least 50 billion euros in annual revenue, and possibly far more.

The EU's own budget for 2011 was 127 billion euros, only a fraction of the sum of its member states' budgets. The largest members have annual budgets approaching 1 trillion euros. Under the Commission's proposal the revenue collected from the financial transaction tax would go to the EU budget, which may also mean decreases in member-state contributions to that budget. The details of the enhanced area of cooperation proposal remain to be seen, but in any case this independent source of

FIGURE 5.1 The more likely the introduction of some form of financial transaction tax has become, the louder the finance industry in London and throughout the world has been in opposing it.

funds would strengthen the position of the EU, and especially that of the European Commission, relative to the member states. How the tax revenue is used will undoubtedly be contentious, since many countries are expecting at least a share – if not all – of it for their own budgets either directly or through reduced membership fees.

The Commission's proposal is an intriguing move in many senses. For years the Commission has opposed proposals by civil society organizations and national parliaments for a currency transaction tax, on the grounds that its implementation would be impossible or at best highly impractical. Now it is pushing through an even more comprehensive, and to some extent even less administrable, financial transaction tax as a fair and practical way of reining in financial markets. The aim is to make the financial sector shoulder its share of the costs of the 2008–09 crisis. At the same time, the Commission has distanced itself from the so-called efficient markets hypothesis, on which the neoliberal economic policies of the IMF, for example, and the EU itself have been based. The Commission is suddenly keen to recognize many 'market disturbances' and 'systematic risks' in financial markets.[14]

According to the Commission, its tax proposal is only one step. The large-scale and technically complex programme of financial market reforms is already under way, and will include at least partial prohibition of speculation on sovereign credit default swaps and of what is termed 'naked' short-selling.[15] Reclaiming the crisis funds solely through financial transaction taxes would be slow, however: at an annual rate of 50 billion euros in tax revenue, it would take over ninety years to reclaim the 4.6 trillion euros committed to handling the crisis. Additional taxes are being considered, such as a tax on financial activities and a value-added tax – which financial actors so far do not have to pay.

Although the Commission has now put some distance between itself and the efficient markets hypothesis, the proposal remains true to the free-market ideal in several respects. One reason given for excluding regular currency trading from the tax base is that in the Commission's view taxing currency trading would violate the central market freedoms guaranteed by the Treaty of the European Union. The unconstrained movement of trans-national capital is addressed by Article 63 of the Treaty on the Functioning of the European Union. What do the constraints on capital mobility mentioned in this article actually mean – would a currency transaction tax really be an obstacle to mobility? On the Commission's interpretation, it certainly would if one trading party were a non-eurozone EU state. All other cases would be left to the discretion of the European Council, which if it saw fit could apply Article 64(3).[16]

The Commission thus seems to remain wedded to the notion that the EU is essentially a free-market project. Further evidence of this is that the tax proposal in effect recommends that derivatives markets be treated with kid gloves. And the proposal of a derivatives tax that is only one-tenth of the tax on spot agreements is a sign that, even after the 2008–09 global crisis, the Commission believes that speculative financial instruments can also be useful for ensuring efficiency and controlling risk. Markets can fail and thus create risks, but properly regulated free financial markets work well.

The Commission's proposal is different from any variation of the Robin Hood tax proposed by civil society movements, according to which the profits would be directed to eradicating poverty, to development, and used more generally for purposes of the global common good. The Commission's proposal is instead more of a step towards European fiscal federalism. The EU and its member states have nonetheless propounded a global financial transaction tax, especially at G20 summits. If the EU's global initiatives came about, each country would retain the tax revenue it collected (the EU itself would count as a single country under this scheme). Would this plan require an international treaty, or would informal mutual agreement be enough? If the latter, then the tax would most likely become only a temporary mechanism that could easily be abandoned or opted out of. This would fall short of any scheme for a global tax proper.

The Commission's proposal is also problematic from a democratic perspective. The tax mechanism would be at least partly independent of the EU member states, and as such would lack democratic justification. It is worth remembering, however, that the demand 'No taxation without representation!' marked the beginning of the North American Revolution, and taxation was a concern for the instigators of the French Revolution also. The present-day European context is entirely different, of course. The financial transaction tax would affect the widely despised financial sector, and the member states and their citizens are

represented at EU level. But the chains of responsibility and
accountability connecting EU citizens to their representatives in
the European Parliament and Council are in the eyes of many so
convoluted and indirect that they have no practical meaning. This
is one reason why the EU has had insurmountable problems in
justifying its development. Without adequate democratic practices
and mechanisms, common taxes and a common budget could
saddle the EU with a legitimation crisis, especially in conditions
of self-inflicted economic woes.

Eurobonds and budgetary discipline

On 22 November 2011 the European Commission published its
proposal for a system of common bonds.[17] According to this plan,
eurozone governments will issue bonds collectively to raise money.
The Commission believes issuing joint eurobonds that would
replace national issuance by eurozone members could ease market
fears about sovereign debt in the region and bring down yields for
those countries under most pressure. The aim of this system is to
enhance financial integration among the member states and at the
same time impose tighter budgetary discipline. According to the
proposal, the government of each member country would present
its budget plans to the Commission for approval before they were
discussed at national parliamentary level. The Commission could
make suggestions and would have the power to demand changes
to the proposed budgets if they were found to be out of line with
EU rules and principles. Not only that, but the eurozone countries
would also be subjected to even more rigorous, year-round inspec-
tions and supervision by the Commission. These checks would
be carried out by new 'fiscal councils', and the budgets should be
based on independently conducted prognoses of each country's
business cycles and growth prospects. If the Commission gets its
way, this process will be constitutionalized:

The introduction of national fiscal rules that are consistent with the budgetary objectives set at Union level should be a crucial element to ensure the respect of the Stability and Growth Pact provisions. In particular, Member States should put in place structural balanced budget rules which transpose into national legislation the main principles of the Union fiscal framework. This transposition should be effective through binding rules preferably of a constitutional nature so as to demonstrate the strongest commitment of national authorities in relation to the Stability and Growth Pact.[18]

It is evident from the proposal that the Commission does not consider budgets to have any bearing on democracy, or vice versa; the word is not mentioned in these texts even once, in any form. In the Commission's statements it is rightly acknowledged that the effect of one euro country's budget can easily spread to other eurozone countries. But the problem is not approached as a question of collective democratic will, but as a task that requires either a technocratic solution or market-based discipline and supervision. The goals have already been set: (i) budgets that are as balanced as possible, largely irrespective of conditions; and (ii) competitiveness on world markets.

The aim of the Commission is thus to further the constitution-alization of disciplinary neoliberalism. Each eurozone country must pursue deflationary policies in order to achieve or maintain balance-of-trade surpluses. This pursuit, furthermore, must be founded on the German model of strict wage discipline. The outcome of this vision for the whole of Europe will be chronically deficient aggregate demand, with knock-on effects for the rest of the world economy.

The other facet of the Commission's proposal concerns common bonds.[19] Making public debt common would guarantee uniform costs of debt in the whole eurozone. In so far as common bonds would increase liquidity, they would also reduce the debt costs of all the member countries. The point of comparison here is the United States, which can borrow at lower interest rates than European states. 'Stability bonds' could be issued by either a new, common operator or national governments, but in a coordinated and disciplined way. The guideline is that the more the risks and costs of public debt are shared, the greater the discipline that must be imposed on economic policy.

The Commission also presents 'political stability and predictability' as a condition for successful stability bonds.[20] This can be taken to mean that, irrespective of electoral results, all policies that could affect the preconditions for growth – as these are understood by the Commission – should be standardized throughout the European Union. The Commission therefore seems to be propounding a sort of one-party democracy: that different outlooks on economic policy are no longer allowed, except at the level of rhetoric (and rhetoric can have harmful effects, which can be seen in the form of negative reactions by the financial markets). The plan offers three options for the establishment of eurobonds:

1. In the Commission's view, the best solution would be the most far-reaching change possible: all the sovereign bonds of the eurozone states would be replaced with common eurobonds, with countries' separate bond systems being abolished entirely. This option would bring the biggest increase to debt market liquidity, and would strengthen the euro as a global currency. Bringing a common bond system into operation would, at the very least, require coordination of member states' borrowing. For the Commission, however, a still better option would be to establish a common debt mechanism for the eurozone. Under this system the member states would in effect act as guarantors for each other's debts, and so to be possible this would first require significant amendments to the EU Constitution. The Commission recognizes that such

amendments would take years, despite the urgent need for a solution to the ongoing crisis.

2. A somewhat more moderate option would be to replace sovereign state bonds with eurobonds, but only up to a certain point. If a state were to exceed an agreed level of debt, it would have to mobilize its own bonds. The Commission's premiss is that the lower the level of common debt, the more certain it is that the markets will impose discipline on states and their economic policies. But a low level of common debt increases the credit risk: the higher the level of common 'stability bonds', the lower the credit risk remains, but this creates a correspondingly greater incentive for some states to attempt to free-ride at others' expense. Because states would assume responsibility for each other's debt, this option would also require amendments to the Treaty of the European Union. Its implementation would thus take years, and would be no help in an acute crisis.

3. The fastest and easiest option would be to replace only some sovereign bonds with eurobonds, and for eurozone states to agree to only partly guarantee eurobonds. In other words, the member states would retain at least formal primary responsibility for their own share of the common debt. (The meaning of 'primary responsibility' is of course open to interpretation, and would be a crucial focus of negotiations.) In any case, in the Commission's view this option would not require amendments to the EU Constitution, and so it could be a relatively quick solution to the ongoing debt crisis. However, the 'stability bonds' in this model would be more fragile than in the others, and there is reason to suspect that financial markets might not have sufficient faith in them. In response to this fear, the Commission has proposed that the stability bonds to be used in this option would be supported with guarantees that could include cash, gold reserves and the earmarking of some taxes for debt repayments.

The Commission has proposed that these options be implemented in reverse order to the one just given (i.e. 3, 2, 1), or, alternatively, that only the third and first options be implemented, in that order. In the Commission's view, deeper European integration is needed in addition to a swift solution to the present crisis. Increased budgetary discipline for the member states was already introduced in March 2011 with the addition of extra implementation mechanisms to the stability and growth pact. Further steps in the same direction are being taken with the introduction of the European Stability Mechanism. But the Commission remains adamant that this is still not enough: stability bonds will increase the possibility of moral hazard, and so additional measures are needed to bring the euro states under control. To this end, it is being proposed that the entire planning and finalization of each state's budget must be subjected to scrutiny and supervision at EU level. It may be that the ESM and the proposed new system will be combined, but they could also be maintained as separate but mutually complementary systems. The same ideas of financial discipline are being established through several different, overlapping new institutional arrangements.

Additionally, a new 'Fiscal Compact' for stability, coordination and economic administration was drafted in early 2012, and was ratified by twenty-five European Union member states on 2 March 2012.[21] This includes the same disciplinary and control mechanisms as the strictest eurobond proposals. The Fiscal Compact resembles in some respects the sort of legislation used in states of exception and states of emergency. The assumption behind the Compact is that member states can decide their own budgets in accordance with standard parliamentary principles, so long as the maximum business-cycle-adjusted, deficit limit of 0.5 per cent of GDP is not exceeded. But when state deficits come close to or exceed that threshold, a state of exception will enter into effect, and the European Commission is then automatically empowered to take control of the indebted state's budget.

The fundamental idea is the same in all three proposals: in order to gain and maintain the confidence of the markets, stability and growth are sought from economic disciplinary mechanisms that are applied to states. The right of national parliaments and governments to devise their own budgets becomes conditional. This is not a trivial aspect of all these proposals: democratic politics concerns not only legislation – which typically has budgetary effects – but also budgets themselves. Budgetary control is now being transferred into the hands of technocratic EU bodies, in the name of 'calming the markets' and promoting European competitiveness.

What does competitiveness mean, then? According to the strategy adopted in Lisbon in 2000, for instance, the promotion of competitiveness in the EU is understood to mean liberalization of markets (including privatization and outsourcing), reduction of economic 'constraints', encouragement of entrepreneurship and innovation (primarily by strengthening the intellectual property rights and copyright protections for large companies), and easier access to funding through improved capital mobility. The Europe 2020 strategy adopted in 2010 contains proposals for job creation, education and transition to a low-carbon economy, but these have not supplanted the earlier free-market doctrines in any way. So under this strategy, job creation and ecological sensitivity are objectives that can be best achieved through growth driven by competitiveness on world markets. To the extent that the Commission's budgetary powers are taken to involve concern for competitiveness, the Fiscal Compact becomes a mechanism whereby even the minutest details of national budgets can be, at least in principle, streamlined to accord with free-market doctrines.

Assessing the proposals

Both the temporary financial stability mechanisms and the more permanent mechanism will bring increased budgetary discipline, irrespective of what other instruments and mechanisms may also be brought into use. The financial transaction tax and regulation of financial markets have yet to be implemented, as has the eurobond system. The implementation of all these depends on many things, and the EU's decision-making procedures can be fairly described as labyrinthine. The system contains many different actors with competing interests and visions, and unexpected twists and turns in EU negotiations and finalization processes are common. The United Kingdom, for one, is opposed to a financial transaction tax and to financial market regulation, and thus they can only be realized within the eurozone or part of it rather than throughout the EU. But the eurozone countries are also divided on many issues: for instance, Germany is forcefully opposed to eurobonds, and other surplus countries have followed this lead. Attempts have been made to bring the eurobond opponents on board by adding even further-reaching budgetary disciplinary measures to the proposals.

The question of 'investor responsibility' has also become part of the EU's multifaceted negotiation games.[22] There is no requirement of investor responsibility in the temporary stabilization mechanisms, but it was planned for the European Stability Mechanism. However, the objections that were made to this proposal reveal a lot about where the real power lies when it comes to determining EU policy. Finland, Germany and the Netherlands wanted a specific reference to investor responsibility for the private sector in the text of the treaty, or, failing that, in its preamble.[23] But the demand was dropped due to the fears of the majority of eurozone states: 'The concern is that forcing the private sector to take losses if a country needs to restructure its debt is undermining market confidence in eurozone sovereign bonds. If clauses on private sector involvement are removed, most [eurozone] countries argue, market sentiment might improve.'[24] Because the debt-ridden eurozone countries are afraid of 'upsetting the markets', they favoured abandoning the requirement of investor responsibility. Germany consented to abandon its demands for private investor responsibility on the condition that essential elements of member states' budgets be put beyond the reach of democratic control. One party to the negotiations wants to increase the moral hazard on financial markets, another wants to suppress democracy. It is striking that both demands are likely to be realized, unless Europe's common economic and monetary union caves in first.

Increased moral hazard could also cancel out the stabilizing potentially created by the financial re-regulation and transaction tax. The combined effect depends on the details of the reforms, and on external contingencies that are impossible to forecast with any accuracy. In any case, the official reform proposals on the EU agenda are problematic for two reasons. First, from the perspective of economic theory their overall effect is conflicting at best. On the positive side, the crisis countries' interest rates are being brought down, and some stability is created through the regulatory reforms. Second, and on the negative side, economies are being recessed and would be subjected to the discipline of financial markets, involving continuing speculation and moral hazard. In short, the eurozone states are simultaneously adhering to both sides of the dichotomy:

control of interest rates on public debt ↔
tendencies towards further economic recession or even depression

stabilization through transaction tax and regulatory reform ↔
deepening dependency on finance and financial system,
maintenance of speculation and moral hazard

The prevailing plans and proposals pay no heed to the paradoxes of the economy, nor do they enable overall demand to be adequately managed on either a European or a global scale. They are powerless against the debt problem, against the root causes of financialization and its effects, and against world economic disparities. To top it all, not only are the reform proposals woefully slow to implement but there are also tensions among them. It may well be that they will not be adopted in time or, because of their inherent contradictions, are not enough to prevent the collapse of the euro.

Economic theory is important, but it is far from being the only thing that must be considered. Each and every proposal on the EU agenda poses deep problems for legitimacy and democracy. The ESM alone removes some budgetary powers from the national parliaments and transfers them to the EU's technocracy, which is neither politically nor legally answerable for its activities: 'The Commission will have the opportunity, in full respect of the prerogatives of national parliaments, to be consulted on the precise fiscal rule before its adoption so as to ensure it is compatible with, and supportive of, the EU rules.'[25]

A financial transaction tax could be the first EU tax. The Union would receive the right of taxation, without well-defined mechanisms of democratic control and accountability. The furthest-reaching proposals, however, are the supervisory, oversight and disciplinary mechanisms that have been attached to the Fiscal Compact and to the proposals for common European bonds. From the Commission's point of view, budgetary powers do not pertain to democracy.

The EU bond proposal contains a passage that restricts the scope for democratic politics to a minimum. If 'political stability and predictability' are conditions for stability bonds, then economic policy in all the member countries should from now on always be the same regardless of election results, at least in regard to the size and sustainability of national budgets and the assumptions on which their estimated future values are based. The same holds at least potentially for all the conditions that relate in one way or another to competitiveness and macroeconomic development. The Commission is in effect imposing one-party rule on member states, without so much as a mention of democracy.

6

European futures

The problems of the European Monetary Union came to light and worsened right after the 2008–09 crisis, and partly as a direct consequence of it. As with the global financial crisis, the euro crisis took many by surprise. Typical of crises and turning points is that they seem to increase unpredictability and chaos.[1] The future may appear very uncertain in the midst of a crisis, as in the eye of a hurricane.[2]

Hurricanes can be forecast, however. They are neither un-caused nor random, and the general conditions under which they occur are now precisely known. They require very high humidity, ocean surface temperatures of at least 26.5°C, and a distance from the equator of at least 500 kilometres. The total number of hurricanes that occur in the world's different maritime zones each year is roughly eighty: the energy in hurricanes always comes from the sun, and there is a stable limit to the amount of solar energy available to create hurricanes in summer seasons in different regions. In recent years human activity has begun to contribute to the incidence of hurricanes, and these effects too can be forecast with reasonable accuracy. Because ocean temperatures depend on the strength of the mechanisms that sustain and reinforce the greenhouse effect, heightened emissions of CO_2 and other greenhouse gases increase the likelihood of hurricanes.

World economic hurricanes can also be anticipated. Here the question is not one of natural phenomena, since financial and debt crises are human creations. Knowledge about financial market practices, the underlying rules and principles on which those practices are based, and their characteristic effects make it possible to anticipate the future, including crises and turning points.[3] Knowing the general pattern does not mean, however, that it is easy, or even possible, to predict the precise timing and location of any particular hurricane or financial crisis. In the case of the latter, this is true not least because many people try to react to the same information in order to reap profits. The more accurate and precise are the forecasts (or predictions) demanded, the more uncertain and chaotic the process appears. The level of chaos varies. The range of possibilities provided at historical nodes and turning points is greater than at normal times, when business-as-usual prevails and forecasts can be more easily extrapolated from the immediate past.[4]

The central distinction between natural and social storms is that the enabling conditions for the latter are historical and institutional. People can modify these conditions, even when they are not the original architects of the systems in question: 'Men make their own history, but they do not make it just as they please; they do not make it under circumstances chosen by themselves, but under circumstances directly encountered, given and transmitted from the past.'[5] Both institutions and history can be shaped through conscious moral and political action, but transformative possibilities are conditioned too.

Actions have unintended consequences. The essential point is that although actors always know what they are doing under some description, they do not always know the real effects of (the outcomes of) their actions. The central goal of future studies is to enable the rational anticipation of the possible and likely effects of current practices and choices. This applies also to the present euro crisis and to the future of the European Union more generally. The question is not primarily one of precise prediction, even though some possibilities are likelier than others. Future studies also involve the moral and ethico-political evaluation of different choices and scenarios. Good future studies enable well-founded and sensible participation in the making of world history.

Critics have consistently argued that the financialized world economy has a tendency to develop crises. Sector by sector and incrementally, instability and volatility have jumped to a higher level since global finance returned to the centre of the world economy. Over the course of the last three decades or so, the world has seen around three hundred significant financial crises. There is also evidence that, through the deepening processes of financialization, price fluctuations on various markets have become more frequent, and gradually larger and more serious.[6] The mechanisms of debt, bubbles and collapses are well known (see Chapter 3). Post-Keynesian economists who have followed Hyman Minsky have theorized the connections between the pursuit of profit through speculation, debt and crises. And investors such as George Soros have learned how to use this information to their own benefit.[7] It is not enough to have evidence and theories that are adequate to explaining it, however.

The difficulty is that different interpretations of how economic mechanisms operate are contested. There are various reasons for why particular theories are endorsed: many prevailing economic models and theories are based on the sort of wishful thinking that could never be true. But still officials and politicians believe them and act in accordance with them. For instance, if one assumes that if all investors know absolutely everything about the future, and that they can also calculate all the possible costs and profits of all the transactions that could ever be made, from here to eternity, it is relatively easy to derive a theorem according to which 'perfectly competitive' markets operate efficiently in the technical, Pareto-optimal sense,[8] and also justly, albeit only in accordance with one narrow conception of justice that is sympathetic to particular interests.[9] If nobody can possibly miscalculate at any point, and if the markets as a whole are nothing more than the sum of their parts (that is, than the sum of the decisions of omniscient and computationally rational investors), and if many other unrealistic assumptions are also made, it can be materially shown that stable equilibrium of the markets is necessarily guaranteed. Some of the assumptions can of course be relaxed to a certain extent, one at a time, and consequently a somewhat more complicated picture can be drawn in various technical-mathematical models, but the basic story of mainstream neoclassical economics tends to remain the same: competitive markets are the best guarantee of stability, efficiency and justice.

If future predictions are based on illusory premises, economic hurricanes will inevitably come as a surprise. All abstract theories are imaginary in the sense that they are constructed upon metaphors, abstractions and idealizations. False assumptions and outright delusions are problematic, however, and ignorance can also be ideological. In mystifying reality from a certain perspective, theories have a tendency to support particular interests. An example is the hypothesis of efficient and just markets that supports the maximum freedom of action for entrepreneurs, investors and capitalists. This hypothesis justifies the right of these groups, operating under conditions of asymmetric power relations, to the income that they manage to organize for themselves through (i) struggles between different hierarchical levels of organizations, and (ii) struggles for the division of income between capital and labour. The hypothesis of efficient and just markets also supports the subjection of other activities to the control of 'free' markets,

and to their being shaped by the dominant operating principles
of the companies involved. As a rule, those whose own interests
are tied up in these kinds of ideologies try to hold on to their
world-views to the very last.

In this chapter I first distinguish various expectations concerning the future of the EMU in light of different economic
theories and theories of legitimation. Even a simple four-square
model helps in understanding why many politicians, researchers
and citizens have expected stable and increasingly prosperous
developments in the eurozone, whereas others have been able to
foresee difficulties, crises even. The distinctions made also help in
developing scenarios about possible and likely futures. What kind
of EU will take shape after its crisis and (likely) partial fragmentation? According to the first scenario, the neoliberal European
project will continue and deepen; in the second scenario, the
EU will develop into a social-democratic federation of states
and a world power; but in the third scenario the EU will pursue
transformations of global governance and promote democratic
and social goals, understanding itself as part of a much wider
dynamic whole.

What grounds expectations about the EMU's future?

Our expectations about the future are shaped and determined not
only by sheer thoughtlessness and a host of forms of fallacious
thinking, but also by theoretical assumptions (see Table 6.1).[10]
Crucial to the EU's future are economic theories and theories
of legitimation ('legitimation' meaning moral, legal and political
acceptability). Economic theories can be roughly divided into
two groups: (i) liberal economic theories, which rest on microeconomic models of equilibrium and on hypotheses of efficient
markets based on neoclassical macroeconomic doctrines; (ii)
post-Keynesian and Kaleckian theories, according to which the

TABLE 6.1   Prognoses for the EU

	Legitimation theory: Schumpeter	Legitimation theory: Habermas
Neoliberal economic theory	(A) The Maastricht Treaty is firmly grounded, the EMU is legitimate and functional	(B) The EMU works, but its legitimacy is unstable
Post-Keynesian economic theory	(C) The Maastricht Treaty is unstably founded: the EMU will strangle Europe economically, and is prone to crisis	(D) The Maastricht Treaty is unjustified, and economic crises will eventually destroy its legitimacy

capitalist market economy is in many ways unstable, including in such ways that processes of uneven growth and inequality have self-reinforcing tendencies.

Theories of legitimation can also be roughly separated into two groups. On one side are those according to which efficient production of goods and services, protection of private owner-ship, and the freedom to choose on the market are sufficient for acceptability and political justification, provided liberal human rights are guaranteed and political leaders can be periodically chosen in elections. These economistic and minimalist concep-tions of legitimation are often connected with the economist Joseph Schumpeter. On the other side are theories of legitimation according to which the normative justification of political rule, and in the longer term also factual acceptability, require ethico-political meanings that are significant to us, human development, social justice, and citizens' active participation in democratic practices. These theories are difficult to reduce to one group, but one important contributor has been the German philosopher and social theorist Jürgen Habermas.

The whole EU, and particularly the EMU, has been built on interpretation A. The European Central Bank sets interest rates, aiming for low inflation. No other common economic policy is deemed necessary. The expectation derived from abstract theory is that if only price levels can be kept stable, income levels in the whole of Europe will over the long term become more balanced. This idea is based on new classical macroeconomic models developed in the 1970s, according to which market actors' perfect knowledge of the future and the rational expectations based on that knowledge inevitably defeat the purposes of public economic policy. Active economic policies can only serve to bring about higher inflation, an undesirable outcome.[11]

Neoliberal doctrine also includes a distrust of politicians, who are held to be maximizers of their own interests and willing to cause undue business cycles generating inflation if it will help get them re-elected. For this reason, their hands must be tied by rules that will prevent inflationary politics.[12] Markets that are free from public interference are the best maximizers of overall production, provided they can operate within the limits of stable and easily predictable rules and institutions. Citizens' political approval stems from material outcomes, and the economic benefits of integration are sufficient justification of the European integration process.

Interpretation B is critical of the Maastricht Treaty and of the EMU, but is agnostic on economic theory. It has no position on whether neoliberal economic theory is correct, but highlights broader legitimation-theoretical perspectives related to community, justice and democracy.[13] The central argument is that although the material benefits of free markets and neoliberal globalization may be real, they are not all that matters. The technocratic nature of EU institutions and the insulation of the ECB from politics are democratically problematic. It is doubtful whether the EU as it presently is can provide the same sort of framework for citizens' good lives as nation-states do. Proponents of interpretation B generally argue that from an ethico-political perspective nation-states are the best guarantor of opportunities for human development, social justice and democracy.

The only genuine alternative to nation-states would be the transformation of the current union into a socially responsible and democratic European federation. The EU as it stands in 2012 is not acceptable, however. Although the support of the majority can be partly bought with material benefits, and although the elites and the media have joined ranks on the EU's side, the legitimation of the EU is on shaky foundations. Precisely for this reason, from the elites' point of view each expression of democratic will brings risks; better, then, to avoid referenda and the like.

From the standpoint of interpretation C also, the future of the EU has always looked uncertain and dubious. However, on this view the reason is not problems of legitimation but the harmful economic effects of the EMU. The convergence criteria of the Maastricht Treaty – low inflation and strict ceilings on budget deficits and on debt accumulation – are in many circumstances deflationary, in effect reducing demand in the whole of Europe, not merely within particular member states or the eurozone. Insufficient aggregate demand leads to lower sales and profits, which further discourages future investments and can also slow technological development, or at least hinder the development of significant innovations. Low levels of investment lessen both future productive capacity and demand at each potential level of production. Deflationary economic developments also increase vulnerability to greater financial crises and steeper business cycles.[14] In a world of many simultaneously operating and mutually conflicting mechanisms and processes that fluctuate at different and only partly synchronized rhythms, these kinds of feedback effects are not necessarily dramatic but rather incrementally deepening. In the end, however, the EMU will collapse under the sheer weight of its own economic impossibility. Disparities in relations of trade and financing within the EU cannot be evened out without a common political community equipped with state-like functions.

Europe's growth rates are often compared to those of the United States, and these comparisons do give some indication of the EMU's negative effects. In the period from 1973 to 1990, private-sector labour productivity in Europe seemed to grow faster than in the USA, and still from 1990 to 1999 Europe had a slight edge. Since European monetary union came into effect, however, things have gone the opposite way, with slightly higher growth in the USA. Unemployment figures in Europe also deteriorated in the early 2000s, whereas unemployment dropped in the USA up until the 2008–09 crisis. (However, the differences in employment levels were in fact mostly down to higher employment among young less-educated and older people in the USA, which are largely explained by that country's greater economic inequalities.[15]) All in all, there have been no significant differences in employment rates between Europe and the USA. Declining rates of economic growth have been the trend in the whole OECD region for some time.[16] Through the EMU, however, this trend has become more visible in Europe than it is in the USA. This is in line with the expectations of field C.

Interpretation D combines the preceding two options' pessimistic outlooks for the EU.[17] On one front, the EU is struggling with continuing problems of legitimation. Peace and technocratic promises of material prosperity have failed to suffice for justifying the European integration processes over the long term, especially considering the EU's constraining effects on democracy and the continuing trend towards growing inequality. In addition, the EMU project was founded on unrealistic economic theories that have in fact aggravated the recessionary tendency and contrib-

FIGURE 6.1 The European debt crisis is still being handled through traditional state diplomacy, despite it being a question of major events that deeply affect the lives of all Europeans.

uted to balance-of-trade imbalances and to economic crises. The economy's downward development and the resulting crisis have brought the legitimation difficulties closer to full-scale crisis. The consequences of the chaos unleashed by the combined economic and legitimation crises could be hard to foresee, but the choice seems clear: either the eurozone fragments, partly or even fully, or the Union is put on a firmer foundation, not only economically but morally and politically.

The 2010–12 crisis has largely been in accordance with post-Keynesian economic anticipations. Nevertheless, the EU's official responses, ranging from the crisis funds and stability mechanisms to the financial transaction tax and common bonds, have so far remained broadly within the range of option-field A. Admittedly, on economic theory some small concessions have been made in the direction of C, most notably with the proposals of financial regulation and the transaction tax, but at the same time deflationary discipline has been stepped up, hitting the member states' economies even harder in the process. From the point of view of legitimation theory the EU has been pushed even further into the technocratic and Schumpeter-style direction. So it is not surprising that Jürgen Habermas is among those who have lost patience with the situation: 'It's simply unacceptable... Enough already!'[18]

In so far as interpretation D is on target, the future of the EU looks bleak both economically and in terms of its legitimacy. Under the European Commission and Germany, Europe is being driven into ever-deeper economic difficulty at the same time as EU citizens are becoming increasingly suspicious of the whole EU project. Because there are not enough prominent movements in the region promoting a post-Keynesian, socially responsible and democratic Union, it is likely that nationalistic opposition to the EU will become more widespread. This trend will not necessarily be channelled only through so-called populist parties; across the party political spectrum outlooks on the EU will be reassessed.

Euroscepticism, obviously, does not support deepening European integration. Mutually reinforcing developmental trends are hard to roll back, and it is through economic development that the crucial 'point of no return' could be reached. What is centrally in question is the support and justification for the European project. If the current situation becomes sufficiently polarized to cause collapse, then after fragmentation all that may remain of the EU, if anything, would be only remnants of the original union. The crisis would then have reached a whole new level of seriousness.

Three scenarios on the EU's future after the crisis

The first scenario on post-crisis Europe is that the neoliberal project of European integration survives for the time being. The surplus countries that have insisted on deflationary economic policies, and some other countries that follow their lead, would try to continue and to deepen the integration project in accordance with the old formula, perhaps for many years. Continuation along this same path would be politically difficult, however; that is, although from an economic perspective even tighter adherence to neoliberal principles could work for a while for a core part of the Union – though with only sluggish or negative rates of growth – the attempt would not have sufficiently broad support from the citizens of the persevering states. The neoliberal project heightens existing antagonisms and creates new ones. This scenario is the most likely option in the short run, but its more extended prospects are fairly desolate.

The second scenario is that of a metamorphosis of the Union. This does not rule out the exit of one or more member states from the eurozone or even from the Union itself; nor does it exclude the continued parting of the ways between the eurozone countries and the other EU members (in the case of Britain, any changes to EU composition would accelerate this divergence). The second scenario, then, is that through crisis, partial fragmentation and a host of political struggles and compromises, the EU remoulds itself as a social-democratic federation. The new union would have at least some major welfare state elements, and construction of mechanisms and institutions of economic governance along post-Keynesian lines. In addition, the revamped EU would be likely to develop a distinctive foreign policy and evolve into a global military power.

In the third scenario, the EU develops a new identity, new institutions, and its democratic potential, as part of a global social-democratic system of governance. The foundations for global social democracy and the various prior conditions and reform movements that could enable it are so far weak, however. A large number of Europe's dissenting intellectuals and civil society movements favour something along the lines of the second scenario, a European federation bent for separate social and democratic solutions. But the alter-globalization movement may yet gain momentum as a reaction to various crises and wars.

SCENARIO 1   The neoliberal European project continues

Even if the euro were to collapse completely, this would not directly entail the end of the EU. What it would mean is a return to a time before the common currency. EU laws and institutions would remain in force. More likely than complete dissolution of the eurozone is partial disintegration. One or more countries would be forced to abandon the euro (and one or more surplus countries, such as Finland, could be among them). The remaining eurozone countries would continue to pursue deepened integration in line with previously agreed plans and current proposals (Chapter 5). Through stability mechanisms, ECB bond acquisitions, common bonds and stringent budgetary discipline, the economic crisis would over time be calmed, since the debt of the remaining eurozone countries may be controllable, especially if the euro group can export some of its problems to other parts of the world. To what extent and how fast recovery would succeed would depend on the overall development of the world economy (China's long-predicted financial and economic crisis would deal a fatal blow to these hopes, however). In any case, the price of adjustment measures would, at the very least, be recession and fairly high unemployment levels, including in the remaining euro countries. At worst there would be deep depression, through which Europe's standing in the world economy would decline further.

The partial failure of the European project and the consequent economic difficulties would further escalate the legitimation short-falls. Growing inequalities and high unemployment in the context of a perceived further influx of immigrants would intensify social antagonisms developing with paranoid, nihilistic or even funda-mentalist characteristics.[19] When neoliberal policies are locked in and social unrest mounts, solutions are not sought in new economic and social policies, but by implementing harsher punishments through the legal system,[20] labelling those who deviate or dissent as existential threats.[21] This is one possible way of attempting to justify the European Union through exclusionary identity politics, since the identification of threats to one's own existence can create unity and acceptance, or at least acquiescence.[22]

In this scenario, the size of the prison system will grow rapidly along the lines of the US and British systems. More and more problems will be treated as security problems; that is to say, they will be approached as threats to private property rights, personal freedoms, life, that can be resolved through technological means – for example through camera, Internet and satellite surveillance, and through the imposition of harsher legal and economic pun- ishments for observed deviations from the norm. Technological means of enforcing law and order are applied in multicultural, and increasingly stratified and polarized, urban centres, or at least in parts of them. Surveillance is extended to all quarters to ensure the observance of property rights and contracts, and also in production, trade and financial spaces, which have by now spread through the entire world. Also military force is used for the same purposes, although on a different scale. In the early phases it is likely that NATO would still be providing most of the military facilities. The neoliberal order is transnational and global.

The more tenaciously neoliberal principles and economic poli- cies are adhered to, the less capable the EU will be of resolving its economic and legitimation problems in ways that are sustainable from a holistic perspective. Increases to effective demand can be attempted by:

(i)   accepting financialization as a given, and encouraging con- sumers and homebuyers to take on more debt so as to in- crease consumption to the extent that this is still possible;

(ii)   creating and opening new markets, for instance by com-
       modifying things that were formerly outside the market and
       making them into globally tradable goods;
(iii) 'beggar your neighbour' policies, i.e. increasing export
       demand and using export mechanisms to transfer one's
       own problems elsewhere in the world economy (this is one
       meaning of competitiveness);
(iv)   increasing security and military capacity, i.e. increasing
       public expenditure through militarized Keynesianism.[23]

The formation of overall demand is a complicated process.
A new and smaller EU comprises countries with taxation levels
that historically speaking are high, albeit in decline. They also
have income distribution mechanisms and automatic stabilization mechanisms, through which aggregate demand is in effect
sustained to some degree. Nonetheless, inherent to the neoliberal
EU model is a drive to commodify everything possible (ii), and
one-sided solutions (iii and iv). It is possible to try to improve
the prognoses for growth through intensified financialization
and commodification, and at the expense of the economic
prospects or security of other countries. Each strategy tends
to engender outcomes that from post-Keynesian economic and
Habermasian legitimation theory perspectives are foreseeable
and problematic.

Economically, the EU with all its new disciplinary mechanisms
is faltering. A crisis-hit EMU is weakening the outlooks for economic growth even more than before, and is prone to intensified
and renewed crisis. High unemployment tends to strengthen
xenophobia. Beggar-my-neighbour politics and expanded security
and armament programmes, while potentially better at generating short-term growth, feed into the processes of constructing
external scapegoats. Financialization and commodification make
uncertainty and alienation more pervasive. For many, everyday

activities and practices involve values and meanings that are denigrated by commodification. People may try to compensate for this loss of meaning through consumerism, but the vacuum can also be filled by one or other shade of fundamentalism or other hard-willed dogma.[24]

Hence the augmentation of the neoliberal EU project creates problems and aggravates antagonisms in Europe, and in the global political economy. Such developmental trends may even be enough to reverse, at least temporarily, the long-term trend of declining violence and consolidating peaceful and democratic means of resolving conflicts. The neoliberal EU, in short, is built on sand; it is likely that it will come to an end within the next ten to fifteen years. The problem is that its end may not come about smoothly, but as part of a deep worldwide crisis or catastrophe.

SCENARIO 2 A (relatively) social-democratic federation of states

Four decades ago Johan Galtung suggested that enlargement of the European Union would alternate with deepening integration until its political capacity corresponded to its economic resources.[25] Switches from one phase to another do not happen without crises, however, especially not when the question becomes one of decisive steps towards the emergence of a federal system. The general meaning of *crisis* is a turning point in a process, which can lead to changes in the nature of the thing in crisis. The occurrence of crisis requires the presence of some threat potentially fateful to the system or its identity, but which at the same time can open up new possibilities for change. Political opportunities then have the chance of grabbing hold of these chances ('opportunism' in this sense is not necessarily selfish, or even self-centred; it can also be principled). Since 2010, the euro crisis has been above all exploited to further privatization and commoditization and to downgrade public services. But these are not the only options.[26]

Crisis can also be put in the service of building a different kind of federation.

At the time of writing (July 2012) the eurozone remains intact; nor has the EU undergone any significant structural change in a social-democratic direction. Nationalism may be on the rise and pessimism as to the Union's future may be taking hold, but the project of a unified Europe still enjoys relatively wide but declining approval. In spring 2011 about half of the EU's citizenry continued to believe, despite the ongoing crisis, that EU membership is useful and should be supported.[27] Unsurprisingly, a year later *Reader's Digest* reports declining trust in the euro (from 51 per cent to 40 per cent) and popularity of the Union (down to mere 30 per cent).[28] Although there is a consensus among the EU political elite that the basic Treaty of the European Union should not be amended for the time being, demands for changes to the EU's founding documents have made headlines throughout Europe, and further afield. The direction of development is roughly in line with Galtung's predictions: after expansion and following emerging problems, efforts are being made to extend and strengthen the EU's executive powers. Galtung's predictions were made at a very abstract level, however, and say very little about the substance of the emerging power system, be it a federation or otherwise.

European integration has been justified by appeals both to peace and to the ability to do some technical and economic things better through integration than they can be done by separate states (the so-called Monnet method). The euro crisis has cast doubt on the neoliberal and Schumpeterian interpretations about what is technically sensible and acceptable from the point of view of justifying the EU. Despite this, the European Commission has been prepared to make only minor theoretical concessions in a post-Keynesian direction, and no legitimation-theoretical concessions whatever in a Habermasian direction. As a rule,

TABLE 6.2   The ideal-type social-democratic federal state

Political economic institutions	Basis of legitimation
European taxes and noteworthy fiscal policy: EU budget larger than member states' (at least 7–8 times 2011 EU budget)	Democratic representation – parliamentary democratic principles at EU level: commission or government directly responsible to parliament; parliament (possibly bicameral) decides on budgets and laws
Main economic policy focus on fiscal means, aimed at full employment as well as economically and ecologically sustainable growth	Full employment and social justice
Monetary policy aimed at supporting fiscal policy (promoting investments and growth); if overcapacity and lack of demand, demand increased with central bank funding	Democratic control extends to European Central Bank: ECB answerable to democratically elected council
Regional policy aimed at reversing self-reinforcing processes of uneven development and guaranteeing the most even possible regional development level throughout the EU	Subsidiary principle: decisions made as close as possible to where they will apply; member states and municipalities levy taxes and establish rules and procedures
Common income, wage and industrial policies, including partial socialization of investments	Social rights and guaranteed basic income for all EU citizens

responses to the crisis have been made through economic liberal means, displacing democratic procedures. The Commission has remained willing to compromise social justice and democracy further in order to increase orthodox economic discipline. Even some economists have begun to warn of an impending democratic crisis and swerve to authoritarianism in Europe, thus recognizing that economy is altogether political.[29]

The political situation could change if and when the eurozone really starts to disintegrate, which would cast doubt on and politicize the EU's basic principles also from a Europeanist angle. The legitimation problems, for their part, could impel the development of a federal system among the core EU countries, more in the name of European welfare and democracy than competitiveness and budgetary discipline. At this point, countries outside the eurozone would have little say in the formation of the federal project, so there would be no need to take British opposition into consideration, for instance. Thus the field would be open to social-democratic federalists also.

The federation would form a single political-economic entity. There would no longer be foreign trade between the member states, for example, with the whole region having a single current account relative to the rest of the world. How far could the EU federation develop in a post-Keynesian direction and in accordance with the Habermas model of legitimation? An easy way of forming an answer to this is to create schematized ideal types, against which realistic possibilities for change are then assessed. Table 6.2 summarizes the main features of this from the perspectives of economic policy and legitimation. (This is intended as an illustrative framework, rather than an exhaustive list.[30])

In parallel with the significant EU budget and tax revenue, new forms of democratic participation and representation will be developed.[31] In economic policy, the aims are full employment and social justice, with the main emphasis on fiscal instruments. Monetary policy is made subject to general economic policy goals, and the European Central Bank is democratized. The EU has active regional policies, and at the same time the principle of subsidiarity is comprehensively applied. The Union guarantees a basic minimum income to all its citizens, implements coordinated and otherwise harmonized income and wage policies, and endeavours to influence the rate, composition and direction of economic growth through active public investment policies.

The federal model presented in Table 6.2 depicts a traditional conception of social democracy. For one thing, in it political community is ordered in a hierarchy of territorial units, from municipalities, through states, to the overall federal system (with decision-making regulated by the principle of subsidiarity). Second, although the basis of legitimation in this model is social and democratic, it resembles the Habermas model only to a certain extent. It lacks the active role for civil societies and spaces for direct, participatory and deliberative democracy. Third, in places it is also static, undynamic. Absent from it is the hope of a better future – that is, movement to the next levels of the good society. A more dynamic interpretation of social democracy would incorporate both social learning and democratization of the various social subsystems and pluralization of forms of property.[32] In this context, however, the crucial point is only to estimate those immediate changes a transfer towards which would demand a social-democratic federation of states. How possible and likely are these changes?

Implementing the model outlined in Table 6.2 would require the rewriting of the EU Treaty. The changes needed would not affect only details of the founding documents; they would also require changes to their underlying philosophy, to their economic theories, and to their theories of legitimation. Approval of a new constitutive treaty would require broad agreement on the new direction of integration. Such a scale of agreement could not be achieved without broad-based, highly visible political movements to work for the foundation of a federal social-democratic EU. Such movements are practically non-existent in Europe, although behind the scenes there are many active associations and their networks. Political parties across the spectrum have internalized neoliberal principles (usually taking them on board as unchangeable facts). Businesses and banks have had, and still have, privileged access to the formation of political agendas in Europe. The EU member countries, struggling with debt, have made their freedom to act conditional on the mechanisms of the global financial system. Political configurations and power relations must be transformed before the transition to an ideal-type social-democratic federal system could be possible.

Adapting Galtung's argument, we can anticipate, however, that the deepening of the euro crisis makes it possible to find compromises between different visions and interests. According to this scenario, a post-Keynesian and democratic left will eventually succeed in establishing the federal project. This project is also supported – but only reservedly – by the part of the political right that is primarily interested in Europe's prestige and power in the world. This pro-European right assumes that the EU must become as powerful as the United States. The neoliberal project has failed to deliver success. Making Europe powerful requires the building of a European nation, at least at the level of elites, which in turn requires at least a moderate level of approval by the broader citizenry, achievable through some measures of welfare and democracy. The idea of the right is that a regional economy must be complemented with a centralized federal state equipped with efficient military capabilities of global reach. Otherwise, the EU would not, on this view, have the necessary political agency or ability to act differently in world politics. As Javier Solana, then High Representative of the Union for Foreign Affairs and Security Policy, wrote in 2003 in reference to an EU membership that was soon to be expanded:

> As a union of 25 states with over 450 million people producing a quarter of the world's Gross National Product (GNP), and with a wide range of instruments at its disposal, the European Union is inevitably a global player. ... The increasing convergence of European interests and the strengthening of mutual solidarity

of the EU makes us a more credible and effective actor. Europe should be ready to share in the responsibility for global security and in building a better world.[33]

One sign of movement in this direction is that the European Commission has established two large new research areas, in the fields of space and security. The various processes thus converge. But although deepening economic crisis can make changes to the EU's basic structure more likely, the probable outcome is not an ideal-type social-democratic federation but an amalgam of different institutional solutions and goals that are in tension with each other.

SCENARIO 3   The EU as part of a social-democratic system of governance

The EU is part of many governance systems in the world economy. Particularly in the areas of trade and investment, the EU already operates as a single actor in worldwide negotiations. Moreover, from a post-Keynesian economic perspective, the Union is just part of the world economy and its processes.[34] Financialization, for instance, has been a worldwide process. Reversing it would require broad international treaties and global institutional reforms. The power of large multinational companies and the effects of worldwide oligopoly markets cannot be tackled by the EU alone. Even more obvious is that the economic paradoxes and contradictions discussed in Chapters 2–4 are not confined to Europe but play out on a global scale. Struggles over income distribution are taking place the world over, at the same time as efforts continue to reduce costs in the name of international competitiveness. If the whole EU attempts to create a balance-of-trade surplus, this could only happen at the expense of other countries and overall global demand. Self-reinforcing processes of unequal growth and development affect all parts of the world economy.

The EU is an important trading partner to other countries, and as a whole comprises an open economy. It is part of many systems of governance in the world economy. And yet the world's population is predicted to be around 9 billion by 2050, of which only about 5 per cent will live in the EU – and if the federal system does not contain all the states currently in the EU, the proportion will be even smaller. Geographically, too, the EU region occupies a fairly modest peninsula on the western side of the Eurasian continent. Global industrial society has brought new kinds of risk that are not isolable to any discrete region. These are not only economic: some of the most prominent other such risks include climate change, genetic manipulation, the spread of diseases, and nuclear weapons. Europe's fate is dependent on the development of global risk society and on the coming turns in world history.

Legitimation theory also points in the same direction: norms are acceptable only to the extent that they are capable of being generalized. The objective is to find norms, a condition that is met only when 'all affected [by the norm] can freely accept the consequences and the side effects that the general observance of a controversial norm can be expected to have for the satisfaction of the interests of each individual'.[35] The aim of this kind of universalization principle is to help in locating norms that can be accepted by all parties irrespective of race, gender, age, nationality, world-view, or even present conditions (so valid norms may, and sometimes also must, take into account future generations). The criterion of perfect generalizability thus applies to all human beings, and maintaining this principle implies world citizenship. Making world citizenship a practical reality requires global domestic policies and world economic policies.[36]

How possible and likely is it that the EU adopts a global Keynesian economic theory and the sort of unbounded moral theory that demands the opening of democratic political spaces and the furtherance of democratic practices in global governance

also? Thus far the EU has represented itself as a civilian power
trying to justify its actions by appeal to universal human rights
– and the EU also frequently appeals to other generalizable
principles, for instance when it comes to trade. The world order
envisioned by the EU reflects the universal norms it has adopted,
but these can also be ideological and favourable to particular
interests. Their real generalizability can be tested only through
global dialogues in democratic forums.[37]

From the perspective of realizing this scenario it is indicative
that a significant proportion of global civil society actors and
cosmopolitan networks are either in Europe or of European origin.
European philosophers and political theorists have developed
post-national ethico-political concepts and models of democratic
global governance. In some EU member countries, as in the
European Parliament, these intellectuals' networks, civil society
organizations and political movements have been able to influence
the substance of discussion, and on occasion even to influence
actual decision-making. Many Members of the European Parliament have, for example, actively supported the campaign for a
global parliament, and the EU and some of its member states have
propounded a universally applicable financial transaction tax.

Despite all this, a swift turn to democratic global Keynesianism
is unlikely. Official EU principles have as a rule been founded
on neoliberal economic theory and technological, materialistic
approval. Unless these internalized principles are changed, the
EU will not be able to promote alternative principles in world
politics. Neither would global democratic Keynesianism follow
directly from the construction of a social-democratic European
federation. A separatist and Eurocentric federation would en-
counter the same economic problems and paradoxes, stemming
from an inadequately generalizable perspective, as any sovereign
state would. The more Eurocentric and short-sighted the new
federation's self-perception, the more likely it is to become a part

of the prevailing conditions of the world economy, with all their inherent contradictions.

Conclusions

The world economic crisis has had two phases. In the first the crisis was just barely contained by the actions of states and central banks. The OECD region sank into an epic recession, but managed to avoid full-blown depression. Although the crisis is global, its effects have not been evenly distributed. Uneven growth is part of the whole story of the development of the world economy, and was also a background factor in the 2008–09 crisis. There was only a small dip in the economic growth of China and some other Asian countries, in part because major resuscitative measures were taken in Asia too. The OECD region started to recover because of such measures, and over the course of 2010 stock market prices began to return to pre-crisis peak levels.

The rescue and resuscitation packages were funded to a large extent with debt, however. Because of the crisis, a significant amount of private debt became public debt. The second stage of the crisis was triggered by the state debt crises in the OECD countries and especially in the eurozone. Cuts to public expenditure also began to be demanded in those countries where public debt had not been a problem as such. When many countries implemented deflationary policies at the same time, overall demand fell both across Europe and in the world economy as a whole. The stronger the drive for public spending cuts and wage cuts for ordinary citizens, the worse the world economic prospects for growth became. This further exacerbated the debt problem, since recession depletes state revenue and increases expenses.

The EMU has from the beginning been a contradictory project, a monetaristic monetary union without political union. The expected benefits of European monetary union created by neoliberal economic theories never came about. Although the EU has a smaller amount of total public debt than the United States, the EU has no federal budget or other mechanisms for balancing surpluses and deficits within the union, and the EU's rules prohibit central bank funding. As such, the eurozone countries are dependent on private debt markets and the (speculative) expectations created on them, which American credit rating agencies also employ in their judgements of creditworthiness. It is under these conditions that the debt crisis became a euro crisis. In addition to its deepening economic woes, the EU is now also threatened by political crisis, and is finding its legitimacy in doubt.

By 2012 the EU had driven itself to a turning point: down one path lies the disintegration of the eurozone, down the other the development of a federal system. Deepened integration could also come about as a consequence of some degree of fragmentation. I have argued in this chapter that if the EU does not disintegrate entirely, one of three possible futures is likely to materialize. A neoliberal EU could try to soldier on in some variation of its present make-up. This may work temporarily, but its longer-term prospects are bleak. Closer union through tighter technocratic budgetary discipline and shared responsibility for debt will not resolve the contradictions of the EMU; nor will it solve Europe's overall economic troubles. In addition, these methods deepen the EU's democratic deficit and erode its ethico-political acceptability. Further deepened neoliberalism creates problems and antagonisms, both in Europe and in the global political economy.

Fragmentation of the eurozone under the weight of its economic difficulties would put the EU's basic principles in question and politicize them. Legitimation problems might spur the core EU countries to forge a more fully federal system, arising out of concerns for their own democratic situation and welfare rather than in pursuit of competitiveness and budgetary discipline. In other words, the EU could become a social-democratic federation, but one inevitably bearing the marks of a compromise between different visions and interests. European federation is also propounded by those on the Eurocentric right, with the aim of turning the EU into a great power with full-spectrum capabilities of traditional great powers, including military capabilities.

The third possible future is that a cosmopolitan EU is able to develop common institutions as part of a far broader global whole. In this scenario, the EU develops its identity, policies and resources as a unified but pluralistic civilian power. This EU is an open political community, and the criterion for membership is respect for certain universal human and civil rights (which are nonetheless historically and politically constructed and transformable, not given by nature). It strives to develop new institutional arrangements, decision-making structures including an empowered Parliament, industrial relations, a taxation system, and so on, but it no longer presents itself as the centre of the civilized world or as a model for others to emulate. In contrast, this EU understands itself as part of a far broader and deeper whole – that is, as part of the planetary whole – and acts accordingly. It actively participates in efforts to democratize global governance and build new global Keynesian elements of governance, with the objective of putting the development of the world economy on a new and more sustainable footing.

History contains turning points that can determine the possible paths of development for several decades into the future. If 1848 had become a successful revolutionary year in Europe, the continent would have democratized more swiftly and in a less nationalistic form than later happened. France would have survived without Napoleon III's reign, and Germany would have unified without the Iron Chancellor Bismarck's wars and militarism. The 1870–71 Franco–German War would not have happened. Although contradictions of political economy, technological developments and the armament of separate sovereign states would have remained problems, the war of 1914–18 would not have occurred, at least not as we know it. Problems of war and peace in the subsequent decades were not entirely dependent on the events of 1848, of course. But, nevertheless, had it been different so too would have been the path of world history afterwards, making the catastrophes of the twentieth century significantly less likely. Choices and turns have consequences.

The choices made in the present decade also have their long-reaching effects. What kind of future is being prepared by the fact that democracy is being replaced with neoliberal technocracies in the EU, and that politically we are moving towards an authoritarian counter-reaction to these developments – in the context where the state of democracy in the United States is so dire that it is widely considered a post-democratic society?[38] The scenario of a continued neoliberal EU project does not promise a long future for that project, but neither does it promise a quick or easy transition to a world beyond neoliberalism. The more firmly and rigorously neoliberal principles are adhered to, and the longer the divisions are allowed to widen and deepen, the more likely it is that the project will end in catastrophe. Future studies are not about prediction, even if they do lean on forecasts of possible and likely developments: 'It is far better to foresee even without certainty than not to foresee at all.'[39]

Good future research also facilitates a well-founded involvement in the making of history. Scenarios for the EU's possible futures also suggest how to act otherwise and what kinds of possible twists in the ongoing crisis to look out for on the way. A social-democratic federal European Union would prevent a repeat of the current EU euro crisis, and would also solve a few other contradictions in the European political economy. The EU is, however, only a relatively small part of the world economy as a whole. Moreover, generalized principles of justification point in the direction of world citizenship and a global political community. A cosmopolitan European Union would act foremost as a builder of worldwide institutions, its immediate goal being the establishment of global Keynesianism. This kind of EU may be the least likely possibility in the short term. But over the long term it is the most justifiable and sustainable option.

7

How should debt crises
be resolved?

The sovereign debt crisis in Europe is only an instance in a long
series of similar crises across the world, including in Europe itself.
Every time the first question seems to be: what should be done
about the acute debt crisis? Alternatives and longer-term futures
are rarely discussed; the focus tends to be on the here and now.
One obvious response to an acute situation is renegotiating the
amount and conditions of debt. Based on historical experiences,
timely controlled debt reorganization is better for all concerned
than delayed emergency measures based on a mistaken diagnosis.
Delays contribute to changing conditions: if problems are mounting up chaotically, even good ideas may not work any longer,
since at every turn one's response will in effect be a reaction to
an emergency.

The kind of pragmatism with a time horizon limited to a few
weeks or months is invariably more of a problem than a solution to
economic crises. A case in point is the deterioration of the Greek
situation. After a critical point it became increasingly obvious
to many observers that even debt restructuring may no longer
be enough to save the Greek economy.[1] Here-and-now reactions
are, in a very literal sense, childish.[2] But, equally, bad decisions

taken too late are choices that condition future choices. There are many possibilities that are never realized; and processes tend to be path-dependent. Also in sovereign debt crises, recurring patterns of typical developments result from closing off the same possibilities and following the same path time and again.

If an acute crisis is not used to open up new, better possibilities and to create new institutional solutions, the scenarios of the past may be replayed, albeit with some variations. Whereas the first time round the result may be a tragedy, the second incarnation of any historic event, as Marx famously remarked on Hegel, usually takes the form of farce.[3] There is something silly about replaying past episodes in new circumstances. Lessons can be learned from historical experiences by creating new institutional arrangements.

The history of the twentieth century offers a wide selection of examples of how debt problems have been handled in international politics. Historical choices and their typical results can be enlightening, even though there is always variation because historical situations are always unique in some ways. In this regard, German history is especially fruitful. Stringent war reparations were imposed on Germany at the Peace of Versailles in 1919. Debt settlements were agreed upon the following decade, but these were insufficient, and at the same time the German federation, member states and municipalities all took on new debt on international markets. After the stock market crash of autumn 1929, Germany sank into a vortex of debt and deflation that culminated in the rise to power of Adolf Hitler. The National Socialist regime quickly began unilaterally restructuring the country's debts, and in a few years' time stopped repayments completely.

After World War II, Germany was again made answerable for its old debts, in addition to the colossal economic burden of reconstruction. In addition to aid, the country was also granted loans. Its debt burden was once again unmanageable, but by the

1950s Germany was treated differently than it had been in the interwar years. A comprehensive programme of debt restructuration was negotiated in London (with only the country's reparations to the State of Israel for the genocide of the Jews being off the table). In stark contrast to the Versailles treatment, the estimate of overall debt and ability to repay that formed the basis of the London negotiations was decidedly favourable to Germany. This debt burden was cut to around half of its recalculated value at the time. Also, there were none of the provisos that would now be called structural adjustment conditions. The payment conditions that were agreed upon were very reasonable, with the country being given thirty years to clear its debt. Some of the debt was deferred for repayment until after the country had become reunified. The London settlements contributed to enabling Germany's spectacular economic resurgence of the 1950s and 1960s, and consolidated the development of democracy in West Germany. In short, the deeply contrasting choices that were made after World War I and in 1953 led to vastly different outcomes. This provides some pointers as to what works and what does not, politically as well as economically.

The lessons of history are easily forgotten, though. Now, in the early 2010s, Germany and other surplus eurozone countries are acting in ways that rather recall the treatment of Germany from 1919 to 1932 by the 'victors' of the First World War than those of the later war.[4] The heavily indebted eurozone countries were left with no option but to cut public spending and take on further debt. In other words, the deficit countries were forced to adopt and implement deflationary policies, which tend to make them less capable of settling their debts in so far as these policies contribute to a recessionary spiral. In an interconnected European and global political economy, policies such as these have effects on the conditions for growth and employment in all countries. From a forward-looking perspective, however, of greatest concern might be the political reaction in places where the consequences of the crisis hit home most forcefully at an everyday level.

There are plenty of other past events to learn from also. The debt crises of many developing countries have been festering for decades. After the oil crisis of the early 1970s, loans were easily available on favourable conditions, and few questions were asked by lenders even when the debts were incurred by corrupt despots. When the United States government and its Federal Reserve decided to raise interest rates in the late 1970s and early 1980s, primarily for domestic reasons, many countries in the global South were suddenly in great difficulty. The resulting debt crisis has taken several fateful turns since then, and in many of the worst-affected countries it continues. To what extent might it be true to say that the doctrines of the International Monetary Fund that are now being applied to Europe have been successful in the global South? What have been the major consequences, both intended and unintended?

The debt crisis in the global South spurred a worldwide campaign with the central aim of establishing an international debt arbitration mechanism. A common and permanent mechanism treating all parties as equal still does not exist, although minor advances towards controlled debt restructurings may have been achieved. The creation of a global system does not have to start from scratch. A possible model is Chapter Nine of the United States bankruptcy law, which regulates debt settlements of public entities with administrative powers, and of municipal authorities in particular.

As the movements in favour of global debt settlement mechanisms have argued, the advantage of Chapter Nine is that it does not force public entities to cut back or close public services in order to pay off debt. According to Article 904 of the law, creditors or courts may not attempt to influence how the public entity uses its assets or income. Chapter Nine also prohibits public entities from raising taxation levels to the extent that would harm their residents' standards of living. Thus, under this legislation debt cannot be a justification of one-sided dictatorial policies any more than it can justify slavery. (The United Nations and international law have prohibited debt bondage since the 1950s, but the practice continues in parts of Asia.)

The crisis that began in 2010 had many different causes. Causes are forces and mechanisms that produce effects. The present euro crisis would not have come about without the structural connections and causal mechanisms discussed in Chapters 2–4. Conversely, the absence of certain mechanisms can in some cases fail to prevent a crisis, and in this sense the absence of a debt arbitration mechanism can be seen as a cause of the euro crisis. Although such a mechanism, had it existed, would not have removed the inadequacies and internal contradictions of the European Monetary Union, it would have been likely to change the course of the beginning of this decade by deferring the worst effects of the EMU's shortcomings, and perhaps also by preventing debt levels from mounting so much and so rapidly. But because the Third World debt campaign was unsuccessful in creating new global institutions, Europe too has now become a target of the International Monetary Fund's structural adjustment doctrines.

The debt problem affects not only states, and neither could public debt restructurings alone reverse the entire financialization process. A notable proportion of the public debt of OECD countries is of private origin and a direct outcome of the 2008–09 crisis. Added to that, two further conditions can make debt arbitration more difficult: when many countries are struggling with similarly severe debt problems at the same time, limiting the room of negotiations for debt concessions, and when investors and banks are themselves indebted, and thus have fragile financial bases. I argue in this chapter for the importance of organizing the overall dynamics of the economy in such a way that consumer and investor demand remain sufficiently high without accumulating private debt. When households, firms, investors and banks have become too heavily involved in debt, methods are needed to relieve this burden. In so far as taking on public debt is sensible, the conditions of debt must be subject to public control.

So the main argument of this chapter is that lessons can be learned from history. Collective learning comes about through institutional changes, for example through the creation of a binding international debt arbitration mechanism. This is not enough in itself, however: institutional means of steering and regulating the entire dynamic of debt are also needed.

Lessons of German history: war debt and its consequences

The First World War had many overlapping causes. The choices of heads of state at turning points in the Second Industrial Revolution contributed to shaping conditions in the late 1800s and early 1900s. Very often, these individuals did not have a very good understanding of the unintended consequences of their actions and of how these consequences combined with those created by others acting at the same time. First the European states slid into a long economic slump from 1873 to 1895, which incited competition for markets and colonies. In these conditions technological development and the forging of strategic alliances escalated the level of competition between the European Great Powers, leading to international tensions and arms races.[5]

By the beginning of the 1910s, the risk of major war was in the air, at least in discussions among foreign policy elites. During the Agadir Crisis of the summer of 1911, for example, Britain's minister of foreign affairs at the time, Winston Churchill, wrote that the likelihood of war was foremost in his mind throughout the

crisis talks.[6] Watershed events of the summer of 1914 could easily
have been otherwise. It was by sheer accident that Gavrilo Princip
managed to shoot dead Archduke Franz Ferdinand of Austria in
Bosnia on 28 June 1914. The decision of various heads of state
to go to war and support their allies resulted from calculations
based on uncertain and fast-changing circumstances. Timing
also had a role in igniting the Great War: above all, if the wave
of democratization and anti-imperialist nationalisms that were
under way at the time had been able to continue developing,
the European political configuration would have been markedly
different by the 1920s. Military technology would have continued
to develop and a real threat of war would have remained in force,
but the 1914–18 style of industrial war might never have been.[7]

Germany surrendered in November 1918, by which time the
blockaded country's economy lay in ruins. Shortages and desperation had taken the population to the brink of revolution. Among
the allied states, Germany was held to be the main instigator
of the war, and at the Paris negotiations was forced to sign at
Versailles the treaty containing this damning admission. Its share
of the reparations for 'war guilt' was set at 226 billion gold marks
– around half of all the known gold in the world at the time.
Paying this debt would have taken most of the century. The debt
was renegotiated several times. During the Great Depression,
serious consideration was finally given to dissolving the reparations. But this change of heart came too late for a country that was
otherwise engulfed in debt at national and municipal levels and
throughout its banking system. These problems led to a debt–deflation spiral, feeding into the popularity of Nazism.[8] In the 1928
elections the National Socialist party received only 2.6 per cent
of the vote, but this shot to over one-third in 1932. Hitler soon
became chancellor of the Weimar Republic, and after a 43.9 per
cent landslide for the NSDAP in March 1933 became chancellor of
the Third Reich. No further elections were held. Although official

EU responses suppress memories of these developments, they are not entirely forgotten. As the head of the Austrian Central Bank and ECB Governing Council member Ewald Nowotny noted quite dramatically in the context of the ongoing euro crisis in June 2012: 'The single-minded concentration on austerity policy led to mass unemployment, a breakdown of democratic systems and, at the end, to the catastrophe of Nazism.'[9]

The historical significance of the war reparations demanded of Germany continues to arouse debate, one that was begun in 1919 by John Maynard Keynes. Keynes was involved in the Versailles peace talks, but resigned from the British delegation in protest at what he saw as the excessively punitive demands made against Germany. His pamphlet *The Economic Consequences of the Peace* was published later the same year, and in it he sharply criticized the vengeful tactics of the Allies, especially the French, and their fear of a German resurgence.[10] His main economic argument was that European political economy is characterized by interdependence: the Great War was a European civil war, and no part of Europe stands to gain by striving for the economic ruin of any other part.[11] Along with Germany's being forced to compensate the victorious states and to export assets and commodities to them, imports to the allied countries from Germany were replacing domestic production. An impoverished Germany, meanwhile, was unable to continue buying allied countries' exports. Consequently, all sides suffered economically. Keynes also predicted – correctly, as it turned out as early as 1923 – that the war reparations would plunge Germany into hyperinflation. This 1923 spiral was dramatic, with prices doubling every two days. Keynes also thought it obvious that the plight of Germany would have grave and far-reaching political effects.[12] During the Paris negotiations, many among the United States delegation feared that the Bolshevik Revolution in Russia would spread to Germany, but here too Keynes was more prescient. Hitler made his first grab at power with what has become known as the Beer Hall Putsch of 9 November 1923, with inflation levels at their peak.

Keynes also criticized the Versailles Treaty morally (and even aesthetically). To be just, principles and rules must be generalizable and equitable. On this ground he found other international political initiatives of the period, such as the principles presented in US President Woodrow Wilson's 'Fourteen Points' congressional address of 1918, to be superior to what the Allies agreed at Versailles the following year. But Wilson himself was not beyond the reach of Keynes's often-portentous criticisms. Keynes was famously scathing of 'this blind and deaf Don Quixote', both for his character and for what Keynes saw as his 'betrayal' at Versailles of the liberal cause of his own Fourteen Points:

> After all, it was harder to de-bamboozle this old Presbyterian than it had been to bamboozle him; for the former involved his belief in and respect for himself. Thus in the last act the President stood for stubbornness and a refusal of conciliations … A sense of impending catastrophe overhung the frivolous scene; the futility and smallness of man before the great events confronting him; the mingled significance and unreality of the decisions; levity, blindness, insolence, confused cries from without, all the elements of ancient tragedy were there. Seated indeed amid the theatrical trappings of the French Saloons of State, one could wonder if the extraordinary visages of Wilson and of Clemenceau, with their fixed hue and unchanging characterization, were really faces at all and not the tragi-comic masks of some strange drama or puppet-show.[13]

Some economists and historians have challenged Keynes's attacks, or at least their broader historical significance.[14] The German state, it has been argued, in any case had a deep deficit by war's end. This, however, misses Keynes's point somewhat: he argued repeatedly for at least partial dissolution of *all* the debts accrued for the purposes of waging the war.[15] But Germany would

FIGURE 7.1   A banknote for ten billion marks, October 1923.
Germany paid for its war expenditures largely by borrowing and
printing money. The reparations, and finally the Ruhr invasion
by France in January 1923, accelerated the pace of inflation to
astronomical levels.

still have been able to pay reparations, according to Keynes's
critics, especially since production and work productivity increased during the 1920s also. The reparations, they argue, were
in no way enough by themselves to pauperize Germany, which at
the same time borrowed on international markets. The country's
hyperinflation of the 1920s had several causes that could not
be laid at the door of Versailles. And once inflation took off, it
may even have been deliberately accelerated (although this is a
controversial conjecture).

Keynes's critics also sometimes argued that events at Versailles
were only tenuously connected to the economic collapse that
began in 1929. (The precarious basis of growth during that decade
is in line with Keynes's predictions, however.) The deflationary
policies of the early 1930s were not forced on Germany from

outside. Prompt dissolution of the war debt may have helped before the chain of bank closures in Germany in 1932, but would that have been enough without changes to economic policy? What precisely were the consequences of the punitive war reparations, and what course might things have taken without them?

These and other objections to Keynes share the premiss that other options are always available in any historical situation, and would affect later developments. For instance, the rise of the National Socialist Party was due to many developments in the Weimar Republic, including new means of mass communications and their powerfully enabling consequences for propaganda, and Hitler's own nationalistic convictions and will to continue the world war by any means.

Although historical episodes are always contextual and never repeat themselves without at least some variations, and although choices of actors always play a role, one can say with reasonable certainty that the reparations demanded of Germany (and some other states) had a harmful effect on the development of the whole European political economy and created problems also within the allied countries. The General Strike in Britain in 1926, for instance, was crucially linked to Germany's war debt. World economic growth in the 1920s, built on debt and speculation, was ripe for collapse, and war debt was part of a wider problem (Germany was not the only country burdened with war reparations). This situation led to the worsening of the 1930s' depression, which was even worse in Germany than in the United States. The 1930–32 centrist Catholic minority government led by Heinrich Brüningen pushed through deliberately deflationary economic policies. With the government's hands largely tied, Brüningen's main aim was to strengthen Germany's international bargaining position regarding the war debts, but another reason for this orthodox austerity approach was that Germans had learnt to fear inflation. Reparation payments were temporarily suspended in summer 1932, but in the elections of July of that year the National Socialist Party reaped 37.4 per cent of the vote.

Historical debate continues over the ideological nature of Brüningen's actions and the extent to which he had other choices, but it is clear that the predominant view in Germany at that time was that the reparations programme ruled out resuscitative economic policies.[16] Some phenomena can be causally overdetermined: altering each individual element would not necessarily change the end result even though necessary conditions would be involved, and even though new, less important individual elements would not leave the end result unaffected. The following conditions and acts were among those that contributed to the Nazi takeover:[17]

- The post-war chaos in Germany, during which many attempts at coups and revolutions were made, some lasting months.
- The 1919 Weimar Constitution, which provided for the creation of ordinances and laws without parliamentary approval, or with only minority support (one effect of which was to enable Brüningen's deflationary policies later).
- The French occupation of the Ruhr from 1923 to 1925, resulting from interrupted payments of reparations to France. This increased support for and membership of the Nazi Party.
- The series of economic collapses that began in New York in 1929, which degenerated into major depression in the following years and increased German unemployment to 30 per cent.
- The decision of Germany's Social Democratic Party in 1930 to stay out of the coalition government, bowing to pressure from its young and radical wing. This allowed the authoritarian aspects of the Weimar Constitution to be fully exploited, first by Brüningen and soon after by Hitler.
- The Reichstag fire on 27 February 1933, which contributed to the suspension of democratic rights in the country.[18]

In summary, Versailles and its punitive war reparations cannot be held as the only reason why Hitler succeeded in taking power and becoming a dictator. Nevertheless, the Versailles Treaty did decisively shape the course of the 1920s and 1930s, both through its economic effects and through the interpretations and expectations of various individuals and movements. Critical assessments of probable causes can in some respects be self-fulfilling, even when this is the opposite of what was intended. The historical irony is increased by the fact that, on coming to power, the Nazis prepared Germany for war through a militarized Keynesian economic regime.[19]

The 1953 London debt agreement

Because Keynes was not heeded in the victorious states' circles, either at Versailles or in the 1920s, he was unable to change the course of history. It was only later, towards the end of the Second World War and in its aftermath that Keynes's arguments began to take hold in the Western states. The Bretton Woods system, agreed in 1944, the 1948–52 Marshall Plan and the reindustrialization of Germany did not perhaps reflect Keynes's most ambitious visions, but they were nonetheless important steps in the direction he hoped for. The debt conference of 1953 crowned this development, which from 1947 on was bolstered by the threatening cold war.

In 1949 the regions of Germany that were occupied by Britain, France and the United States became West Germany. One obstacle to full sovereignty was the German debts that had been left unpaid during the 1930s. Chancellor Conrad Adenauer officially accepted responsibility for the debts in 1951, but on the condition that new terms of repayment were arranged that took into account the country's economic situation and new political conditions. The new agreement finalized in 1953 covered the inherited debts from before the war (13.5 billion marks, of which a bit less than half was public debt) and debts arising from reconstruction (16.2 billion marks). Determining the debts from the pre-war years was a conceptually and technically difficult task. Interest rates were among the elements that were arranged on terms highly favourable to West Germany, and also favourable was the delinking of the old debts from the gold standard. Under the terms of the London Agreement, West Germany would repay debts of 11 billion marks on a thirty-year plan, and for the first five years would have to pay only interest on the debt. Part of the debt outlasted the partition of the country, and the final instalment was paid in 2010.[20]

The 1953 debt settlement facilitated the German economic miracle, as did the high level of education in the country and the roads, buildings, machines and other very modern facilities built during reconstruction. Through exports West Germany achieved a surplus economy, and payment of the debts on schedule brought no difficulties. However, the meaning of the export surplus began to change once Germany had paid off its main debt (the small outstanding amount of debt after reunification had no practical importance). Germany's export surpluses of the 1990s and 2000s have been a consequence of the sort of deflationary economic policies that function only so long as some other countries continue to increase their debt. The German economic expansion and surplus benefited various parties up until the early 1980s, but since then have gradually become a burden for the rest of Europe, and to some extent for the whole world economy.

Learning from developing countries' debt problems

State debt problems have by no means been confined to Germany, however. During times of deep crisis sovereign debts have so often become such a major burden that managing them without serious or unsustainable political consequences becomes impossible. For example, in all the major Latin American debt crises of the 1800s and 1900s the indebted countries at some point suspended repayments and declared themselves insolvent, which in some instances led to military interventions by the creditor countries. In federal systems also, such as in the United States, it was common in the 1800s and 1900s for some states to suspend payments and declare insolvency. But whereas legal mechanisms have been developed within countries for resolving such situations, no such systems were developed at the international level, and are still lacking.[21]

The colonial regimes of Africa, the Middle East and Asia were dismantled in the decades following the Second World War. Many of the resultant sovereign states became indebted during the 1970s, and the Third World debt crisis became an international concern in 1982. First and foremost the International Monetary Fund, and later other institutions also, began to present methods of resolution that were based on the premiss that the indebted countries were alone responsible, or at least primarily responsible, for the crisis. This being so, the costs of whatever system was implemented were principally placed on the debtor countries for repayment. Many South-based activists and economists raised objections.[22] In their view, any solution must be based on shared responsibility.

The most common argument for shared responsibility for debt has been moral. In many cases, and especially in the 1970s (when Western banks became flush with money from oil), lenders offered easy money to governments that were frequently military dictatorships. The loans were largely spent on arms, on the elites' own consumption habits, or transferred to the Swiss bank accounts of the military leadership. It is clear that if money is lent in the knowledge that it will be spent on obviously non-productive purposes, the lenders themselves should take a correspondingly larger share of the risk. The debtor countries, of which many have since become democracies, and their citizens should not be held responsible for such debts; nor should they have primary responsibility for their repayment.[23]

Shared responsibility can be justified on mere economic grounds also. Uncertainty has a negative effect on productive investments also. There are many situations that are independent of those involved that affect the sustainability of long-term productivity and financing. Sudden changes in market conditions or interest rates can make productive investments loss-making, and eventually insolvent. A similar, albeit less dramatic and immediate, outcome can result from weakened terms of trade for raw materials and low-processed goods relative to industrial products. Within countries it has become a well-established principle that creditors and debtors are both responsible if the inability to meet repayments has been caused by unforeseeable changes.[24]

What is also essential in assessing responsibility for debt is the fact that beyond a certain point debt levels begin to grow in accordance with their own independent logic, even if no additional loans are taken for consumption or investment. When debts have grown to the extent that repayments become practically impossible, automatic mechanisms for the accrual of nominal debt come into effect (Table 7.1). This simple example takes no account of inflation, debt amortization, or of the fact that a country with continuously worsening economic problems will very likely have to pay higher interest rates on new loans. The insolvent country in the example can only pay half of the interest on each year. The total debt at the start of the first year is $1,000, and the interest rate remains at 10 per cent. The due amount of debt at the end of the first year exceeds the amount actually paid off by $50. This is added to the debt capital, bringing the next year's debt to $1,050. Because the debtor is permanently insolvent – the question is not one of merely temporary debt difficulties, but of structural problems – the problem cannot be solved by itself.

TABLE 7.1   The accumulation of phantom loans

	Capital debt	Due interest	Tended fees	Additional debt
Year 1	1000.00	100.00	50.00	50.00
Year 2	1050.00	105.00	52.50	52.50
Year 3	1102.50	110.25	55.13	55.13
Year 6	1276.29	127.63	63.81	63.81
Year 10	1551.81	155.18	77.59	77.59

The longer-term result is very simple mathematics: the interest is simply added to the debt. Although the debtor pays off a larger real sum each year than in the preceding year, the debt capital grows all the time. After ten years it has grown by more than 50 per cent on the original unpayable amount of debt, to $1,551.81. A continually growing proportion of the debt that accrues in this way is such that the debtor will never be able to pay it off. These are 'phantom loans', which were not originally even intended for any other purpose than for nominal debt service (nominal, because the debtor remains continuously insolvent).

When the country is close to insolvency and finds it difficult to receive any more credit, it can turn to the International Monetary Fund. Since 1989 the IMF has also loaned to countries that get into difficulty servicing their private debts. IMF loans function as a signal to other creditors that they can continue lending to the country. But IMF loans come with tough conditions, concerning the national economy (how and on what the state can spend both its income and the money it borrows) and the organization of state institutions (for example, the decentralization of state administration, increased transparency and surveillance, and privatization).

The idea is that countries in need of credit must 'adjust their structures' in the name of technical efficiency, above all through cutting public spending and increasing exports. The demanded measures include the liberalization of trade and markets for the benefit of transnational companies, and privatization – which also usually puts state assets in the hands of transnational companies. State outlay on food subsidies, education, health care and social insurance is cut, or fees are introduced for these services. The IMF has typically also demanded devaluation measures, which reduce the prices of exports but make imports more expensive. Another, invariably tacit, condition that may be imposed is that the state behaves 'sensibly' in international political forums, meaning acquiescence to the dominant economic policy consensus and to the primacy of Washington.

How have the IMF structural adjustment programmes broadly construed, covering the theme with all its variations, succeeded in resolving debt problems? There is no simple answer to this, for many reasons. In many developing countries import trade is heavily dependent on world market prices for raw materials and agricultural products, and prices can fluctuate strongly. IMF debt crisis packages over the past fifteen years or so have usually included also some debt restructuring, in the course of which the amount of nominal debt has decreased. Development aid has been made conditional on structural adjustment programmes, so that compliant countries have usually received more aid than comparative countries.

Furthermore, states vary in the extent of their dependence on the IMF. There may have been easy alternatives to the Fund's and Western banks' loans – for example, in the 2000s the Asian surplus states and China in particular have provided loans at reasonable interest rates, and without political conditions attached. Countries in trouble have been able to resort to currency and monetary policies of their own devising; for instance, in the last decade some countries succeeded in substituting domestic for international debt, which gave them control over interest rates. Strong-willed governments, such as Argentina in the early 2000s, have been able to negotiate better conditions in direct negotiations with the IMF. Every debt crisis occurs in particular circumstances and has its own distinctive features, and thus the making of decisive and general conclusions would require analysing the many different possible paths of developments.[25]

An added problem is that there are different criteria for assessing success. Is the goal solely to have debt repayments continue without interruption, reduction in the amount of debt, or perhaps increased gross domestic product; or development in some general sense, including citizens' welfare, democracy and justice?[26] Evaluations of success according to more precise criteria would require counterfactual analysis also: what would have been the alternative to the IMF style of 'structural adjustment', and what would have been the likely consequences of this alternative? Would it have succeeded on the terms of the chosen criteria?

On a general level something can be said, however. Structural adjustment programmes carried out with one-sided adherence to IMF conditions and without significant debt restructurings do not work. According to studies done by the United Nations Conference on Trade and Development (UNCTAD), in the 1980s and 1990s in particular even when countries managed to control their debt, the levels continued to rise still further. Countries in the IMF programme were given significantly more loans and development aid, and on some occasions direct investments followed these. Nevertheless, they failed to develop. Although it is understandable that the IMF itself attempts to present the results of structural adjustment programmes in the most optimistic possible light, evidence of the improvements they bring is hard to find. In the words of a report by UNCTAD, when it comes to the precarious economic growth of highly indebted countries

FIGURE 7.2   Bono and German chancellor Angela Merkel discuss developing country debt in 2007, before the global financial crisis and European debt crisis.

'the efficacy of the economic reforms, on which so many lives and livelihoods now hang, is, and must remain, an act of faith.'[27] Structural adjustment has also had a tendency to channel income and wealth to the upper income levels in a society, and to transnational firms. When more wealth than in the past is taken out of the country, there is less left to support residents' domestic consumption, even if the country's GDP level does rise as a result of structural adjustments. And in so far as the little money that does remain in the country is less evenly distributed than before the IMF intervention, the end result tends to be a fairly bad one for the majority of the country's populace.[28]

The IMF's structural adjustment programmes have not created a single economic miracle; the levels of GDP per capita of the very poorest development countries were more or less the same in 2000 as they were in 1970. The first notable attempt by lending institutes at reducing debt was in 1996, with the creation by the IMF and the World Bank of the Heavily Indebted Poor Countries (HIPC) initiative. Debt relief measures began to be implemented as part of the two Bretton Woods institutions' own poverty relief programmes. The measure was widely criticized, and in 1999 a revised version was unveiled, often called HIPC II. The new effort amounted to an admission by the IMF and the World Bank that simply drawing up new repayment schedules was not enough. Significant cuts to debt levels were also essential, but even these have not sufficed to make the subsequent experiences of IMF programmes especially positive in any way.

The HIPC and other debt settlement programmes that include structural adjustment conditions have come under continuous fire throughout the 2000s also. Although debt relief has helped somewhat, the structural adjustment programmes have not. Also, responsibility for debt has been transferred in ways that create moral hazard: first multi-centred finance institutions help private lenders to offload their problem loans, then OECD states use development aid funds to pay off the problem debts of the IMF and other multi-centred institutions.

The positive impact of debt relief has been significant for some developing countries. It contributed to improving some of these countries' external balances during the 2000–2007 period, when the prices of raw materials and the amounts of Chinese and other direct investments rose rapidly. And yet many developing countries continued to experience fragile finances. These countries, which over the past four decades have experienced as many downturn years as years of economic growth, are especially vulnerable to the effects of crises in the world economy. Drops in export revenue and other effects of the crisis that began in 2008 have again raised the debt levels of these states.[29]

Debt arbitration mechanism

According to economist Joseph Stiglitz, many individuals and companies profit financially from deferring the resolution of debt crises, including in countries in which markets are subject to clear public regulations.[30] It is economically beneficial for individual lending banks or states to believe that the debts will indeed be paid some day. As long as the lending system remains functional somehow, the growth of ghost loans could turn out to be profitable for banks: loan sizes increase continuously, and interest rates are high. Revenue from debt servicing or interest payments are not the only benefits that lending institutions reap from this system, however. Debt dependency provides the economically powerful countries and the Bretton Woods institutions with a means of keeping indebted countries under their control. If risks grow, they can attempt to transfer the problem to the IMF countries and to their development aid budgets.

Efficient and complete resolution of the debt problem may well be against the interests of the lenders. As Stiglitz notes,

> The existence of such negative incentives is why bankruptcy law in [the United States of] America allows bankruptcy judges discretion to force recalcitrant creditors to accept a resolution that is in the broader interest. Why should principles that make sense within countries – like the US – not be applied in the international arena?[31]

But the rule of law is still not applied to international financing. Creditors have managed to set their own conditions for debt servicing, and to control how the situation is handled even when the debtor is insolvent. The lawyer and economist Kunibert Raffer, a leading researcher of debt, has pointed out that no 'civilized' legal system allows only one party to influence the outcome of the legal process.[32] Only in international debt settlement negotiations do lenders function simultaneously as plaintiff, judge and jury.

At the beginning of the 2000s it looked like the Bretton Woods institutions were beginning to bow to pressures for the creation of some sort of insolvency mechanism or international bankruptcy procedure. Even the George W. Bush-led United States government at the time seemed open to the idea of international bankruptcy laws. In September 2001, finance minister Paul O'Neill spoke publicly of the need to create such a mechanism on the lines of Chapter 11 of the US bankruptcy legislation. In November of the same year, the IMF's deputy managing director Anne Krueger made a similar proposal.[33] The situation changed rapidly, however. The 'war on terror' stole the limelight from the alternative globalization movement, at the same time as a new wave of optimism took hold about the global debt problem. During the 2003–07 financial boom, it seemed like the debt problems were almost solving themselves. Export prices of raw materials and agricultural goods rose swiftly, and middle-income developing countries were increasingly turning to China and other Asian surplus countries for easy, no-strings-attached credit.

The idea of a country going bankrupt is not necessarily a good one, however. No country could possibly be keen on the idea of being declared bankrupt and put at the full mercy of its creditors. Countries want the kind of legally binding international debt arbitration mechanism that would simultaneously give them the opportunity for comprehensive debt restructuring and freedom from the conditions imposed on their economic policy.

As has already been indicated, Chapter 9 of the United States bankruptcy laws could be a suitable model for the creation of a general framework within which willing countries would have the possibility of going even further through establishing various kinds of temporary tribunal or unofficial negotiations for even more radical debt restructuring. A substantive goal could be general debt relief programmes and the kind of debt repayment system that would incrementally reduce the amount of outstanding debt at a realistic pace without allowing ghost debts to accrue. This system would be a significant step towards emancipation from the unnecessary and undesirable powers of the Bretton Woods institutions, which have been used more for the further- ance of special interests than sensible economic policy. A debt arbitration mechanism alone is not enough, though.

Requirements for debt settlement: undoing both mounting debt and financialization

Controlled and legally binding debt arbitration offers the pos- sibility of swift debt restructurings as soon as a country's leaders notice the country is in serious difficulty. Debt arbitration is a sensible choice in individual situations, and can help prevent one country's debt difficulties worsening and spreading to other countries. However, it would be an instance of the whole–part fallacy to assume that what can work for one party in one instance could work for everyone simultaneously. Special problems arise if a sufficiently large number of big economies get into difficulties with debt all at once, and arise also if creditors' own financial base is fragile due to them having debts of their own. In both the USA and Europe the combined amount of debt in the financial sector is much larger than these countries' combined public debt.

In other words, although the development of an international debt arbitration mechanism would be progress, it would not be enough, because effective debt restructuring depends cru- cially on the broader economic policy context within which the negotiations are conducted. For debt arbitration to have a reason- able chance of success, overall financing must have sustainable foundations. At the same time, there must be possibilities to intervene in the mechanisms of the world economy that create debt. Above all, there is a need for means of evening out trade deficits and surpluses, since chronic deficits tend to lead to debt accumulation.

It is not possible in this chapter to examine in detail all the practices and mechanisms needed (but on the economic theory behind these reforms, see Chapters 3 and 4). Instead, the aim is to outline the broader context within which a global debt settlement could remain functional in the longer run also. Some of the main steps required include:

- restriction, taxation and, in some cases, abolition of speculative activities;
- closure of tax havens and regulation-free zones;
- dissolution of accrued debt, starting with households;
- use of central bank funding to support citizens and public budgets;
- the creation of global mechanisms to control current account deficits and surpluses.

Reforms of the speculative economy would apply both to actors and to forms of activity. The basic function of banks is to channel savings into fixed real investments, and banks would still be able to focus on this. By contrast, they could be prohibited outright from participating in speculation and insurance activities, as the Glass–Steagall Act did in the USA from its establishment in 1933 until its gradual repeal in the 1980s and 1990s (which contributed to the 2008–09 crisis). In 2010, the US Congress and the Obama administration passed the Dodd–Frank Wall Street Reform and Consumer Protection Act. This contains a section called the Volcker Rule, which prohibits regular banks from making speculative investments that do not benefit their customers. The Rule does provide for exceptions, however, and it does not prevent banks from speculating on behalf of customers.[34] Enforcing a clear distinction between different forms of activity, and prohibiting the description 'bank' from being used by any institution except regular banks would markedly reduce the amount of speculation, leveraging and related causes of debt accumulation. The financial sector as a whole would thus become more stable.

The goal, or at least the actual effect, of most financial innovations is to circumvent regulations, increase the opportunities for taking risks, and transfer risks to others in such a way that these others are not aware of the fact. Although risk financing can sometimes be useful for technological development, this sort of financing can be organized in several other ways too. The function of almost all financial instrument innovations has been to make the overall system harder for the uninitiated to understand, less transparent, and more susceptible to risk.[35] In this light, a new principle could be brought into use: only certain, predefined forms of financial trading would be allowed, and all others would be illegal. The new principle would increase the freedom and welfare of all in a consistent and generalizable manner, while also preventing authorities and other investors from being deliberately misled. Predictions would be easier to make in a simple and transparent financial system, and for this reason it would be less costly for all involved. There would be a drop in the amount of pointlessly risky gambles, and of high-risk leveraging, and thereby also in the amount of speculative debt. This in turn would make the financing system more stable and sustainable.

A financial tax would make it possible to influence financial activity and to distribute profits and risks fairly.[36] Fees for stabilization could be levied on banks and investors, and public insurance funds and buffers could be created to ensure the stability of the financial system. These would be funded from tax revenue collected from the financial sector. High-rate taxes would markedly increase the costs of financial activity, and would deter speculation significantly. (In contrast, the financial transaction tax for either the whole EU or the eurozone that was proposed by the European Commission in September 2011 would be set at a rather low rate.) The tax revenue could be used for many national and global public goods. In addition, when it is known in advance that the risks are shared and socialized in the event of a crisis, the basic principles underlying the financial system as a whole must be reconsidered. If risks are partly socialized, then assets and profits would also have to be shared and publicly accessible to some extent. For example, at least partial public ownership of the major financial players could be justified, as could a high tax rate on the profits of banks and investors. A ceiling could be placed on both salaries and bonuses (i.e. maximum income law), which would contribute to preventing excessive saving.[37]

Offshore centres provide regulation-free and tax-free investment zones for highly mobile transnational money, and make it possible to evade domestic regulations and taxes. In doing so they contribute to and facilitate high-risk speculative activity and investments. When so-called 'high-net-worth individuals' and companies transfer their wealth and profits to tax havens, the result is a loss to state tax coffers and currency reserve. This is one cause of state deficits and debt, and in the case of Greece and Portugal, for example, it is a serious problem. Tax havens also give large transnational firms and banks an unfair competitive advantage over smaller domestic and local companies. The institution of sovereignty shields offshore centres by allowing them to be self-legislating.[38] The activities of tax havens can be restrained through increased transparency and taxing money flows to and from them at a high rate (for example 25 per cent).[39] Vigorous constraints on the activities of tax havens would reduce what Rasmus calls 'the global money parade'.[40]

Furthermore, many accrued debts that are directly connected to consumption and investments should be renegotiated. Financial stability depends both on the level of debt and on its nature: when the former rises and the latter deteriorates, dissolution is called for. Reducing the amount of disposable income that households spend on servicing debts has an immediate stimulatory effect on consumer demand, and thereby also on the formation of fixed real investments. The situations of many of those in the worst financial difficulties would improve if credit-card interest rates alone, including all their administrative costs, were capped at between 8 and 10 per cent. Private, debt-funded owner-occupied housing markets are susceptible to boom-and-bust cycles, and to relieve this difficulty mortgage renegotiations could be made possible for small- and middle-income owners.[41] Reducing the amount of mortgage debt over the longer term, however, would also require the creation of alternatives to private home ownership, such as the provision of partly owned houses, social and price-regulated homes, publicly produced and rent-controlled apartments. In general, any measures that would increase employment and make the distribution of wealth more egalitarian would add to financial stability and help maintain effective aggregate demand.

Keynesian economic policy does not mean living in debt indefinitely, or increasing the long-run state debt burden.[42] During times of growth, debts should be paid off and reserves established for the next downturn. When the stimulation of economy requires increased public expenditure, however, organizing such funding may become a problem, particularly during a downturn or if the state is already in debt. When growth is slow or negative and there is clearly excess capacity, it is possible to resort to partial central bank funding of the state budget without thereby triggering a self-reinforcing increase in inflation levels. One way of doing this is for the central bank to create money for the state budget by issuing low- or zero-interest-rate sovereign bonds and 'buying' many of them from the state with money the central bank issues.[43] Fiscal measures should be used for the development of the basic infrastructure of the economy in particular, and for improving long-term financial, social and ecological sustainability. The creation of money for supporting the speculative get-rich-quick

economy is a short-sighted strategy, but the financial base can be
strengthened and demand can be increased through timely and
controlled use of central bank financing for supporting low- and
middle-income household consumption, housing construction,
infrastructural development, and acceleration of fixed real investments, especially during economically difficult times.

The practical possibilities for international debt arbitration and
restructuration thus depend on the nature of the overall global political economic framework. The list of necessary measures that I
have sketched is abstract, however, and provides no precise speci-
fications as to relevant time or scale of reforms. To what extent
could an individual country implement these measures, and to
what extent would the participation and support of larger bodies
such as the EU be needed? To what extent would the measures
require new worldwide institutional arrangements? Going one's
own way within one state with new ideas is possible, but it has
its limits, and often only broad-scale, concerted action can bring
about the desired effects. It is clear at least that tax havens can be
closed only through joint and coordinated efforts, and limiting
speculative activities would require worldwide political action.

Also the managing of trade deficits and surpluses requires
new, global institutional mechanisms. The most systematic and
detailed proposal for controlling deficits and surpluses remains
Keynes's blueprint for an International Clearings Union, ICU,
which he outlined in the 1940s.[44] It would be a global central
bank of sorts, with a common central bank currency, the 'bancor'.
This currency would be used for international trade, and the
exchange rates of other currencies would be fixed relative to it.
Deficits and surpluses would be visible in each country's central
bank account, and when any country's surplus exceeded a certain
level the central bank would retain part of it to fund the needs
of the global community. Under this system states would have
a strong incentive to avoid the accumulation of large surpluses,

and would be more likely to use their surplus to import goods and services from deficit countries.

Conclusions

The history of the past century offers plentiful examples of debt crises and of the kinds of outcomes the attempts to handle them have typically produced. The experiences of Germany between the world wars, and the experiences of economically developing countries from the early 1980s onwards, exemplify the sorts of measures that can easily prolong and exacerbate crises. By contrast, the London negotiations on German debt in the early 1950s demonstrate how things can be done differently. At that time, the global political economy was in any case favourable to sustainable debt restructurings, and in the Bretton Woods era as a whole financing was on a more stable footing than it has been in the neoliberal era.

Germany's chief negotiator during the London talks, Hermann J. Abs, also mediated in negotiations on the restructuring of Indonesia's debt in 1969. The government of General Suharto was granted a debt relief package that was very similar to the one Germany had received sixteen years earlier. In both cases, the debt burden was cut to roughly half its value at the time of the negotiations, and neither country was subjected to 'structural adjustment conditions'.[45] The German economic miracle coincided precisely with the years immediately following the debt settlement, and in Indonesia too the economy began to recover quickly after 1969. The average annual growth rate was between 5 and 8 per cent, and the country's GDP doubled roughly every ten years. In 1970, 60 per cent of Indonesians lived below the poverty line, but by 1996 this proportion had dropped to 12 per cent, despite extremely rapid population growth. Over the same period the child mortality rate dropped by half, average life expectancy rose by almost twenty years, and literacy rose to almost 90 per cent.[46]

But debt restructurings do not have to be dependent on transient political situations or on the goodwill of specific decision-makers. A permanent global debt arbitration mechanism that upholds the rule of law would offer possibilities for swift debt conciliation for countries that find themselves in difficulty. It would not be enough by itself, especially if more than one large economy got into debt problems at the same time. Problems also arise if creditors' own financial base is unstable on account of their being in debt themselves. There are also structural reasons for increasing involvement in debt.

The number-one prerequisite for debt arbitration is a stable financial system. This requires the sort of measures and institutional mechanisms that are only partly realizable within nation-states. For this reason, solving the euro crisis demands not only structural reforms to the EU system, but also new systems of global governance.

8

Towards democratic
global Keynesianism

Europe has not only been on the receiving end of globalization, as in the case of the global financial crisis of 2008–09 and its aftermath. It has also been a major actor in the globalizing world that it has actively contributed to creating.[1] But what does globalization mean? In its general social-scientific meaning, 'globalization' refers to the expansion of the field of societal relations, and to the decreasing significance of physical and temporal expanses.[2] Goods, ideas and technologies have travelled and have been transported over long distances relatively quickly for centuries, and more circuitously for millennia. Since the Second Industrial Revolution, in particular, means of transport and communications have developed dramatically. People's everyday experiences have become increasingly intertwined through world economic mechanisms and interdependencies.[3] Nowadays real-time simultaneous communications from almost any part of the world to anywhere else are affordable and easy for many, and intercontinental flights are entirely routine for the wealthy classes. For these and related reasons, relations of power and dependency in society have become increasingly transnational and transcontinental. Globalization in this abstract spatial sense is not primarily dependent on any dominant ideology.

Globalization in its second, economistic sense refers either to the interests and visions of transnational corporations or to the neoliberal ideology. The term 'globalization' itself began to be used in various senses in the 1980s, and its economic meaning in particular quickly became widespread in the mainstream media. When Harvard Business School professor Theodore Levitt published an article on this theme in 1983, over a thousand companies quickly ordered a total of 35,000 copies of it.[4] Since then, the article has been purchased and downloaded around a million times. It is a superlatively worded advocacy of truly global market strategies, as opposed to the traditional decentralized strategy of transnational corporations. At this time, historical developments favoured neoliberalism. In the 1980s, states had less and less success with leftist economic and social policies: in France, for instance, socialist president François Mitterrand's programme on taking office led to capital flight. In 1983, two years after his election, Mitterrand made an almost complete U-turn on economic policy. Increasingly many journalists, political leaders and also citizens began to believe British prime minister Margaret Thatcher's slogan that 'there is no alternative'.[5]

Thatcher's neoliberalism is a doctrine of governance according to which competitive markets, or their administrative simulation within organizations, are the best guarantees of efficiency, freedom and justice, or all of these.[6] Globalization is treated as being synonymous with the so-called Washington Consensus, a ten-point economic plan that for decades the International Monetary Fund, the World Bank and the United States Department of the Treasury have thrust on all the countries that have been forced to turn to them for economic help.[7] The programme has included liberalization of trade and investments, privatization, deregulation, strengthening of private property rights and of market mechanisms and market discipline, and various reforms related to taxation and the use of public funds. Also built into the programme has been the process of financialization, in which financial markets, financial institutions and the financial elites steadily increase their hold over company activities, economic processes and economic policies.

Conformity to these doctrinal demands has, however, been unrewarding: in the area of finance in particular, crisis has followed crisis in quick succession. In October 1987 world markets came close to complete collapse, and in the early and mid-1990s there were many financial crises, such as the banking and currency crises in Finland, Sweden and Norway; the 1992 crisis of the European Exchange Rate Mechanism; and the so-called Tequila Crisis of the Mexican peso in 1994. When the Asian economic crisis of 1997–98 made headlines throughout the world, the editor of the left-wing French newspaper *Le Monde diplomatique*, Ignacio Ramonet, called for 'disarmament of the markets'.[8] Ramonet caused a furore with his proposals: closure of tax havens, higher capital gains tax and a 'global solidarity tax', the Tobin tax on currency transactions. Ramonet's aim in writing the piece was to decrease the sense of social insecurity felt by ordinary citizens, and to improve the conditions for equality and democracy. The *Le Monde diplomatique* office was soon awash with correspondence, with many readers, worried by the developments of the 1980s and 1990s, writing to ask what they could do. When no one else took the initiative, the 'le Diplo' journalists themselves formed Attac (Association pour la taxation des transactions financières et pour l'action citoyenne; Association for the Taxation of Financial Transactions and for Citizens' Action), a citizens' organization that would go on to develop networks throughout Europe and later worldwide. Attac rejects both Thatcher's dogmatism and the Washington Consensus. 'A better world is possible!'[9]

FIGURE 8.1   Keynes's comparison of financial markets to casinos has implications for regulation and taxation: in many countries gambling is tightly regulated and heavily taxed, with a large amount or even all of the profits being used for the common good.

Economic theory is at the heart of debates on the direction of development. The reform proposals put forward by Ramonet and Attac draw on the economic theories of John Maynard Keynes and Michał Kalecki, and on revised and expanded versions of these (post-Keynesian theory). In the conditions of an irreversibly interconnected world economy, these theories cannot adequately be applied solely at national level; a global perspective is needed. One such perspective, though limited in scope, was presented in the 1970s by economist James Tobin, in the form of a proposal for a global tax on currency exchanges.[10] Tobin generalized Keynes's proposal for stock exchange taxes ('When the capital development of a country becomes a by-product of the activities of a casino, the job is likely to be ill-done ... It is usually agreed that casinos should, in the public interest, be inaccessible and expensive. And perhaps the same is true of Stock Exchanges').[11]

Tobin's brief but important step towards new worldwide solutions and institutions can and must be generalized to apply to other activities and mechanisms also. As a follower of Keynes, Tobin was well aware that the formation of effective aggregate demand in a single country is dependent on what happens elsewhere.[12] My argument for global Keynesianism goes further than Tobin's. Mere coordination of economic policies between states or the implementation of a currency transaction tax, for example, is not enough to make the governance of interdependence sustainable. The euro crisis is also an indication of the importance and urgency of thoroughgoing reforms to the system of governance of the world economy. Because the EU is intertwined with worldwide political economic processes, including financialization, global reforms would also contribute to the metamorphosis of the EU. Needed are the sorts of global governance mechanisms that can shape the supply of money in the system, balance surpluses and deficits on an equitable basis, and direct the formation, composition and distribution of economic growth.

Economic governance is an essential part of democracy, as Tobin emphasized in his own proposal. However, Tobin remained tied to the traditional nationalistic world-view. But in an interconnected world, democracy can also be applied transnationally and globally. In increasing measure, transnational and global realities conflict with the assumption that decision-makers are – or should only be – held accountable to the enfranchised citizens of their own country, and with the assumption that the effects of political decisions remain confined to within the territorial borders of states. Even if increased autonomy for states in economic policymaking could – and indeed sometimes can justifiably – be a crucial ethico-political goal, initiatives for new institutional arrangements point in a rather different direction, namely towards global democracy.[13]

When these two views are combined, the result is a vision of democratic global Keynesianism. The central problem for making this vision a reality is the prevailing social imaginary, which does not sufficiently correspond to real-world social conditions. Imaginaries comprise metaphors, mental frames and stories that enable understanding of things that are abstract and removed from quotidian experience. At the end of this chapter I sketch some new metaphors, frames and stories that help in forming sensible solutions both to key problems of global political economy, and to other big questions about the future, concerning for example security and the environment. The prevailing identities and political communities can be modified through both imaginaries and common institutions. This kind of transformation requires new answers to the perennial questions: who are we, to what communities do we belong, and where are we going?

Global Keynesianism: the holistic viewpoint

As an economist Tobin considered himself 'an old Keynesian'.[14] He first proposed an international currency exchange tax in 1972, at the time the Bretton Woods system was crumbling and the world was shifting to an era of floating exchange currencies and free movement of capital. Tobin's initiative was based on Keynes's proposal in the 1930s of a sizeable government transfer tax on all equity transactions. Keynes also made many other proposals, including for a tax on currency reserves, and these too may have influenced Tobin.[15] He generalized Keynes's proposal and applied it to currency markets. After several decades and financial crises, a currency exchange tax has become a central demand of the alter-globalization movement. The idea is still relevant, not least because foreign exchange has been left out of the European Commission's proposal for a financial transaction tax.

In 1978 Tobin suggested that a currency exchange tax would
be only a second-best solution to the problems created by acutely
fluctuating currency exchange rates and, more crucially, by rapid
movements of capital. The better solution would be integration. If
there were only one global currency in the world and one central
bank, there would be no need for a currency transaction tax. As
the example of the euro has now shown, the creation of a common
currency is a complicated and demanding undertaking. In order
for the global currency project to be realizable, many other things
would also be necessary, including a global monetary policy and
a common fiscal policy. And for both of these prior requirements,
far-reaching economic integration is essential. From the perspective of political possibilities also, a common global currency
remains a far-fetched aspiration: 'however appealing, [it] is clearly
not a viable option in the foreseeable future, i.e., the twentieth
century'.[16] In the new century the time for a world currency and
central bank may come sooner than we think, but not without
extensive changes to prepare the ground for them.

Following Keynes, Tobin stressed the importance of coordinated economic policy between states, with a far-reaching
and more global outlook on the shared responsibilities of states.
Regardless of whether the governments of the largest industrial
countries acknowledge it or not, together they and their central
banks 'are making fiscal and monetary policy for the world'.
Tobin warned that this system could easily create vulnerability to
'the burdens of much more damaging protectionist and autarkic
measures designed to protect economies, at least their politically
favoured sectors, from the consequences of international financial shocks'.[17] In other words, an uncoordinated free-trade and
financial system can create financial crises, unemployment and
other problems that in a later phase lead to the rise of economic
nationalism and measures of self-sufficiency or even autarchy,
with harmful consequences for worldwide wealth creation. The

whole is dynamic: in weighing up the options one must take into account the likely historical consequences, both economic and political.

Free-floating currency exchange rates are not stable. Transnational flows of capital react too sensitively to even small interest rate and other differences, and hamper autonomous and sustainable economic policies. Tobin's proposed solution to excessively fast and massive flows of capital was a currency transaction tax that would decrease and slow worldwide financial flows. This would increase the autonomy of state monetary and economic policies by 'throw[ing] some sand in the wheels of our excessively efficient international money markets'.[18] This departure in outlook from orthodox neoclassical economic theory – and also from the European Commission's proposed financial transaction tax – is significant. From an overall economic point of view, large and overly 'well-greased' financial markets are a cause of inefficiency, and make sensible economic policymaking difficult.[19]

The goals of a currency transaction tax – efficiency, justice and democracy – are widely understood, as is the way in which their realization is dependent on specifics of the taxation regime.[20] In this connection it is crucial to know why Tobin placed such a high priority on coordination between states' economic policies and on their shared cosmopolitan responsibilities. These priorities follow directly from Keynesian economic theory and the holistic perspective on which it is founded, according to which the formation of demand is seen from the standpoint of all actors and countries at once. Applying this perspective methodically is the very basis of global Keynesianism.

Throughout the 1930s Kalecki and Keynes developed theories of effective demand and of the so-called multiplier effect. Any increase in demand will increase the degree to which overall production capacity is utilized. Investments have a very special role, however: fixed real investments increase long-term productive capacities, while at the same time creating immediate multiplier effects on aggregate demand and on how current capacity is utilized. For instance, if a firm builds a new factory, it gives plentiful employment and increases the demand for raw materials and intermediate product, which provides further employment and strengthens demand for goods and services. To absorb the increased productive capacity, however, more demand is needed in the future.

Increasing private or public consumer demand also has multiplier effects. Cleaning streets or maintaining public gardens, for instance, increases the demand for goods and services and provides employment, which increases others' income and profits, which in turn creates further multiplier effects. All these activities increase effective demand, with a gradually weakening impact. The dynamic of growth and investments in the capitalist market economy tends to be cyclical. An upward spiral (the fast growth phase) dominates up to a certain point, but when the turn comes the same mechanisms start to pull in the opposite direction (depending on the conditions, towards recession or even depression).[21] Demand can also be created or maintained through public measures.

One major problem, however, is that national economies are not closed systems but parts of an integrated world economy. The more connected economic activities within the borders of a state are to the processes elsewhere in the world economy, the more the effects of public policies will spread elsewhere. Already Keynes acknowledged that 'in an open system with foreign-trade relations, some part of the multiplier of the increased investment will accrue to the benefit of employment in foreign countries, since a proportion of the increased consumption will diminish our own country's favourable foreign balance.'[22] Depending on the country's position in the world economy, this can easily decrease interest in pursuing Keynesian economic policies. In addition, if the timings of expansionary or contractionary economic policies of different states are contradictory, or, even worse, if states attempt to transfer their economic difficulties abroad by increasing their exports (relative to imports), the end result can be bad or even catastrophic for many countries, or for all. What is crucial, therefore, is that all participate fairly in maintaining adequate domestic demand, which creates export possibilities for the others. In this way, all countries create the common conditions needed for growth.[23]

This is the logic according to which Tobin came to find coordination among economic policymakers so important. In the prevailing conditions, therefore, Tobin espoused the use of two strategies at the same time: increased autonomy for state economic policymaking, and extensive cooperation between the economic policymakers of different countries. There may be no direct contradiction between these two strategies. From Tobin's perspective, most important of all is that politics controls the economy and not the other way round. Still, there is some tension between the two strategies: how can coordination of autonomous national economic policies succeed without common institutional arrangements that are binding on all? Tobin did not consider the politics of such coordination in any depth, instead giving his recommendations as an economic theorist researching economies as 'separate' from politics and power relations.

The problematic of an intertwined world economy affects the conditions for economic policy not only through trade relations or through their governance by the World Trade Organization, but also in many other ways.[24] Trade requires a global monetary and credit system, and must always be conducted in some currency or other. Since the end of the Second World War the US dollar has occupied this central role, but it is not the only trade currency. In a world of many currencies, currency exchange proceeds in accordance with certain principles, and these principles have changed over time. The same applies to credit. Deficits can be bankrolled with credit, which is always granted in some currency and subject to certain conditions. A state's possibilities for managing its economy are crucially influenced by its position in the international division of labour, its balance-of trade deficit or surplus, and the institutional mechanisms of the global monetary and credit system. The fates of countries are intertwined through the prevailing institutional monetary and credit arrangements, which can be more or less fair or one-sided, legal or obscure, functional or crisis-prone, sustainable or fragile. All institutional arrangements are amenable to change.[25]

In addition to trade and money, the interconnectedness of the world economy can be understood from a third perspective, through relations of production. Industrial production has always been dependent on the supply of energy and raw materials. In the 1800s and 1900s trading companies and empires were active in ensuring the reliability of raw material supplies, and since the late 1800s transnational firms have extended production and sales processes from country to country. The more complex the finished product, the more likely it is that processes involved in its manufacture and sale have been divided into different phases. Subcontractors are also commonly used. A mobile phone, for instance, can contain the work of hundreds of companies. Completion of the final product is dependent on the entire supply and production process. Increase in the demand of the final product, apparently produced in one country, affects the economic prospects of numerous firms and their employees across the world.

The high mobility of production and money, and advances in transportation and communications, have made it possible to decentralize production processes to different parts of the world. At the same time as the multinational nature of production intensifies the interdependence of different regions of the world economy, it lessens the multiplier effect of domestic demand. And at the same time as production chains are increasingly dispersed throughout the world, the domestication of profits for tax-related considerations – often meaning simply tax evasion – becomes correspondingly easier, almost anywhere in the world and especially in tax havens. These developments have effects on states' economic policies and tax revenue, and on power relations, which also partly determine the limits of economic policy. Mega-companies have significant structural power over national governments.[26] When production and its components can be easily dispersed geographically, the bargaining position of domestic workforces relative to transnational capital becomes weaker. Monitoring, regulation and steering of how relations of production are formed and of their effects are only possible through worldwide concerted actions and common institutions.

Towards global Keynesian institutions

Global Keynesianism is an approach that frames questions of public economic policy and politics more generally on the world economic scale.[27] Global Keynesianism aims to regulate global interdependencies in such a way as to produce stable and high levels of growth, employment and welfare for everyone and everywhere, simultaneously. Global Keynesianism is an ecologically responsible doctrine: governing interdependence could not otherwise be sustainable. The main themes of global Keynesianism are public administration, democratic politics, mixed economy, global taxation, global redistribution of wealth, global aggregate demand, joint management of investments and financing, ecological sustainability, and the many levels and contexts of governance and their interconnections.

The term 'global Keynesianism' entered the literature in the early 1980s, and to start with was mainly used by critics of the Brandt Report, published in 1980.[28] Soon advocates of the approach also adopted the term.[29] The Brandt Report developed the idea of a world civilization for the new millennium, and proposed a new international economic system. Among the mechanisms that this would include are global taxes, the revenue from which would be used in efforts to eradicate poverty and to promote economic development of the global South. At the time, soon after the 1970s' oil crisis, concern about world economic problems was widespread. The Report warned, in the spirit of Keynes, of a repeat of the developments of the 1930s, the likelihood of which could increase with dwindling supplies of raw materials and energy.[30] It also noted that the accumulation of debt in the developing countries of the global South following the oil crisis had contributed to maintaining demand in the industrialized northern countries.[31] The problem is that accumulation of debt by the poor countries is not a sustainable way of ensuring sufficient levels of overall demand, as has been shown by the global debt crisis that started in the early 1980s. Interdependency is irreversible, but better methods and mechanisms are needed to govern it.

The Report included consideration of how transfer of global resources could contribute to the South's economic development and industrialization, and at the same time act as a common stimulus package for the entire world economy (by means of development aid, transfer of funds through taxation, and debt arbitration). Expansion of balanced markets would contribute to growth in all parts of the world economy, but not without problems of adjustment in the affluent North. The import of products from the global South replacing domestic industrially produced equivalents – in later years, above all from China – most harshly affects residents of the poorer regions of OECD countries, particularly those with fewer skills and lower levels of education. The task of states is to actively facilitate adjustment to these changes by maintaining full employment, supporting alternative sources of employment, and implementing or maintaining active regional policies.[32] Other suggestions made in the Report include:

- price stabilization mechanisms for primary products, benefiting above all the developing countries;
- a controlled and actively supported transition towards renewable energy sources;
- common legally binding regulations on the investments and other activities of transnational companies.

The Commission also recommended a new world monetary and credit system.[33] According to the Report, regional arrangements such as the European Monetary System require a functional global monetary and credit system.[34] The Special Drawing Rights system set up by the International Monetary Fund in 1968 was the first step towards a genuinely international currency.[35] This system should be developed and extended: the monetary system of the future cannot be based on the currency of any particular country, but should rather be founded on a jointly approved global currency. This future currency would form the basis for currency reserves, and could also be used to help control the amount of liquidity (the combined total supply of money) in the world as a whole.

Surpluses and deficits would be counted in the global currency. Adjustment mechanisms that apply in the same ways to all parties could prevent the accumulation of surpluses and deficits, for instance through reallocation and redistribution of SDRs. A function of the IMF is to lend money to deficit countries when necessary. Although in the view of the Brandt Commission some loan conditions are understandable – as a bank, the IMF must ensure that it gets its money back – the dominant IMF conditions typically have effects that are the opposite of those intended, and are particularly harsh to the most vulnerable debtors. If the IMF demands deflationary structural adjustments from a state, the onus is on the organization itself to show that these are justified, as it must assume responsibility for the effects of these measures on solvency, income distribution, employment and social services. Irrespective of the content of the conditions, the time allowed for implementing the adjustments must be sufficiently long (the use of Earth's orbit around the Sun – a year – as the basic time-unit of economic processes is arbitrary and highly problematic). Also, power should be distributed more evenly by giving a greater role in decision-making to developing countries.[36]

The Brandt Commission's proposals awoke widespread discussion, but they led to no practical measures. Over three decades later, the most far-reaching of the Report's proposals remain unrealized. In the early 1980s, the world was increasingly pushed onto the path of the neoliberalism espoused by Thatcher and Reagan. But the neoliberal world order itself also tacitly contains some global Keynesian elements. In practice, the United States has had the role of the main engine of demand in the world economy. The country's chronic deficit, except for a few years during the 1990s, and ability to pay off its debts by printing dollars and by mobilizing dollar-valued sovereign bonds have bridged the gaps in global aggregate demand. Demand has been maintained through increasing the levels of debt more generally too, which is a central element of the financialization process. This state of affairs came to an end with the 2008–09 crisis and its aftermath, however.[37]

Even if Europe's stability facilities and mechanisms of the austerity programmes of the USA and Britain were to succeed in stabilizing the situation in the short term, which is unlikely, there are no grounds for assuming that the world economy can return to the pre-2008–09 growth path, which in any case was leaning more and more downwards. Financial fragility constrains private deficit consumption, and increasingly stringent conditions are now being imposed on public deficit consumption. The USA is unable to serve as the global demand engine any longer.

Global Keynesianism offers an alternative to following the neoliberal path to the bitter end.[38] By intervening in the immediate and fundamental causes of the economic crisis that began in 2008, global Keynesian redistribution would prevent the future development of the same conditions that have led to the present crisis. By influencing the conditions for economic growth and its sustainability, the redistribution would reduce the amount of social antagonisms and would at the same time create conditions for effectively tackling the major future challenges facing industrial civilization. Such a New Deal would be a large stride towards the sort of world that could come to terms with its own interconnectedness in an ethico-politically meaningful way. The following are just some of the elements that belong to an ecologically sensitive global Keynesian programme of reform:

- an expanded role for SDRs, or alternatively the establishment of a new global currency, and the creation of a mechanism by means of which world trade deficits and surpluses could be automatically balanced (based on Keynes's International Clearing Union, the Brandt Commission proposals, and other more recent proposals);[39]
- a debt arbitration mechanism and reform of the money and credit system in order to put financing on a sustainable basis (see Chapter 7);
- support for workers' rights and trade unionization on a planetary scale, both out of solidarity and to increase global aggregate demand;
- global taxes, such as an armaments tax and various financial transaction taxes, and a greenhouse gas emissions tax;
- an adequate basic level of education for all, implemented in such a way that funding for realization of the universal right to education would also be seen as part of the global redistribution of wealth;

- regulation and maintenance of demand at a universal level, which presupposes the coordinated institutionalization of economic policies between nation-states and functional international organizations – coordinated, for example, through a world parliament.

Global Keynesianism rests on an economic theory that holds that within a continuously changing world economy, two general tendencies nonetheless hold: uneven and contradictory trajectories of development that can be self-reinforcing, and development and inequality gaps that are often prone to widen.[40] Through tackling the contradictions and inequalities of the world economy and creating a new, planetary institutional framework, this whole entity can be made to work more sensibly, sustainably, fairly, and with more foresight than the present system. Crucial for overall development of the world economy is to build up efficient demand at a level corresponding to ever-increasing productive capacities – in a world characterized by increasing ecological limits to growth.

A central Keynesian idea is that a relatively even distribution of wealth is beneficial from the perspective of aggregate demand, not least because less-well-off consumers consume the bulk of their income. Within many countries and also globally, rising inequalities between groups and classes are a problem.[41] For this reason, the goal must be to raise real wages and other income, especially in the global South, which would also lessen pressures to cut wage levels in the global North and expand the southern markets for northern goods.[42] This cannot be brought about without broad political support for trade-union movements and organization of labour power throughout the world. As such, workers' rights and systematic worker organization could become the central goal of planetary economic policy for states and international organizations.

Registration and taxation of the arms trade would have many simultaneous objectives.[43] First of all, arms registration would bring transparency to states' military capacity, and to its direction and pace of development: it would become clear to all what weaponry each country is buying and selling. Arms taxation, for its part, would claim a portion of the profits on the arms trade for other purposes, such as poverty eradication and development. This source of tax revenue could be channelled especially to those parts of the world where there is acute risk of civil war. Various proposals in this vein have been made since the 1980s. In 2003, French president Jacques Chirac and his Brazilian counterpart Luiz Inácio da Silva proposed an arms trade tax as part of their efforts to reduce poverty and to create innovative new funding mechanisms.[44]

The European Commission's 2011 proposal for a Europe-wide financial transaction tax contains no proposal for taxing currency exchanges. In June 2012, a group of nine EU countries proceeded on the basis of this proposal. Because of the exclusion of currency trade, the proposal leaves open the possibility of working for a global currency transaction tax in tandem with the European financial transaction tax. The aim of a currency exchange tax would be to impose some much-needed calm and stability on the global financial system, and at the same time generate revenue for global initiatives for the common good. A global greenhouse gas emissions tax, for its part, would provide an incentive to reduce the use of fossil fuels and to step up development of more energy-efficient technologies and other sources of energy. This tax would be aimed at influencing company investments and also individual consumers, and the revenue raised could far outweigh that generated by a global currency transaction tax. The best way to realize these or other global taxes would be to assemble like-minded coalitions for negotiating and implementing a treaty and a functional international organization for implementation of the system first among themselves.[45]

A certain proportion of global tax revenue could be used to fund a universal basic education system for the whole world. A well-functioning system of this kind, motivated by cosmopolitan solidarity, would be one means of simultaneously promoting growth and peaceful politics for the future. Education is an essential condition for industrial development, and education for girls in particular helps to hurry all the world's countries and regions through swift demographic transition and to bring population growth (an ecological problem) to a head as soon as possible. Basic education cannot work unless local actors and conditions are centrally involved in organizing it, and neither can development come about without a sustainable local tax base. With the aid of a global fund, however, education could be actively advanced everywhere there are difficulties in providing equitable basic education to all.

A global Keynesian programme also includes the establishment of many new functional organizations, such as tax organizations, and each of these would have multiple times larger funds than any international organization currently extant. From the standpoint of regulating global aggregate demand, the key question is how to create the kinds of institutional arrangements that would allow coordination between the economic policymakers of states and international organizations. One possible solution to this is a world parliament. This would not need to have legislative powers, nor need it be the sovereign centre of the world community; it could be a conglomeration of various coordinating bodies, and the highest interpreter of international and later cosmopolitan law.

The argument for global democracy

At this stage it is useful to return to James Tobin's ideas. When Tobin presented his idea for a worldwide currency transaction tax, his most important goal was to safeguard the economic policy autonomy of sovereign states.[46] Tobin did not consider the monetary system from the perspective of economic theory or economic policy, but rather saw that the question was also one of democracy, which has inherent value irrespective of economic effects. In the same spirit Tobin argued in 1999 that '[t]o claim, as some right-wing ideologues did, that the victory of the West in the Cold War was the victory of economic liberalism was ridiculous: it was the victory of democracy and the mixed economies.'[47] Despite Tobin's understanding of democracy as a value in its own right, he was not prepared to apply the democratic principle beyond the borders of nation-states.

Tobin's argument on democratic grounds for a global currency exchange tax can be generalized into an argument for global democracy. Tobin's ambition was to reduce the size, volume and power of excessively 'efficient' transnational financial markets in light of their many undesirable consequences, including to national autonomy. In some sense he also understood that the present institutional arrangements could be transformed, although this would not be politically easy. The argument for transforming unnecessary and undesirable worldwide power relations is fundamentally an argument for global democratic emancipation.[48] The present institutional order is not natural or inevitable, nor even very effective. On the contrary, its various elements are in many respects founded on mistaken theoretical and ideological assumptions.

Global finance has become an established part of transnational power relations. There are good reasons for making the relations between finance and credit more equitable and democratic. The creation of a currency transaction tax could well be one part of the sort of ethico-political response that would open the dominant hierarchical power relations to political conflict and change. But for this goal to be attained consistently, both the means and the ends must be democratic. This idea can be further generalized to apply to all the areas of governance to which the global Keynesian argument also applies. When the processes are intertwined and in conditions of deep interdependence, relations of power are necessarily involved. Emancipation from non-essential and undesirable power relations is possible through common democratic governance, or even through government. Democratization can be brought about either by changing existing systems, or by creating new ones.

Too often, democracy is treated as being synonymous with elections and parliamentarianism. Global democracy refers to a complex and multi-level network of different systems of governance, within which democratic principles can be combined in different ways.[49] But a world parliament could also have a significant role in this system in the future. It would be a global body, with representatives elected on the principle of one person, one vote. Yet a world parliament would not otherwise need to replicate the institutional frameworks of already-existing parliaments.

The central function of the world parliament could be to coordinate economic policy and other activities between states and functional organizations. A second reason for the creation of a world parliament derives from the contradictions and indeterminacy of international law. Law is always vague, but this usually does not cause problems of legality when legislators, judges and citizens share many of the same background assumptions and values, and when approved and legal procedures exist for resolving interpretive conflicts. In world politics, by contrast, different parties can be radically at odds as to how to interpret laws. There is for this reason a need for a legitimate body that can solve interpretive conflicts and clarify what the law is. Such a proposal could give real powers to a world parliament, but on the other hand it would avoid the familiar problems and dangers of proposals for world federalism based on the idea of a sovereign legislative centre.[50]

Towards planetary politics and a global imaginary

Democratic global Keynesianism is a cosmopolitan doctrine. It does not approach matters from the standpoint of any single group, nation or state, but rather takes as its starting point the global political economy as a whole, with all its ecological and other consequences. Democratic global Keynesianism also rejects the assumption that the world has a centre – Eurocentrism is as bad a starting point for understanding the world economy as Sinocentrism. From a holistic perspective it is clear that the euro crisis is also a manifestation of neoliberal globalization and worldwide financialization. The European Monetary Union has its origins in the collapse of the original Bretton Woods system in the early 1970s. The EMU's founding ideas are rooted in precisely the same economic theories as the neoliberal ideology itself. The global financial crisis of 2008–09 triggered the EMU crisis. Although the EU itself could in principle resolve the ongoing euro crisis, at least for the time being, the key to a sustainable solution lies in reform of the system of governance of the world economy.

Democratic global Keynesianism can also explain why and how a world economy that rests on traditional orthodox economic liberal doctrines and their neoliberal variants are easily driven to one-sided and parochial reactions and counter-reactions. Mere market globalism is on no more stable a footing than nationalism, and both are part of the same mutually dependent system of sovereign states and capitalist market economy. In place of this combination we need global Keynesianism.

But even if cosmopolitanism is theoretically correct, can it work in practice?[51] Are people not by nature communal animals in the Aristotelian sense? Isn't our thinking based on language – in a world full of different languages? The conflict between communitarians and cosmopolitans began in the city-states of antiquity. Cynics and heliocentrists opposed the Aristotelian city-state-centric and geocentric world-view. Much later, the scientific revolution in Europe returned heliocentric and cosmopolitan thinking to the fore. Enlightenment philosophers criticized and ridiculed those who believed their own city, country or civilization to be the centre of the world, or even superior to others.[52]

During the Enlightenment, however, almost everyone was in practice still confined by poor means of transport and communications within a relatively narrow geographical scope. Practically no Enlightenment-era philosopher had ever ventured beyond Europe. The most famed proponent of ethico-political cosmopolitanism, Immanuel Kant, spent his entire life, from 1724 to 1804, in the Prussian town of Königsberg where he was born. Though Kant never travelled more than 15 kilometres from the town, he had an extensive philosophical and scientific library at his disposal. At the time he was producing his cosmopolitan writings in the late 1700s, the capitalist press and the revolutionary wars were fostering the rise of nationalism. The period from the Napoleonic wars to the Second World War and the independence of the former Great Power colonies was the golden age of nationalism. Each nation trumpeted its distinctiveness and excellence on the basis of the same ideas.[53]

The Second World War was the first genuinely global war. New communications technology enabled immediate reporting from all fronts across the globe, while enabling intensive domestic propaganda campaigns on a massive scale.[54] Globalization has created an everyday awareness of the world's interconnectedness, even though new technologies can also increase divisions and fragmentation. In any case, the foundations of a planetary imaginary have been laid through the development of new technologies and world economic interdependency.

In social theory, the concept of an 'imaginary' refers to the parameters within which people can develop mental pictures or maps of their own social existence.[55] In order for an envisioned social reality to be realized in social practices and institutions, it must first be imagined. This is in accordance with the principle *verum esse ipsum factum*: the true is precisely what is made.[56] Because people are always born into already-existing practices and institutions, the social world appears to us to be given as an objective reality. And indeed in many ways it is, since in social realities that are constructed in this way there are also many relations, connections and mechanisms that people cannot (fully) understand or control. This includes power relations to which they often adapt, even despite their opposing them.

Social reality is made possible by the imaginative capacities of human beings, and it rests on the prototypes, categories, frames and metaphors that are present in, but particular to, every language and historical period. Through tacit background assumptions and structures of meaning, plausible stories can be told of who we are, where we have come from, and where we are headed – and what our common interests are. Nationalistic thinking is structured this way, but it is also possible to create and advance a global imaginary.[57]

Cosmopolitan prototypes, frames and metaphors were developed already during the Copernican revolution: if the Earth is not after all the centre of the universe and everything else does not orbit it, how could any arbitrarily chosen point on Earth – itself a sphere – be a 'centre' of the world? Giordano Bruno, Christiaan Huygens and Voltaire went even further, by conceiving of myriad solar systems that each had worlds similar to our own, but that were possibly more technologically and morally advanced. Kant began his philosophical career by developing the concept of a galaxy and a naturalistic theory of the origins of the solar system.[58]

The League of Nations, the United Nations and the Bretton Woods institutions could never have come into being without a

FIGURE 8.2   In the Internet era the planet itself is seemingly becoming virtual. Real-time communication is now routine, especially in the wealthy parts of the world, and distances have shrunk to the length of a click.

cosmopolitan consciousness. Since the end of the Second World War market globalism has given rise to many planetary proto-types, frames and metaphors for commercial purposes. Many are familiar with the photo taken from Apollo 17 on the journey to the Moon: the Earth illuminated by the Sun is the stuff of countless logos, book covers and Internet images. Environmental and aid organizations were the first to make use of the photo. And later it was resorted to by many intellectuals, who rather than treating the planet as a twenty-four-hour shopping centre relate to it as their home.[59] In the 1960s and 1970s many alternative movements adopted the slogan 'Act locally, think globally' – but why should thought and action be shackled to any one place on the planet's surface? Shouldn't we think cosmically and act globally?[60] Don't shared problems demand global solutions?

Visual prototypes and metaphors are not enough, however, to create a global imaginary. Also needed are prototypical stories and their role models, so as to provide the whole with meaning. H.G. Wells launched the idea of real world history almost a century ago, and this has since become part of both global and universal history, or Big History. In these stories, the history of humankind is naturally linked to the history of the human species, through an incremental transition from biological to cultural evolution. The history of the human species becomes part of biological evolution through systematic increases in diversity and complexity. In turn, the history of life forms part of the history of the solar system and the galaxy. This is the transition from cosmic to biological evolution. Through these developments, world history is framed as part of an immensely broader process, which offers the possibility of seeing activists and politicians as role-players in a cosmic drama.

From this angle, Wells's assessment of Woodrow Wilson, for example, at the Versailles peace negotiations in 1919 is very similar to that Keynes: 'The worldwide outbreak of faith and hope in President Wilson, before he began to wilt and fail us, was a very significant thing indeed for the future of mankind.'[61] At Versailles, Wilson's cosmopolitanism wilted in the face of primitive nationalism and the urge for discipline and revenge. 'The first attempt to create a world law faded like laughter at an inn.'[62] To Wells, this was, however, merely an attempt on the journey towards a unified and democratic world community. Things were taken further after the Second World War, and since then there has been a steady proliferation of international treaties and organizations.

In his 'Big History' developed in the 1990s and 2000s, David Christian emphasizes the success of diplomats and environmental activists in reversing some environmental trends. Many endangered species have been saved from extinction through cooperative efforts, and air pollution in Europe has been mark-edly reduced through international treaties. The 1989 Montreal Protocol on Substances That Deplete the Ozone Layer has had some success.[63] These achievements also can be understood as early steps towards a more functional world community (on the cosmic scale, a few decades or centuries are vanishingly small periods of time).

Warren Wagar has outlined some of the role models that may become central to the historical developments of the coming several decades. In his 'short history of the future', the capitalist world economy drifts into a major depression in the near future, simultaneously with the worsening of climate change.[64] A number of students form a study group that over time develops into a global political party. After the global catastrophe this party becomes the central political force in the world, and it eventually succeeds in creating a democratic socialist global republic. This in its turn turns out to be only an intermediate phase, since through the development of human capabilities centralized states become redundant. These kinds of stories are prototypes: they frame topical historical events and offer expectations and behav-ioural models for the future. In product development, a prototype is an early model that is used to test and further enhance ideas or processes.[65]

What comes after globalization?

Globalization in the first sense of the term refers to the historical situation in which the world is irreversibly intertwined and in which a basis for a planetary imaginary has already been built via the development of technologies and world economic prac-tices and institutions. In its second, political sense, globalization denotes the project of the liberalization of profit-seeking private capital from all constraints. The EU has been an active contributor to this project, which came to a head through the 2008-09 crisis and its aftermath. Aggregate demand in the world economy can no longer be maintained with the aid of the United States' overconsumption, financialization and accumulation of private or public debt.

The process of European integration could also tumble, unless there is a successful change of direction. The fragmentation of the EMU as a result of the ongoing economic difficulties would cast doubt on and politicize the basic principles of the EU, while legitimation problems could prompt the core EU countries to develop a social-democratic federation. The main conclusion of Chapter 6 was that the more Eurocentric and short-sighted is this federation's self-perception, the more prone it would be to merging with the prevailing conditions of the global political economy, with all their contradictions. A better possibility would be for the EU to be able to develop common institutions as part of a broader global whole. This would also enable and ease the EU's own reformation.

In Chapter 7 I argued that a permanent debt arbitration mechanism that upholds the rule of law would enable swift and timely response to debt crises before they get out of hand. This mechanism would not be enough by itself, for instance if several large economies got into economic trouble simultaneously. Problems also arise if creditors' own finances are fragile due to their being in debt themselves. For debt arbitration and restructuration to work, finance as a whole must be sustainably based. Making it so demands the sort of institutional measures and mechanisms that can be only partly created within limited territorial states.

In this final chapter, I have outlined a global Keynesian New Deal. By tackling the immediate and fundamental causes of the economic crisis that began in 2008, this New Deal would prevent the repeat of such serious economic crises in the future. By shaping the conditions for economic growth and its sustainability, the new common institutions would reduce the amount of social antagonism and at the same time create the conditions for solving the problems of industrial civilization. The global Keynesian New Deal would also be a long stride towards a world with a self-understanding that adequately reflects the intertwined reality of the world economy.

When processes are intertwined and interdependency is the norm, relations of power and asymmetric dependency also develop. These can be democratized either by changing existing systems of governance or creating new ones. Global democracy requires, however, that a sufficiently large proportion of actors think and act cosmopolitically. The idea of an 'imaginary' refers to the parameters within which people create images or mental maps of who, what and where they are. The global imaginary arises from prototypes, metaphors, framing and stories that derive from the world as a whole, its history, and the future that is only beginning.

An interwoven world requires the ability to grasp the dynamic and historically evolved wholes of which we ourselves are parts. This could be called a *holoreflexive* understanding.[66] The term refers to the ability to see things, such as ourselves and our daily lives, as parts of worldwide developments and social structures. The spread of holoreflexivity entails the politicization of the world economy, and the forging of new systems of governance. A different kind of globalization is possible.

And yet the disintegration of the EU could set the world further down the path of increasingly myopic responses to the problems of the liberal world economy. Attempts to export one's problems elsewhere can easily lead to rounds of tit-for-tat responses and to the rise of movements that prefer hard will, even the unilateral use of violence, to building better common institutions for common problems. Thus it is possible that the global Keynesian New Deal will finally arise from the ashes of the old world, following a worldwide catastrophe. Thus a lot hinges upon whether Europe can learn from its own history and act consistently, within and without, to bring about a more holoreflexively responsible world.

Glossary of key terms
and acronyms

BALANCE OF TRADE   The difference between exports and imports (services included) measured in money terms. A *trade surplus* is a positive balance, and a *trade deficit* is negative. Over the long run, countries with trade surpluses tend to have savings surpluses, whereas countries with trade deficits tend to accumulate debt. In the world as a whole, deficits and surpluses cancel each other out.

BUBBLE   A situation where market prices are unsustainable. The process leading to a bubble involves positive feedback loops: rising prices generate increasing interest in investing in that market, which further increases prices. Moreover, higher values can be used as collateral to raise funds for further investments in the (apparently) profitable market. So the process resulting in a bubble is self-reinforcing up to a point. Although the eventual bust is the only conclusive proof of a bubble, typical warning signs in a given market include the level and quality of debt of the financial investors, households and others involved.

CAUSATION   Cause and reason are both terms for things that can be taken as responses to 'why' questions. More specifically, to ask about causes is to ask what 'makes it happen', what 'produces', 'generates', 'creates' or 'determines' something, or, more weakly, what 'enables' or 'leads to it'. Such terms are metaphors, often based on our everyday experiences of bringing things about. Nonetheless, in a scientific realist view, causation is an active process that involves real causal powers, liabilities and mechanisms. Nothing happens without a cause, or rather multiple causes, but these vary and can be variously categorized. The distinction between fundamental, enabling and contributing causes hinges on the necessity of a certain thing for producing or generating the outcome or change to be explained.

CONTRADICTION   Actions may be contradictory if they are likely to be or are self-defeating. Contradictions in this sense can arise from incorrect beliefs about how things work (e.g. if one mistakes a poisonous substance for medicine) or from a lack of generalizability (e.g. if everyone wants simultaneously to avoid losing money by withdrawing all their savings from a failing bank). The latter is a *fallacy of composition*, which can become a self-fulfilling prophecy (in this case, by making the bank more likely to fail). Contradictions can also occur at a society-wide level, if there are organizing principles that work against each other (e.g. a Keynesian welfare state can be contradictory in an open and liberal world economy, where corporations can move their tax base elsewhere). Real-world contradictions are not categorical, since whether the contradicting forces cancel each other out or whether one force eventually annuls the other depends on contingent circumstances (e.g. how many people withdraw their savings simultaneously; what else determines investment decisions apart from taxation levels).

CREDIT DEFAULT SWAP (CDS)   An agreement that the seller of a credit default swap will compensate the buyer in the event of a loan default or other credit event. A CDS can be treated as a form of insurance, but it is also a security that can be bought and sold for speculative profit. The market for CDSs can thus become part of a system of positive feedback loops, in which an upward spiral of CDS prices can reinforce a downward spiral of increasingly negative risk perceptions and unfavourable risk assessments and vice versa.

CREDIT RATING AGENCY   Credit ratings are used by states and other financial actors to conveniently assess relative credit risk. The higher the risk assessment, the lower the credit rating will be, thereby raising the price of debt (interest payments). Like many other increasingly common global indicators, credit ratings simultaneously set norms of behaviour and affect the perceptions of success of different actors, thus shaping the conditions of actions in various ways. The three major

credit rating agencies – Standard & Poor's, Moody's Investors Services
and the Fitch Group – are private corporations based in the USA.
Since the global financial and euro crises there has been widespread
apprehension about relying on these agencies, and proposals have been
made for alternative systems of assessing credit risks.

CRISIS   Crisis most generally connotes a turning point in a process.
This can be so momentous as to change the very nature of the being
or society in question. Very often what is at issue with crisis is not
prediction about the outcome, but the etymologically related concept of
critique, which is directed at the cause of the crisis. Although the causes
of any particular crisis will almost invariably be controversial, the crisis
itself can indicate that previously dominant theories have been faulty.
Crisis also means the opportunity to learn, but can provide a pretext
for realizing reactionary agendas also. Social, political and economic
crises are inherently occasions for power struggles.

CURRENCY TRANSACTION TAX (CTT)   A tax levied on every currency
exchange, set at a level low enough not to hinder any transactions that
are needed to finance trade in goods and services or long-term capital
investments. Such a tax was first proposed in 1972 by James Tobin after
the demise of the Bretton Woods system of fixed exchange rates. Tobin
argued for a reform of monetary markets by increasing the transaction
costs for foreign exchanges. This would stabilize volatile financial
markets and increase state autonomy, particularly over monetary policy.
For some, the CTT could also be, or mainly be, a redistributive measure
for funding development and poverty eradication. Institutionalizing a
global currency transaction tax could also facilitate democratic control
of financial markets and related social forces.

DEFLATION   A decrease in price levels affecting goods and services,
wages or assets. For instance, the price level of goods and services may
be rising slightly, while the wage level is declining somewhat and various
asset markets are collapsing. Deflation means declining incomes for some
or many, while the notional value of their debts remains intact. This
tends to destabilize their finances, increasing the risk of default with
repercussions elsewhere in the system. Such developments can become
self-reinforcing and lead to deflationary or debt–deflation 'spirals'. Historical precedents suggest that simply channelling central bank money
into the financial system is unable to overcome deflationary spirals.

DEMOCRACY   Democracy is best conceived of as a process rather than
a stable condition or model. Without any movement towards further democratization, strong tendencies to corruption and accumulation of power
can easily take over, even within a supposedly stable state of democracy.
It is sometimes thought that true democracy is the rule of all citizens
participating directly in every discussion and decision, but this would
drastically limit the size of functional political communities (a meeting
of a mere thousand citizens, each having one minute to discuss the single
issue on the agenda, would take about seventeen hours; and a similar
meeting with a million citizens about four or five years). Understood
as a process of democratization, involving different and democratically
contestable criteria and principles, democracy is not limited by scale. The
relevant criteria include franchise (the number of participants), scope (the
range of areas of social life under democratic control) and authenticity (the
degree to which democratic control is real rather than symbolic, informed
rather than ignorant, and competently engaged). Democracy also requires
a wide range of principles, such as those governing fair participation,
representation, divisions of power, the rule of law and publicity.

EFFECTIVE AGGREGATE DEMAND   Effective aggregate demand can be
defined in relation to continuously changing real production potential.
Allied with modern science and engineering, capitalist market society
constantly creates what Marx called 'new objectified powers of human
knowledge and work', including facilities formed by real fixed investments, the planning horizon for which is often protracted. Without
mechanisms to ensure a sufficiently high level of effective demand for
the goods and services produced, these developments will result in
excess capacity and unemployment. Demand is always monetized, so
what matters is whether the interested consumers and investors can
afford to buy the goods and services – that is, whether they have access
to liquid money or debt. This depends also on income distribution.
A further complication is that, due to degrees of monopoly as well as
financial and various other fixed agreements and commitments, prices
do not easily decrease so as to match insufficient demand. When prices
do fall, the risk of a deflationary spiral increases.

EUROPEAN CENTRAL BANK (ECB)   The successor to the European
Monetary Institute (EMI), which was created to facilitate the transition
to the euro. The ECB was established by the Treaty of Amsterdam in

1998, with headquarters in Frankfurt. According to the EU treaties, which insulate the ECB both from democratic politics and from non-monetary areas of economic policy, the main task of the Bank is to keep inflation low. It thus embodies the basic ideas of Milton Friedman's monetarism and the new classical macroeconomics of the 1970s, which both expect free markets to be self-stabilizing always.

EUROPEAN FINANCIAL STABILITY FACILITY (EFSF) The EFSF was created by the euro area member states in May 2010, in response to the first phase of the euro crisis. It was authorized to borrow more than €400 billion, over half of which immediately went to the Irish and Portuguese bailouts. The Facility can lend to financially troubled eurozone countries, recapitalize banks and buy sovereign debt. The Eurozone countries provide guarantees for the money the EFSF raises on financial markets. This violates Article 122 of the EU Treaty, according to which EU member states cannot divide responsibility for debt among themselves.

EUROPEAN FINANCIAL STABILISATION MECHANISM (EFSM) The EFSM is another emergency funding programme established in May 2010, which also relies on funds raised on financial markets. Unlike the EFSF, the money it raises is guaranteed by the European Commission, using the European Union budget as collateral. Given the relatively small size of the EU budget, the EFSM can raise no more than €60 billion on financial markets, and so is relatively insignificant compared to the EFSF and ESM.

EUROPEAN MONETARY SYSTEM (EMS) The EMS was established in 1979 to prevent large currency rate fluctuations between the member states of the European Economic Community. This was done by linking their currencies through the European Currency Unit, a basket of currencies that prevented currency movements above 2.25 per cent (6 per cent for Italy) in bilateral exchange rates with other member countries. The EMS was supported by various mechanisms and funds, but in autumn 1992 financial turmoil and speculation forced Britain and Italy out of it. In the same year the Maastricht Treaty was ratified, which included a three-stage blueprint for a single European currency.

ECONOMIC AND MONETARY UNION OF THE EUROPEAN UNION (EMU) The idea for the EMU dates to the 1920s, but lay dormant until the downfall of the original Bretton Woods system at the turn of the 1960s and 1970s. Since the 1980s the EMU has been a key goal in the European integration project, which has its own dynamic revolving around peace, identity politics, member–state relations, the ethico-political and power-political aspirations of various European movements and leaders, and so on. However, these dynamics came to be fused with neoliberal ideas and related economic theories in the 1980s and 1990s.

EUROPEAN STABILITY MECHANISM (ESM) As the euro crisis deepened, the German government won support in late 2010 for a minimal EU treaty amendment to replace the EFSF and EFSM with a more potent and permanent mechanism that was in line with the EU treaties. The strict conditions this proposal contained follow the standard neoliberal formula of 'structural adjustment'. In March 2011 EU leaders agreed to a separate eurozone-only treaty that would create the ESM itself. The base capital of the ESM is €80 billion, and is intended to create a lending capacity of up to half a trillion euros. The ESM's Board of Governors has the authority to increases these sums if it sees fit. Because the ESM transfers budgetary powers to the Commission, its constitutionality has been challenged in several eurozone countries.

EUROBONDS In November 2011 the European Commission suggested tackling the financial crisis with bonds jointly issued by the seventeen euro countries. Three versions were proposed, with varying degrees of joint responsibility for public debt and requiring different EU Treaty amendments in order to be implemented. Germany has strongly opposed the idea, and so far the eurobond idea has not moved forward.

EUROPEAN COMMISSION The Commission is responsible for proposing legislation, implementing decisions and upholding the European Union's treaties. The Members of the European Commission, the Commissioners, are charged with pursuing the common good of all EU states and their citizens. The 'common good' has typically been understood in terms of the so-called Monnet method, meaning good performance in various technical tasks that justify EU rule and enable further transfer of authority to the European level. In practice, this good performance has been largely equated with the effects of market liberalization. The Commission is thus a technocratic body whose legitimacy largely rests on its claims of the superior performance of economic (neo)liberalism.

EUROPEAN COUNCIL   The Council is an intergovernmental body that defines 'the general political directions and priorities' of the Union. Its legislative powers are limited but in practice it determines many developments in the Union. The Council comprises the heads of state or government, along with the president of the European Commission and the president of the European Council.

FALLACY OF COMPOSITION   The fallacy of composition, or whole–part fallacy, occurs when a conclusion is drawn about a whole based on the features or capacities of its parts. In society, the fallacy typically arises from the assumption that what is possible for one actor at a given moment must be possible for all (or many) of them simultaneously. Many paradoxes of economic theory stem from this fallacy.

FEDERAL RESERVE SYSTEM (Fed)   The Fed, as the United States central Bank is commonly called, was established in 1913 in response to a series of financial crises and consequent recession. It became an effective lender of last resort during the 1930s' Great Depression, when a new design for the shape and structure of the overall financial system was implemented. Waves of deregulation in the 1980s and 1990s meant a partial return to the past, but did not reduce the functions or powers of the Fed itself.

FEDERATION (federal state)   The EU embodies elements of statehood without being a state. It has its own legislative bodies and legislation; it has also a legal personality established in the Lisbon Treaty in 2007. Moreover, various EU bodies serve state-like regulatory and other functions. Every federation has both a central government and principles that distribute powers among its constituent territorial parts. European federalists argue that the EU needs a common federal government, with distributed powers at regional, national and supranational levels. However, some political thinkers during the past century have favoured strengthening elements of common or world statehood in a non-territorial way, most typically organized along functionalist lines (authorization based on particular functions).

FINANCIAL MULTIPLICATION   Financial actors and especially their powers, including money, are generated by a complicated process of multiplication of loans, assets and transactions. Investors leverage investments by borrowing in order to invest more and thereby create greater revenues from small margins (differences between selling price and cost). Financial assets can be used as collateral in obtaining loans. The borrowed funds are invested, in turn, in other assets, possibly in shares in other investment funds such as investment banks, mutual funds or hedge funds. The tendency towards asset price inflation is further reinforced by a multitude of interconnected social processes, which tend to draw more economic resources to financial markets (e.g. through creating and privatizing pension funds). Financial multiplication breeds bubbles that eventually burst, but even financial crises can aid the growth of the financial system, provided public funds are used to bail out banks and investors in trouble.

FINANCIAL TRANSACTION TAX (FTT)   A levy placed on all or specific types of financial transactions. A currency transaction tax is a tax of this sort, and its aims can be generalized to cover, with appropriate modifications, all types of transaction. The otherwise comprehensive September 2011 FTT proposal by the European Commission excludes 'primary markets' (insurance contracts, mortgage lending, consumer credits and payment services as well as spot currency transactions), on the grounds that these activities are important for citizens and non-financial businesses. The EC further specifies that 'currency transactions on spot markets are outside the scope [of the] FTT, which preserves the free movement of capital.' Nonetheless, the UK and some other EU members have strongly opposed the idea. In a summit in June 2012 it was agreed that since the FTT proposal will not be adopted by the Council within a reasonable period, several member states will request enhanced cooperation in this area.

FINANCIALIZATION   Financialization is a process in which financial markets, financial institutions and financial elites gain an increasing hold over economic process and economic policy decisions in capitalist market society. Financialization is associated with rising social inequalities, shortening timescales in corporate decision-making, reduction of values to financial instruments and their derivatives, and with state policies focused primarily on lowering inflation and promoting business confidence and external competitiveness.

G20 (The Group of Twenty Finance Ministers and Central Bank Governors)   G20 is a group of finance ministers and central bank governors from twenty major countries, covering 80 per cent of world

GDP. The group has been effective since 1999. It studies, reviews and promotes policy discussions and organizes annual summits. This group should not be confused with the G20 of developing nations that was established in 2003.

INTERNATIONAL MONETARY FUND (IMF)   The IMF was established in Bretton Woods, New Hampshire, in 1944, following negotiations between the British delegation led by John Maynard Keynes and the US delegation led by Harry Dexter White. The original Keynesian elements were soon annulled by other tendencies. The Fund was designed to be an organization that would help member states with their short-term balance-of-payment problems. Despite the opposition of all the other IMF member states, conditionality was introduced in 1952 under pressure from the US government, which was then the main creditor of the world financial system. In clear contrast to Keynes's original plans, conditionality shifted the burden of adjustment to the deficit countries, and involved ideas that were later developed into so-called structural adjustment programmes. Conditionality contains various prescriptions for how a debtor country must improve its balance of payments. These include anti-inflationary measures like cutting government spending, raising interest rates, and controlling wage rises (often by attacking trade unions); liberalization of import controls, foreign exchange and financial markets in general; and greater openness to foreign direct investment.

INFLATION   The term 'inflation' comes from Latin, *inflatio* meaning 'expansion' or 'blowing up'. In economics, inflation means a rise in price levels, especially in relation to goods and services, although it can also occur in salaries and asset prices. It affects different groups in different ways, which is one reason why theories about causes and consequences of inflation are disputed. In general, inflation benefits debtors (e.g. new homeowners or entrepreneurs) and is disadvantageous to the creditors and owners of various assets (e.g. individuals with excess incomes, financial investors and lenders). Producers generally gain from moderate inflation in markets for goods and services. If price levels remain stable but wages rise, workers gain; if prices remain stable but asset prices rise, those owning or controlling financial capital benefit. Different theories of inflation are not necessarily mutually exclusive: in some historical and institutional contexts inflation may stem from cost pushes, in others more from expanding monetized demand beyond productive capabilities. Authorities may expand money supply for good reasons, or resort to paying bills by printing more money because taxation is difficult or politically costly (whether this causes productive expansion or inflation is also contingent upon a variety of circumstances). It is widely agreed that low or moderate inflation is good for economic growth, but how much is 'low' or 'moderate' is controversial.

KEYNESIAN   For (post-)Keynesian economic theories, the mutual dependency of the parts and whole works out through effective demand and the multiplier effect. Aggregate effective demand (total spending capacity in the economy) does not usually equal aggregate supply (the total productive capacity of the economy). Instability of speculative finance is a key cause of instability in capitalist market economy, but there are also several other mechanisms through which economic activities tend to oscillate and fall short of their real potential. It is the task of public authorities to ensure full employment and stimulate and shape investment and growth. A key condition for sustainable growth is egalitarian income distribution. Keynesian responses are usually posed only, or primarily, in the national-statist context. There are limits, however, to thinking about policy ideas in limited territorial-statist terms, although the simultaneity of responses may in some situations mean, in effect, coordinated actions by different states and international organizations. Global Keynesian views about economic governance surpass mere policy coordination, envisaging new worldwide institutions to tackle the contradictions and paradoxes of global economic developments.

LEGITIMATION   Legitimation is the process of making something acceptable and normatively warranted to a community, group or audience. Legitimacy is not only a matter of institutionalized prejudices and behavioural dispositions, as seen by some social scientists, but is also based on normative validity claims. Normative reasons for the validity of a rule can translate into 'public opinion' supporting or at least accepting the rule, although various other considerations and assumptions play a role as well. The concept of 'public opinion' is itself multilayered and complex, not least because it is used reflexively in public discussions as a reason to support or criticize a policy, regime or rule.

METAPHOR   Metaphors involve the understanding and experiencing of one kind of thing in terms of another (e.g. 'affection is warmth', 'important is big', 'more is up', 'time is motion'). Recent cognitive science has provided critical insights into the metaphorical nature of reasoning: thought is embodied and mostly unconscious, and abstract concepts such as corporation, state or justice are largely metaphorical, often in complex ways. Most of human reason is based on prototypes, framings and metaphors, and so our judgements of truth are always mediated by our understanding and imagination.

NEOLIBERALISM   Neoliberalism is a programme of developing and resolving the problems of human society through competitive markets. These are assumed to be efficient, just, and to maximize freedom of choice – claims which are closely connected to the 'efficient market hypothesis' of neoclassical economics. More nuanced versions of neoclassical economics may allow for various exceptions. Competitive markets can also be simulated within private or public organizations; this is the programme of New Public Management. The term 'neoliberalism' is controversial and mostly used by its critics rather than supporters. However, it has an established meaning in large social-scientific literature (in the social sciences citation index, the term can be found in more than 10,000 article titles and abstracts). Neoliberalism emerged in the late twentieth century as an attempt to return to the economic liberal ideals of the preceding century, but in contemporary contexts it is rhetorically easier to represent neoliberal ideas as pragmatic attempts to increase efficiency or freedom of choice.

NEW DEAL   Franklin D. Roosevelt launched this term as part of his 1932 election campaign as a response to the Great Depression. The 1933–38 New Deal programme involved '3 Rs': Relief, Recovery and Reform. Roosevelt's New Deal was neither unique (similar social reforms and economic policies were enacted in many countries in the 1930s) nor particularly effective (the USA recovered fully only during the war 1941–45). Nonetheless, the term has become a popular symbol for a drastic turn towards socially oriented Keynesian economic policies, which in one particular manifestation characterized the Bretton Woods era (1944–73).

ORGANISATION FOR ECONOMIC CO-OPERATION AND DEVELOPMENT (OECD)   In its current form the OECD was established in 1960 (its predecessor was set up in 1948 to help administer the Marshall Plan for the reconstruction of Europe after World War II). The OECD defines itself as a forum of countries committed to democracy and the market economy, providing a setting to compare policy experiences, seek answers to common problems, identify good practices, and co-ordinate domestic and international policies. It is often associated with the diffusion of ideas and practices underpinning neoliberal globalization, although it can be argued that it has at least in some limited areas moved beyond the straightforward neoliberal prescription of welfare cuts and structural adjustment.

OFFSHORE   Pirate radio stations have used seaborne broadcasting as a means to circumvent national broadcasting regulations, being literally offshore. The first post-war financial offshore facilities were established in the Caribbean islands and similar statelets. Nowadays major cities or, more precisely, certain activities within them have also been legally defined as 'offshore', meaning that standard national laws, regulations and taxes are not applicable there. Offshore financial centres and tax havens are used to avoid regulations and taxes. Estimates of the size of offshore assets, funds and flows vary greatly. But it seems that assets held beyond the reach of effective taxation are equal to about a third of total global assets, and that over half of all world trade passes through tax havens.

PARADOX   A paradox is a statement that is seemingly contradictory or opposed to common sense, and yet is perhaps true (a paradox can also be a self-contradictory statement that at first seems true). In economic theory, a paradox is a conclusion that seems to go against common sense but upon closer inspection turns out to be perfectly sensible.

SPECULATION   To speculate is to review something idly or casually, often inconclusively. Speculation in this sense is a frail form of rea-soning based on little or no evidence. When Keynes distinguished between enterprise and speculation, he had something similar in mind. Enterprise is 'the activity of forecasting the prospective yields of assets over their whole life'; whereas speculation is 'the activity of forecasting the psychology of the market'. While a review of the prospects of an investment can be based on solid evidence and reasoning, speculation amounts to anticipating what the average opinion expects the average opinion to be, when one knows that everybody else is trying to guess the same thing. Like gambling, financial speculation tends to involve excessive risk-taking.

WORLD TRADE ORGANIZATION (WTO)   The General Agreement on
Tariffs and Trade (GATT), established in 1947, was meant to be a
temporary arrangement and to be subsumed under a trade organization with broader scope, namely the International Trade Organization
(ITO). It took half a century and a turn to neoliberalism before a successor to GATT was finally established. The WTO came into operation
on 1 January 1995, and provides a framework for rule-making and rule
supervision governing a multilateral trade system. The WTO's tasks
include the implementation of the Uruguay Round (and the previous
rounds) and administration of further trade negotiations. It also provides
a permanent forum for the discussion of trade policy and a binding
procedure for the settlement of disputes. The successive expansion of
the area of 'free trade' has constituted a movement from the classical
international trade of material goods to far-reaching liberalization and
deregulation. Ultimately, trade is absolutely and perfectly free only in
a world where free capitalist markets reign everywhere. The current
round of negotiations, the Doha Development Round that began in
2001, has failed to achieve any further movements in this direction. The
USA and the EU have resorted to bilateral agreements with numerous
countries to further the 'free trade' agenda.

Notes

PREFACE

1. Dani Rodrik, *The Globalization Paradox: Why Global Markets, States, and Democracy Can't Coexist*, Oxford: Oxford University Press, 2011.
2. Ibid., p. 203.

CHAPTER 1

1. 'Un Entêtemant Suicidaire. Entretien Exclusif avec Milton Friedman', *Geopolitique* 53 (Spring 1996): 58–66.
2. The fiscal policies of the European Central Bank and the principles of the EMU are grounded in neoclassical economic theories, and in particular in so-called rational expectations theory. Among the most important studies of these theories are Robert E. Lucas, 'Expectations and the Neutrality of Money', *Journal of Economic Theory* 4 (1972): 103–24; Robert Barro, 'Are Government Bonds Net Wealth?', *Journal of Political Economy* 82(6) (1974): 1095–117; T. Sargent and N. Wallace '"Rational" Expectations, the Optimal Monetary Instrument and the Optimal Money Supply Rule', *Journal of Political Economy* 83(2) (1975): 231–54.
3. Charles P. Kindleberger and Robert Z. Aliber, *Manias, Panics, and Crashes: A History of Financial Crises*, 6th edn, Basingstoke, Palgrave Macmillan, 2011, p. 47. The precise details of Newton's involvement and words are open to historical interpretation. From this citation, I have replaced 'people' with 'men', to avoid anachronistic political

correctness (thanks to James O'Connor for pointing this out).

4. Rasmus, Jack, *Epic Recession: Prelude to Global Depression*, London: Pluto Press, 2010.

5. See George Soros, 'The Crisis and What to Do about It', *New York Review of Books* 55(19), 4 December 2008, www.nybooks.com/articles/22113; George Soros, *The Crash of 2008 and What it Means: The New Paradigm for Financial Markets*, New York: Public Affairs, 2008.

6. On the history of 'high' or 'grand' (*haute*) finance and its reinstatement at the centre of the global economy, see Heikki Patomäki, *Democratising Globalisation: The Leverage of the Tobin Tax*, London: Zed Books, 2001, especially ch. 2, pp. 39–71.

7. The word *crisis* is of Greek origin (κρίσις, *krisis*), denoting both a difference of opinion or controversy and the action or decision that overcomes the difficulty. *Critique* is a judgement or decision concerning a conflict or clash. See Seyla Benhabib, *Critique, Norm and Utopia: A Study of the Foundations of Critical Theory*, New York: Columbia University Press, 1996, p. 19.

8. For a more detailed account of the extent to which mainstream economic solutions contain Keynesian elements and the degree to which they contributed to the continuation and consolidation of neoliberalism, see Heikki Patomäki, 'Neoliberalism and the Global Financial Crisis', *New Political Science* 31(4) (2009): 431–42.

CHAPTER 2

1. George Lakoff and Mark Johnson, *Metaphors We Live By*, Chicago: University of Chicago Press, 2003 (1980); George Lakoff and Mark Johnson, *Philosophy in the Flesh: The Embodied Mind and Its Challenge to Western Thought*, New York: Basic Books, 1999.

2. Many collective agents nowadays have the status of *legal* personhood, but few would find it reasonable to grant them any more extensive form of personhood than this.

3. The subject of the moral and legal responsibility of collective actors is, of course, a many-sided and difficult one. My point here is only to highlight the difficulties of everyday moral reasoning, not to suggest that companies and states cannot be held responsible for their actions. See, for instance, Toni Erskine (ed.), *Can Institutions Have Responsibilities? Collective Moral Agency and International Relations*, Basingstoke: Palgrave Macmillan, 2003.

4. Neoclassical economics does use mathematical models and statistical tests that appear to have the objectivity and technical sophistication of methods used in the natural sciences, which they mimic also by

naming theorems, corollaries and so on. The majority of mainstream economic theory trades on this appearance of objectivity and technicality. However, as Donald McCloskey and others have argued, when one looks more closely it becomes clear that economics, like other fields, bases its arguments on metaphors, analogies, appeals to authority, and everyday experience; and very often the ways these devices are used are anything but realistic. Markets, supposedly, are guided by 'an invisible hand', the organization of labour has a 'productive function', and coefficients are 'meaningful'. The language used by economists has real consequences, as it legitimates particular ways of perceiving and ordering the social world. Basic concepts and their interrelations, the analogies and metaphors behind them, and the rhetorical devices used in conjunction with them determine what is acceptable economic discourse, what is admitted to the economic language game and what is excluded from it. See Donald McCloskey, *The Rhetoric of Economics*, Brighton: Harvester Wheatsheaf, 1986; Heikki Patomäki, *Democratising Globalisation: The Leverage of the Tobin Tax*, Appendix 1, 'Monetarism and the Denial of Reality', London: Zed Books, 2001, pp. 223–31.

5. Lakoff and Johnson, *Philosophy in the Flesh*, pp. 161–9.
6. See Stephan Kaufmann, *Sell Your Islands, You Bankrupt Greeks: 20 Popular Fallacies Concerning the Debt Crisis*, Berlin: Rosa Luxemburg Foundation, 2011, www.rosalux.de/fileadmin/rls_uploads/pdfs/sonst_publikationen/Broschur_Pleite-Griechen_eng.pdf (accessed 5 June 2012).
7. Despite the budget deficits Greece's debt per GDP ratio did not increase, since the country's GDP rose rapidly throughout the 2002–07 period. But it is possible and reasonable to argue, of course, that budgetary deficits should not be allowed to accumulate during the economically good times. In Chapter 7 I argue that Keynesian economic policies do not sanction 'living in debt', nor do they condone increases to the debt burden: when the economy is going well, debts should be paid off and funds put in reserve for the next downturn. On this count, Greek economic policy during 2002–07 was not on a firm footing.
8. See Steven Luckert and Susan Bachrach, *State of Deception: The Power of Nazi Propaganda*, New York: W.W. Norton, 2009.
9. Steve Keen, *Debunking Economics: The Naked Emperor of the Social Sciences*, London: Zed Books, 2001, p. 86.
10. Karl Marx recognized the self-defeating tendencies of market capitalism long before Kalecki and Keynes, but he failed to theorize the fundamental significance of money, and remained content instead

with the classical theory of labour value. Kalecki, for his part, published his ideas on overall demand and the multiplier effect before Keynes. Although Keynes's idea of economic 'revolution' is usually attributed to his major work, *The General Theory of Employment, Interest and Money* (1936), 'Keynesian' ideas on economic policy were already in circulation before that. For a range of interpretations from different perspectives and periods on the meaning of Keynes's 'revolution', see Roger E. Backhouse, 'The Keynesian Revolution', in R.E. Backhouse and B.W. Bateman (eds), *The Cambridge Companion to Keynes*, Cambridge: Cambridge University Press, 2006, pp. 19–38.

11. For a simple but effective presentation of the central paradoxes I am referring to here, see Philip A. O'Hara, *Encyclopedia of Political Economy*, Volume 2: *L–Z*, Routledge: London, 1999, pp. 829–32. See also Marc Lavoie, *Introduction to Post-Keynesian Economics*, Basingstoke: Palgrave Macmillan, 2009, pp. 91–6, 110–11, 117–19.

12. The distinction between micro- and macroeconomics was introduced soon after Keynes, and as a reaction against his theory. Keynes's position was labelled macroeconomic on account of its focus on large aggregates and its holistic approach to the economy, whereas the traditional neoclassical economic theory of the late nineteenth century came to be considered microeconomic theory due to its concern with the decisions of individual actors and with equilibrium. This dichotomy neutralized Keynes's criticisms, by leaving untouched the neoclassical theory that he had attacked. Later it was suggested that microeconomics had to have 'microfoundations', which is roughly equivalent to saying that the geosciences have to have a foundation that holds that the world is flat. Neither are there any convincing ontological reasons for the distinction between micro- and macroeconomics. The context of any given action by an individual or collective agent consists of a range of components and aspects of the whole in question; the question of the relationship between actions and their context is the agency/structure problem in social theory. See Margaret S. Archer, *Realist Social Theory: The Morphogenetic Approach*, Cambridge: Cambridge University Press, 1995, pp. 7–12; John K. Galbraith, *A History of Economics: The Past as the Present*, London: Hamish Hamilton, 1987, pp. 77, 235–6. See also Keen, *Debunking Economics*, pp. 154, 188–213.

13. See Jon Elster, *Logic and Society: Contradictions and Possible Worlds*, Chichester: Wiley, 1978, pp. 97–106.

14. This paragraph is a generalization and condensation of the theories of Kalecki, Keynes and some others. It does not prescribe any specific theoretical connections or mechanisms, since these will in any case

depend on historical institutional arrangements (there exist no universal regularities with which these essential particulars could be substituted). For example, the theory of how very large companies set prices is in line with Kalecki's outlook, whereas for the interpretation of effective aggregate demand I have drawn on Keynes and on the Marxian–Aristotelian conception of productive potential. See Michał Kalecki, *Theory of Economic Dynamics: An Essay on Cyclical and Long-Run Changes in Capitalist Economy*, New York: Augustus M. Kelley, 1969, pp. 13–31; J.M. Keynes, *The General Theory of Employment, Interest and Money*, London: Macmillan, 1961 (1936), pp. 25–8; Karl Marx, *Grundrisse: Foundations of the Critique of Political Economy (Rough Draft)*, trans. M. Nicolaus, London: Penguin/New Left Review, 1973 (1939), p. 706.

15. On the concept of cumulative and self-reinforcing causation, see Nicholas Kaldor, 'The Irrelevance of Equilibrium Economics', *Economic Journal* 82(328) (1972): esp. 1244–6; on the general theory of path dependency and self-reinforcing positive feedback, see Paul Pierson, *Politics in Time: History, Institutions, and Social Analysis*, Princeton NJ: Princeton University Press, 2004.

16. This paradox was known before Keynes, and in his use of it Keynes himself cited Bernard Mandeville's *The Fable of The Bees: or, Private Vices, Publick Benefits* (1714).

17. See Lavoie, *Introduction to Post-Keynesian Economics*, pp. 13, 16, 58; Malcolm Sawyer, 'Towards a Post-Kaleckian Macroeconomics', in Philip Arestis and Thanos Skouras (eds), *Post-Keynesian Economic Theory: A Challenge to Neoclassical Economics*, Brighton: Wheatsheaf 1985, pp. 168–9.

18. Joan Robinson, *The Accumulation of Capital*, London: Macmillan, 1956, p. 78.

19. This paradox is most frequently credited to Josef Steindl, *Maturity and Stagnation in American Capitalism*, New York: Monthly Review Press, 1952.

20. Paul Krugman, 'The Paradox of Thrift', *New York Times*, 3 February 2009, http://krugman.blogs.nytimes.com/2009/02/03/paradox-of-thrift (accessed 6 June 2012). There is no Nobel Prize as such for economics; the prize was inaugurated in 1968 (and first awarded the following year) by the Bank of Sweden in memory of Alfred Nobel. Some critics have argued that the Nobel Memorial Prize in Economic Sciences was created by the Bank in order to lend an air of scientific credibility to American mainstream economics.

21. Keynes, *General Theory*, ch. 23, pp. 333–71.

22. Philip A. O'Hara, *Growth and Development in the Global Political*

Economy: Social Structures of Accumulation and Modes of Regulation,
London: Routledge, 2006, p. 204.

23. According to basic neoclassical theory, money can be defined in terms
of utility function, which in turn is defined in terms of a bundle of
commodities. Neoclassical economic theory can also be extended to
cover situations in which money has a stronger role, but the starting
point of the theory is still the simple exchange market. Marx's writings assign money a more significant role in capitalist economy than
is assigned to it by neoclassical theory, and in the later parts of Friedrich Engels's compiled *Das Capital* both money and finance markets
are theorized. In general, however, Marx took as the starting point
the concept of commodity, and understands money in light of the
simple exchange of commodities. See Hal R. Varian, *Microeconomic
Analysis*, 3rd edn, New York: WW. Norton, 1992, pp. 109–10; Karl
Marx, *Capital: A Critique of Political Economy*, Volume 1, intr. Ernest
Mandel, trans. Ben Fowkes, Book One, ch. 3, 'Money, or the Circulation of Commodities', London: Penguin, 1990 (1867), pp. 188–244.

24. Many neoclassical economists have tried to demonstrate that (i) despite the possible increase in volatility, prices usually follow basic
economic indicators; (ii) although financial markets can sometimes
'overshoot', long-term equilibrium does exist. But because there is no
way of knowing what the equilibrium is, this is simply presumed! See
e.g. Rudi Dornbusch, 'Expectations and Exchange Rate Dynamics',
Journal of Political Economy 84(6) (1976): 1163.

25. The classical equation of the quantity theory of money is MV = PT,
where M is the amount of money, V the speed of circulation of the
money, P the price level, and T the volume of transactions. In Milton
Friedman's version of the equation, T is directly dependent on the
national product, Y. If V is stable, T is directly dependent on the
national product and M is dependent only on central bank policy.
Increases in money supply in excess of growth rate ultimately always
result only in price increases.

26. The seminal statement of the general theory of money is Keynes,
General Theory, ch. 17, pp. 222–44.

27. On the theory of money, see Geoffrey Ingham, *The Nature of Money*,
Cambridge: Polity Press, 2004.

28. Although money is in a certain sense generalized and abstract debt,
and although it is the granting of debt that creates money, it is important to keep in mind that money is in fact many things at once
– most obviously a measure of value, a repository of value, an object of
trust, a source of security, a link between the present and the future,
and more. Money and the institutional arrangements for its creation

are central questions from the perspective of politics and democratic theory also; see Frances Hutchinson, Mary Mellor and Wendy Olsen, *The Politics of Money*, London: Pluto Press, 2002.

29. Jack Rasmus, *Epic Recession: Prelude to Global Depression*, London: Pluto Press, 2010, esp. pp. 73–4, 215–16.

30. This is the core of Hyman Minsky's hypothesis of financial instability, and I discuss it in more detail in Chapter 3. An excellent summary of the theory can be found in Hyman Minsky, 'The Financial Instability Hypothesis: A Restatement', in Arestis and Skouras (eds), *Post-Keynesian Economic Theory*, pp. 24–55.

31. See, for example, the following entries in O'Hara, *Encyclopedia of Political Economy*: 'Monetary Theory of Production', pp. 759–61; 'Velocity and the Money Multiplier', pp. 1226–8.

CHAPTER 3

1. The black swan was once a byword for impossibility in philosophical discussion, until the first one was reported in Australia in 1790. During the 2008–09 crisis the example provided the title and central theme for a major bestseller: Nicholas Taleb, *The Black Swan: The Impact of the Highly Improbable*, London: Penguin, 2007.

2. The concept of moral hazard was in common use in the 1800s, usually in relation to the operations of insurance firms, and originally it did have the strong moral connotation that its name suggests. However, this changed in the 1960s and 1970s, when positivist economists began using the term to refer to situations in which the incompleteness of information, asymmetry, guarantees or insurances affect agents' behaviour so as to create inefficiency (or sub-optimal results assessed, in economics jargon, in terms of Pareto-optimality). Along with George Akerlof and Michael Spence, the Nobel laureate Joseph Stiglitz is well known for his work on moral hazard: see e.g. J.E. Stiglitz and A. Weiss, 'Credit Rationing in Markets with Imperfect Information', *American Economic Review* 71(3) (1981): 393–410.

3. G20, 'Leaders' Statement: The Pittsburgh Summit', 24–25 September 2009, http://ec.europa.eu/commission_2010-2014/president/pdf/statement_20090826_en_2.pdf (accessed 8 June 2012).

4. See Heikki Patomäki, 'Neoliberalism and the Global Financial Crisis', *New Political Science* 31(4) (2009): 431–42; Heikki Patomäki, 'What Next? An Explanation of the 2008–9 Slump and Two Scenarios of the Shape of Things to Come', *Globalizations* 7(1) (2010): 67–84.

5. Minsky's most important book, originally published in 1986, was republished during the crisis. Hyman Minsky, *Stabilizing an Unstable Economy*, New York: McGraw-Hill, 2008 (1986).

6. International Monetary Fund, *World Economic Outlook*, October, Washington DC: International Monetary Fund, 2007.

7. The investor George Soros was one of the few in his field who was able to foresee the coming crisis, and made investments on the basis of his predictions. These are documented by journalist John Cassidy, 'He Foresaw the End of an Era', *New York Review of Books* 55(16), 23 October 2008, www.nybooks.com/articles/21934 (accessed 8 June 2012); see also George Soros, *The Crash of 2008 and What it Means: The New Paradigm for Financial Markets*, New York: Public Affairs, 2008. Economist Nouriel Roubini came to prominence through his assessments of the crisis and its handling, and in many cases his predictions proved prescient. See e.g. Stephen Mihm, 'Dr. Doom', *New York Times*, 17 August 2008, p. MM26; and Nouriel Roubini, 'The Coming Financial Pandemic', *Foreign Policy* 165, March–April 2008. The coming mortgage and financial market crises were predicted even earlier by Dean Baker, 'The Run-up in Home Prices: Is It Real or Is It Another Bubble?', Washington DC: CEPR (Centre for Economic and Policy Research) Briefing Paper, 2002, www.cepr.net/documents/publications/housing_2002_08.pdf (accessed 8 June 2012); Gabriel Kolko, Weapons of Mass Financial Destruction', *Le Monde diplomatique*, October 2006: 1–3; Paul Krugman, 'Greenspan and the Bubble', *New York Times*, 29 August 2005, www.nytimes.com/2005/08/29/opinion/29krugman.html?_r=1 (accessed 8 June 2012); Ann Pettifor, *The Coming First World Debt Crisis*, Basingstoke: Palgrave Macmillan, 2006; Heikki Patomäki, 'The Long Downward Wave of the World Economy and the Future of Global Conflict', *Globalizations* 2(1) (2005): 61–78.

8. An excellent background analysis of the US crisis is provided by Jack Rasmus, *Epic Recession: Prelude to Global Depression*, London: Pluto Press, 2010, esp. ch. 7, pp. 201–44.

9. Neoclassical economists who have theorized the occasional instances of 'overshoot' on the financial markets have also assumed that there is perfect information about the future and that the markets by and large exhibit stable equilibrium. Neither of these assumptions can be proven theoretically or shown empirically, however, simply because neither perfect information nor stable, knowable equilibrium exists. If no individual market actor is in reality capable of gauging the future, it must follow that predictions by the 'markets' (as a whole) are based merely on the combination of adopted mechanical criteria of calculating risks and the effects of multilayered anticipations, whereby actors are anticipating (or guessing) the anticipations of others. In addition, the theory of securitization contains a fallacy,

since transferring responsibility from one actor to another does not in
any way remove risk from the system as a whole. On the contrary, securitization encourages market operatives to take greater risks, which
in an uncertain world will sooner or later inevitably come home to
roost. See Patomäki, 'What Next?', pp. 72–3, 82.

10. Figure 3.2 shows the trends in US National Index Levels for house
prices in the United States on the Case–Shiller Home Price Index,
using seasonally adjusted data from the first quarter of 1987 to the first
quarter of 2012 inclusive, set against the Dow Jones Industrial Share
Price Index. The data set is available for download from Standard
& Poor's website using the search term 'S&P/Case-Shiller Home
Price Indices': www.standardandpoors.com/indices (accessed 8 June
2012).

11. CIA World Factbook, 'United States', www.cia.gov/library/publica-
tions/the-world-factbook/geos/us.html (accessed 8 June 2012).

12. All these and countless other details have been pored over in the
media. On investigations into the bonus system, see e.g. 'Bonus Culture to Blame for Banking Crisis, say MPs', *Telegraph*, 15 August
2009.

13. Here I roughly follow, with some modifications, Rasmus's distinction
between fundamental, enabling and contributing causes. Effects
also take place through broader causal complexes. A cause is a
non-redundant component of a complex that on its own is not
sufficient to produce the effect, but in conjunction with other, non-
necessary components can form a whole of sufficient causal power to
bring about a given effect. In addition, each causal component has a
history of its own, and often several different causes are interwoven
through their respective histories. Deeper explanations of complex
phenomena require the unearthing of these causal chains and their
histories. See Rasmus, *Epic Recession*, esp. pp. 14–16, 24, 48; and on
the concept of causal complexes, see Heikki Patomäki, *After International Relations: Critical Realism and the (Re)Construction of
World Politics*, London: Routledge, 2002, pp. 78–9, 119–20.

14. Charles Kindleberger, *Manias, Panics, and Crashes: A History of Financial Crises*, 4th edn, New York: Wiley, 2000 (1978), p. 73.

15. 'The Corporate Savings Glut', *The Economist*, 7 July 2005, www.
economist.com/node/4154491?story_id=4154491 (accessed 8 June
2012).

16. OECD, *Economic Outlook* No. 82, December 2007, preliminary edition, ch. 3, pp. 7–11, www.oecd.org/dataoecd/60/0/39727868.pdf (accessed 8 June 2012).

17. See e.g. Till van Treeck, 'The Political Economy Debate on

'Financialization' – A Macroeconomic Perspective', *Review of International Political Economy* 16(5) (2009), pp. 907–44.

18. The development of income distribution and the growth of economic inequality in the United States have been widely documented and analysed, and more researchers are recognizing a connection between inequality and the growth of the speculative economy. See e.g. Rasmus, *Epic Recession*, pp. 73–4, 215–16; Michael Lim and Hoe Ee Khor, 'From Marx to Morgan Stanley: Inequality and Financial Crisis', *Development and Change* 42(1) (2011): 209–27; Jon D. Wisman and Barton Baker, 'Increasing Inequality, Inadequate Demand, Status Insecurity, Ideology and the Financial Crisis of 2008', American University Working Paper 1-12-11, www.american.edu/cas/economics/pdf/upload/2011-1.pdf (accessed 8 June 2012).

19. Lim and Khor, 'From Marx to Morgan Stanley', pp. 209–27.

20. On Minsky's view, the gradual changes to financial relations and institutions led to the expansion of speculative activity and began to create economic instability in the United States as early as the 1960s. From this perspective, it can well be asked whether the 2008–09 crisis and its aftermath are only a continuation of this long-running chain of developments that started in the USA. Or has the progressive onset of financialization in the global political economy been part of a conscious geo-economic strategy aimed at strengthening the United States' position in the world economy, including as part of its security policy? See Hyman Minsky, *Stabilizing an Unstable Economy*, New York: McGraw-Hill, 2008, pp. 5–11.

21. Inflation is, however, a critical issue in the sense that from the perspective of the owners of capital and of creditors it entails the reduction in the value of money and debts relative to wages, commodities and services. It is in the interests of the owners of capital and especially financial capital to aim for the lowest possible level of inflation in both goods and services and wages; that is, for the maximum retention of the value of money and debts over time. So we can assume that through financialization, economic policy changes so as to make the battle against inflation its top priority. Indeed, monetarism did become the central economic policy doctrine of the 1980s, while the 1990s' new macroeconomic synthesis brought in some additional elements. In open systems there can be several different causes for a complex outcome such as inflation. In oligopoly markets, rising costs in salaries, raw materials and rising energy prices are converted, with a markup, into rising prices of goods and services; changes in the country's position relative to other states can also create pressures towards inflation; irresponsible money printing practices can reduce

general confidence in the value of the currency or create overde-
mand (the state's budgetary funding of the central bank, however,
if carried out properly, would not necessarily trigger inflation); and
expectations concerning inflation, once set in motion, can become
entrenched and even create an accelerating spiral. On the historical
development of macroeconomic theories of inflation and economic
policy practices over the course of the twentieth century, see Chris-
topher Taylor, *A Macroeconomic Regime for the 21st Century: Towards
a New Economic Order*, London: Routledge, 2011.

22. For a more detailed development of this interpretation, see Heikki
Patomäki, *Democratising Globalisation: The Leverage of the Tobin
Tax*, ch. 3, 'Geoeconomics and Beyond: The Structural Power of
Global Finance', London: Zed Books, 2001. Compare also Minsky's
interpretation (*Stabilizing an Unstable Economy*, pp. 5–11). It is possible to synthesize these interpretations, but this would require a
detailed historical analysis that is beyond the scope of the present
work. See, however, Heikki Patomäki, *The Political Economy of Global Security: War, Future Crises and Changes in Global Governance*,
London: Routledge, 2008, in I take steps towards such a synthesis.

23. See Stephen Gill and David Law, 'Global Hegemony and the Struc-
tural Power of Capital', in Stephen Gill (ed.), *Gramsci, Historical
Materialism and International Relations*, Cambridge: Cambridge
University Press, 1993, pp. 93–124.

24. Patomäki, *The Political Economy of Global Security*, pp. 124–45.

25. Thomas I. Palley, 'Financialization: What It Is and Why It Mat-
ters', *IMK Working Paper* 4/2008 (2008), Düsseldorf: Hans Böckler
Stiftung, www.boeckler.de/pdf/ p_imk_wp_04_2008.pdf (accessed 8
June 2012); Till van Treeck, 'The Macroeconomics of "Financialisa-
tion", and the Deeper Origins of the World Economic Crisis', *IMK
Working Paper*, 9/2009 (2009), Düsseldorf: Hans Böckler Stiftung,
www.boeckler.de/pdf/p_imk_wp_9_2009.pdf (accessed 8 June 2012);
Till van Treeck 'The Political Economy Debate on 'Financialization'
– A Macroeconomic Perspective', *Review of International Political
Economy* 16(5) (2009): 907–44.

26. See e.g. Philip G. Cerny, 'Paradoxes of the Competition State: The
Dynamics of Political Globalization', *Government and Opposition*
32(2) (1997): 251–74.

27. On the development of offshore centres, their effects and the strug-
gles for the future of offshore financing, see Ronen Palan, Richard
Murphy and Christian Chavagneux, *Tax Havens: How Globalization
Really Works*, Ithaca NY: Cornell University Press, 2010.

28. The data in this table have been compiled by Jussi Ahokas from

statistics from Statistics Finland and the Bank of Finland.

29. Veblen's best-known work is *The Theory of the Leisure Class*, intr. A. Wolfe, annotated by J. Danlyn, New York: The Modern Library, 2002 (1899). For an explanatory model partially in the spirit of Veblen, see Rasmus, *Epic Recession*, pp. 70–74, 113–21, 220–21; for a more explicit use of Veblen's ideas, see Wisman and Baker, 'Increasing Inequality', pp. 19–28. Rasmus emphasizes that the question is not so much one of cultural change but an attempt to retain an established standard of living in a situation in which most people's wage levels and incomes are declining. However, he does not sufficiently explain why people would try to maintain or even increase their consumption levels even though it would cost them more of their free time or retirement time, and even though they are taking conscious risks in getting into debt.

30. The concept of the philosophy of futility was introduced by Paul H. Nystrom, *Economics of Fashion*, New York: Ronald Press, 1928.

31. Joseph Schumpeter, Edward Chamberlin, Joan Robinson, Joe S. Bain, John Kenneth Galbraith and many critical economists who were influential in the decades between the Great Depression and the neoliberal turn of the 1970s developed theories of advertising, product development and product differentiation, and their relations to monopolistic profits and the centralization of businesses. Research on advertising has been largely left to business school researchers and proponents of game theory, and their investigations have usually focused on specific marketing niches. These studies also very often tend to be strategic; that is, they rarely question the goals that advertisers have set for themselves. But for an exception to the general trend, see John Sutton, *Sunk Costs and Market Structure: Price Competition, Advertising, and the Evolution of Concentration*, Cambridge MA: MIT Press, 1991.

32. John Kenneth Galbraith *The New Industrial State*, London: Hamish Hamilton, 1968. The long-developed style of consumerism in the United States is helpful in partly explaining, for example, the striking imbalance in trade relations between the USA and China. Many Chinese save because they know that otherwise they will be unable to meet the cost of illness or other contingencies, but that is not the only reason; they also save because they see virtue in doing so. Consumerism, both of the conspicuous kind and otherwise, has gained ground in China only among the richest. In the USA, by contrast, consumerist mania has been well rooted for decades, and already pervades all sectors of society and all economic and social classes. See Keith Cowling, Stephen P. Dunn and Philip R. Tomlinson, 'Glo-

bal Imbalances and Modern Capitalism: A Structural Approach to Understanding the Present Economic Crisis', *Journal of Post Keynesian Economics* 33(4) (2011): 575–96.

33. Thorstein Veblen, *The Theory of Business Enterprise*, New York: Scribner, 1923 (1904), pp. 290–300.

34. Karl Marx, *Capital: A Critique of Political Economy*, Volume 1, intr. Ernest Mandel, trans. Ben Fowkes. London: Penguin, 1990 (1867), Book One, ch. 4, pp. 141–67 ff.

35. Theoretically Marx was forced to wrestle with the implications of his labour theory of value and his theory of money when he turned to theorize the functioning of credit and monetary systems. Although he was many times on the right track, he was not able to fully accept the spontaneity of money and its causal role in the cycles of the capitalist economy. Engels, writing in 1895, noted at the end of Volume 3 of *Capital* that 'since 1865, when the book was written, a change has taken place which today assigns a considerably increased and constantly growing role to the stock exchange, and which, as it develops, tends to concentrate all production, industrial as well as agricultural, and all commerce, the means of communication as well as the functions of exchange, in the hands of stock exchange operators, so that the stock exchange becomes the most prominent representative of capitalist production itself. ... Since the crisis of 1866 accumulation has proceeded with ever-increasing rapidity, so that in no industrial country, least of all in England, could the expansion of production keep up with that of accumulation, or the accumulation of the individual capitalist be completely utilised in the enlargement of his own business.' Friedrich Engels, 'Supplement to *Capital*, Volume Three' (1895), in Karl Marx, *The Collected Works of Karl Marx and Friedrich Engels*, ed. Eric Hobsbawm et al., various translators, vol. 37: *Capital: A Critique of Political Economy*, Volume 3, London: Lawrence & Wishart, 1998 (1894), pp. 873–97; 895.

CHAPTER 4

1. 'Brussels Proposes £170bn Spending Plan', *Guardian*, 27 November 2008, www.guardian.co.uk/business/2008/nov/27/europe-union-spending-recession-tax-recovery (accessed 29 June 2012).

2. 'Ireland's Gross Debt Ratio Set to Rise Further According to Bank of Ireland's Monthly Bulletin', Bank of Ireland, 6 May 2011, www.bankofireland.com/fs/doc/press-releases/may-bulletin-2011.pdf (accessed 12 June 2012).

3. 'Greek Economy Slumps 6.9% to Second Quarter', *RTÉ News*

(Ireland), 12 August 2011, www.rte.ie/news/2011/0812/greece-business.html (accessed 12 June 2012).

4. 'A Greek Exit? Europe May Be Ready', *New York Times*, 18 May 2012: B1.

5. Committee for the Study of Economic and Monetary Union, *Report on Economic and Monetary Union in the European Community*, Luxembourg: Office for Official Publications in the European Communities, 1989.

6. Eurostat, *External and Intra-European Union Trade: Data 2002–07*, Brussels: European Commission, 2009, p. 44, http://epp.eurostat.ec.europa.eu/cache/ity_offpub/ks-cv-08-001/en/ks-cv-08-001-en.pdf (accessed 12 June 2012).

7. 'The New Endangered Species: Small Currencies Vanishing as Big Bucks Take Over', *Guardian*, 14 January 2000, www.guardian.co.uk/business/2000/jan/14/9 (accessed 12 June 2012).

8. The European Monetary Union is part of the European integration project, which has its own dynamic revolving around identity politics, member state relations – particularly between Germany and France – the ethico-political and power-political aspirations of Europe, and so on. On another level is the question of hegemonic struggles over the organizing principles of global political economy and the problems of legitimation of modern political communities. See P. Minkkinen and H. Patomäki (eds), *The Politics of Economic and Monetary Union*, Dordrecht: Kluwer, 1997.

9. Robert A. Mundell, 'A Theory of Optimum Currency Areas', *American Economic Review* 51(4) (1961): 657–65.

10. For commentary on this during the lead-up to European monetary union, see Teivo Teivainen, 'The Independence of the European Central Bank: Implications for Democratic Governance', in Petri Minkkinen and Heikki Patomäki (eds), *The Politics of Economic and Monetary Union*, Dordrecht: Kluwer, 1997, pp. 55–75.

11. See e.g. Martin Feldstein, 'Europe's Monetary Union: The Case Against EMU', *The Economist*, 13 June 1992, p. 26, available from the US National Bureau of Economic Research website at www.nber.org/feldstein/economistmf.pdf (accessed 12 June 2012).

12. There has been a widespread belief that convergence could develop within the system once economic and fiscal union had been established. Jeffrey A. Frankel and Andrew K. Rose, 'The Endogeneity of the Optimum Currency Area Criteria', *Economic Journal* 108(449) (2001), 1009–25. Indeed, in the economics literature the debate has revolved around the question whether further economic integration and the single currency may result in a higher or lower degree of

synchronization between national business cycles. For relevant references and argument that the EMU is in fact increasing the degree of synchronization, see Carlo Altavilla, 'Do EMU Members Share the Same Business Cycle?', *Journal of Common Market Studies* 42(5) (2004): 869–96.

13. At issue also is the hegemony of a certain economic mindset, which can be summarized in three aims: 'sound money, inflation, and public funding'. This doctrine spread to different countries at different paces. In the smaller European countries in particular, its uptake was more likely: (i) the stronger the position of the financial sector in those countries was; (ii) the weaker the trade unions were, and the less interested the business class was in keeping its part of the social bargain; (iii) the less independent the country's central bank was; (iv) the greater the country's dependency on the German economy. See Martin Marcussen, 'The Role of 'Ideas' in Dutch, Danish and Swedish Economic Policy in the 1980s and the Beginning of the 1990s', in Minkkinen and Patomäki (eds), *The Politics of Economic and Monetary Union*, pp. 76–101.

14. Paul de Grauwe, 'The Enlarged Eurozone: Can it Survive?', Wassenaar, the Netherlands: Netherlands Institute for Advanced Study in the Humanities and Social Sciences, 2003, www.nias.knaw.nl/Content/NIAS/Publicaties/Jelle%20Zijlstra/JelleZijlstraLecture2.pdf (accessed 12 June 2012). Contrary to the expectations of de Grauwe and others, however, the facts contradict the expectations generated by Mundell's theory about the most likely problems of the euro. On this debate, see e.g. Ambrose Evans-Pritchard, 'Professor Mundell, Euro, and "Pessimal Currency Areas"', *Telegraph*, 25 August 2011, available from the *Telegraph* website (accessed 12 June 2012).

15. The data are from the World Bank Development Indicators, http//data.worldbank.org. The graph was originally produced by Jussi Ahokas and Lauri Holappa.

16. Mundell, 'A Theory of Optimum Currency Areas'. Mundell's argument is a perfect example of pure economic theory in the neoclassical and Ricardo mould. He presents no empirical evidence to support his arguments; he uses a minimalistic model containing two countries, two products and two areas; and he refers to only a few previous writings, the most important of which is Milton Friedman's 'The Case for Flexible Exchange Rates' (1953). The principal purpose of Friedman's 'positive economic' methodology, on which Mundell also leans, is to promulgate and defend classical conservative laissez-faire orthodoxy. The ultimate justification for the theory is that the majority of 'competent economists' and 'the long Anglo-American

economic tradition' are in agreement on the core of the theory. Only those who have received training and developed competence in 'the right scientific environment' are entitled to evaluate the theory. Out of respect for this tradition, the positive methodology holds, a theory must always be assessed in light of that tradition. This conservative epistemology of orthodox neoclassical economics is directly opposed to the critical scientific spirit, which refuses to take any authority for granted and is opposed to epistemic closures of any kind. See Heikki Patomäki, 'Appendix 1: Monetarism and the Denial of Reality', in H. Patomäki, *Democratising Globalisation: The Leverage of the Tobin Tax*, London: Zed Books, 2001, pp. 223–31.

17. Heiner Flassbeck, 'The Euro – a Story of Misunderstanding', *Inter-economics* 4 (2011): 180–87, www.ceps.eu/system/files/article/2011/07/Forum.pdf (accessed 12 June 2012).

18. Pekka Sauramo, 'Saako EMUssa nuijia naapureita?' ['Is Beggar-My-Neighbour Allowed within the EMU?'], *Talous & yhteiskunta* [*Economy & Society*] 3 (2011): 70–76; p. 71. Available (Finnish only) at www.labour.fi/TjaYpdf/ty32011.pdf (accessed 12 June 2012).

19. See Philip Grierson, 'The Origins of Money', *Research in Economic Anthropology* 1 (1978): 1–35, www.anthrofoology.com/post/4550568332/philip-grierson-the-origins-of-money (accessed 12 June 2012); Geoffrey Ingham, *The Nature of Money*, Cambridge: Polity Press, 2004, pp. 89–106.

20. I have presented one hypothetical model of these possibilities and of the likely basic metaphors that can be used to form complex metaphors. These enable the abstract valuation of law, justice and money through the development and use of bookkeeping metaphors. Heikki Patomäki, 'Global Justice: A Democratic Perspective', *Globalizations* 3(2) (2006): 99–120, esp. 105.

21. The term comes from the Latin *fiat*, 'let it be done'. The use, or overuse, of paper money in China occasionally led to inflation, or even hyperinflation. During the Ming dynasty in the fifteenth century there was a return to the use of coins, the supply of which was dependent on the amount of metal available. Soon European colonizers began to increase the supply of metal for minting in China. They used slave labour in South America to mine the ores, and shipped the refined metals to China in order to be able to buy valuable goods for sale in Europe. Historians are divided on how important the supply of South American silver really was for the Chinese money supply. The downfall of the Ming dynasty may, however, have been due in part to drops in the silver supply to the country. See e.g. William S. Atwell, 'Another Look at Silver Imports into China, ca. 1635–1644',

Journal of World History 16(4) (2005): 467–89.

22. Several examples can be found in Charles P. Kindleberger and Robert Z. Aliber, *Manias, Panics and Crashes: A History of Financial Crises*, 6th edn, Basingstoke: Palgrave Macmillan, 2011. Geoffrey Ingham (*The Nature of Money*, 2004, pp. 211–12) argues that many well-known examples of monetary catastrophes were in fact preceded by various other social and political problems that at least co-caused these catastrophes.

23. Charles A.E. Goodhardt, 'The Two Concepts of Money: Implications for the Analysis of Optimal Currency Areas', *European Journal of Political Economy* 14(3) (1998): 407–32.

24. Ibid., pp. 420–24.

25. A useful, if somewhat technical, account of the external and internal components of debt and how their sustainability is assessed is given by Alison Johnson, *Key Issues in Analysing Domestic Debt Sustainability*, London: Debt Relief International, 2001, www.dri.org.uk/pdfs/EngPub5_DomDebt.pdf (accessed June 12 2012).

26. For more detailed argument on this point, see Chapter 7; and e.g. Kuniber Raffer and H.W. Singer, *The Economic North–South Divide: Six Decades of Unequal Development*, Cheltenham: Edward Elgar, 2001; Kuniber Raffer, *Debt Management for Development: Protection of the Poor and the Millennium Development Goals*, Cheltenham: Edward Elgar, 2010.

27. Article 122 of the Maastricht Treaty prohibits the Union from sharing responsibility for debt among member states. Article 123 prohibits the European Central Bank from directly purchasing bonds and other budget-supporting debt instruments from member states. Article 124 specifies that all public institutions must operate on the credit market according to purely competitive market principles. The common purpose of these articles is to constitutionalize anti-inflationary policies. The theoretical justification for this view was Milton Friedman's monetarist economic theory, and the ideologically similar so-called rational expectations macroeconomic theories developed in the 1970s.

28. John M. Keynes, *General Theory of Employment, Interest and Money*, London: Macmillan, 1961 (1936), pp. 155–8.

29. 'Newsletter – EU Financial Reforms', part of the project 'Towards a Global Finance System at the Service of Sustainable Development', July 2011, pp. 3-4, available from the website of the Centre for Research on Multinational Corporations: http://somo.nl/dossiers-en/sectors/financial/eu-financial-reforms/newsletters (accessed 12 July 2012).

30. A good examination of how credit-rating agencies work and the
power the wield is provided by Timothy Sinclair, *The New Masters
of Capital: American Bond Rating Agencies and the Politics of Creditworthiness*, Ithaca NY: Cornell University Press, 2008.

31. Adapted from Patomäki, *Democratising Globalisation*, p. 12.

32. This circular logic follows directly from neoclassical economic theories and their formulaic ideas. The model of 'perfect competition' is
used both as the premiss of the explanation and as its implicit normative ideal. All disturbances, crises and other unexpected outcomes
are explained away as the failure of reality to live up to the ideal.
These kinds of explanations have nothing to do with causal explanations, since the perfect competition world is, almost by definition,
nowhere – the literal meaning of utopia. Using neoclassical economic
theory's own tools of explanation, it is easy to show, as the economists
Richard Lipsey and Kelvin Lancaster did in the late 1950s, that if one
accepts that some markets in the world are not 'perfectly competitive', then increases in stability and efficiency can mean moving away
from the recommendations of the ideal model. In other words, even a
single imperfection or failure of the market can lead to the pursuit of
the utopian ideal actually making things worse. This is an inevitable
consequence of imagining an 'ideal world' of stagnant equilibrium
in the allocation of resources, in which, for example, all actors and
products are homogenous (there is in fact only one 'representative'
actor), all actors can predict everything about the future, and there
are no economies of scale. The implications of the orthodox ideal
have been understood for sixty years, but this seems to have no effect on those who espouse it. See R. Lipsey and K. Lancaster, 'The
General Theory of Second Best', *Review of Economic Studies* 24(1)
(1956–57): 11–32.

33. The estimate is by Barclays bank, 'Ecb Smp: Marking To Market',
Barclays Capital Interest Rates Research, Europe, 6 January 2012,
www.teinteresa.es/dinero/Informe-Barclays-Capital-compra-BCE_
TINFIL20120109_0007.pdf (accessed 12 June 2012).

34. Marshall Auerback 'Europe's Non-Solution: The 'Bazooka' Turned
on Itself', *Real-World Economics Review* 58 (2011): 69–76, www.
paecon.net/PAEReview/issue58/Auerback58.pdf (accessed 12 June
2012).

CHAPTER 5

1. European Commission, *Executive Summary of the Impact Assessment,
accompanying the document Proposal for a Council Directive on a Common System of Financial Transaction Tax, and amending Directive*

2008/7/EC, 2011, p. 2, available from the website of the European Commission's Taxation and Customs Union, http://ec.europa.eu/taxation_customs/index_en.htm.

2. 'G20 Fails to Endorse Financial Transaction Tax', Reuters, 4 November 2011.

3. In early 2012 France began actively lobbying for the tax to be implemented as soon as possible, even if it were only adopted by a small number of EU countries.

4. 'ESM Cloud Partly Lifts', Reuters, 24 June 2011; 'Bank Chief Hints Help for Europe Is Possible', *New York Times*, 2 December 2011:B1.

5. European Council, *Revised Version of the Conclusions of the European Council, 24 and 25 March*, EUCO 10/1/11 REV 1, Appendix II, 2011, p. 21, www.consilium.europa.eu/uedocs/cms_data/docs/pressdata/en/ec/120296.pdf (accessed 14 June 2012).

6. Stephen Gill, *Power and Resistance in the New World Order*, 2nd edn, London: Palgrave Macmillan, 2008 (2003), pp. 78–9, 168–74.

7. In addition and prior to ESFC and ESM, the EU countries also agreed on several loan facilities, for example to Iceland, Latvia, Greece and Ireland.

8. European Council, *Treaty Establishing the European Stability Mechanism* [between the euro area member states], T/ESM 2012/en 1, 2012, Article 4, www.european-council.europa.eu/media/582311/05-tesm2.en12.pdf (accessed 14 June 2012).

9. Ibid., Article 32(3) and (4).

10. Ibid., Article 35.

11. The proposals are available at http://ec.europa.eu/taxation_customs/resources/documents/taxation/other_taxes/financial_sector/com(2011)594_en.pdf (accessed 14 June 2012).

12. The conclusions of the European Council (28/29 June 2012), CO EUR 4 CONCL 2, p. 12, http://consilium.europa.eu/uedocs/cms_data/docs/pressdata/en/ec/131388.pdf (accessed 3 July 2012).

13. On the Tobin tax, see Heikki Patomäki, *Democratising Globalisation: The Leverage of the Tobin Tax*, London: Zed Books, 2001.

14. *Proposal for a Council Directive on a Common System of Financial Transaction Tax and Amending Directive 2008/7/EC*, Brussels, 28 September 2011, COM(2011) 594 final; and *Commission Staff Working Paper Executive Summary of the Impact Assessment accompanying the document Proposal for a Council Directive on a Common System of Financial TransactionTax and Amending Directive 2008/7/EC*, Brussels, 28 September 2011, SEC(2011) 1103 final. Both documents are available from the website of the European Commission's Taxation and Customs Union, http://ec.europa.eu/taxation_customs/index_en.htm.

15. Whereas traditional short selling involves selling borrowed bonds at the going market price and repurchasing them once the price has dropped, and then returning them to the seller, '[N]aked short sellers sell shares of stock they haven't borrowed, have no intention of borrowing, and that may not even exist.' Often, naked short sellers have no intention of ever delivering the actual shares that the unfortunate buyer on the other end of the transaction thinks he has purchased. Therefore, unlike a traditional short sale, a naked short sale results in a failure to deliver the actual shares sold, and the shares eventually received by the buyer in the original transaction represent nothing more than an electronic book entry.' James W. Christian, Robert Shapiro and John-Paul Whalen, 'Naked Short Selling: How Exposed Are Investors?', *Houston Law Review* 43(4) (2006–07): 1033–90; 1038, footnotes omitted.

16. *Executive Summary Of The Impact Assessment*, p. 8.

17. The proposal and many documents related to it are available at http://ec.europa.eu/commission_2010–2014/president/news/documents (accessed 14 June 2012).

18. *Proposal for a Regulation of the European Parliament and of The Council on Common Provisions for Monitoring and Assessing Draft Budgetary Plans and Ensuring the Correction of Excessive Deficit of the Member States in the Euro Area*, Brussels, 23 November 2011, COM (2011) 821 final, 2011/0386 (COD), p. 2, para. 7, http://ec.europa.eu/commission_2010–2014/president/news/documents/pdf/regulation_1_en.pdf (accessed 14 June 2012).

19. *Green Paper on the Feasibility of introducing Stability Bonds*, Brussels, 23 November 2011, COM (2011) 818 final, http://ec.europa.eu/europe2020/pdf/green_paper_en.pdf (accessed 14 June 2012).

20. 'Any type of Stability Bond would have to be accompanied by a substantially reinforced fiscal surveillance and policy coordination as an essential counterpart, so as to avoid moral hazard [on the part of the member states] and ensure sustainable public finances and to support competitiveness and reduction of harmful macroeconomic imbalances' (*Green Paper*, p. 4). Although it states forthrightly that these changes will impinge on state sovereignty, the Commission does not at any point consider the matter from a democratic perspective.

21. The Fiscal Compact is the informal title of the *Treaty on Stability, Coordination and Governance in the Economic and Monetary Union*. A long memorandum on the Fiscal Compact (EU/2011/1935, Finnish and Swedish only), dated 19 January 2012, that was circulated by the Finnish Parliamentary Finance Committee to the Finnish Parliament carried the following tortuous title, summarizing the contents of the

Compact: 'Letter from the Finance Committee to Parliament regarding the proposed regulations of the European Parliament and Council
proposal pertaining to tighter supervision and assessment of budget
proposals and [also regarding] the shared rules for rectification of
the excessive budgetary deficits of the Eurozone Member States, the
economies and public finances of which are currently experiencing,
or are currently seriously vulnerable to, serious difficulties with their
financial stability.'

22. The difference between the concepts is that the term 'investor
responsibility', which was coined during the euro crisis, is ad hoc
in nature – created for a particular case without consideration of its
wider application – whereas the debt arbitration mechanism is founded
on generally applicable legal and moral principles. The principle of
divided or shared responsibility also comprises the idea for a debt conciliation mechanism, but one of a permanent nature that would operate
according to the rule of law. On this proposal, see Chapter 7.

23. 'Investor Responsibility Divides Euro Countries', *Helsingin Sanomat*
(International Edition), 25 May 2011, www.hs.fi/english/article/Inves
tor+responsibility+divides+euro+countries+1135266291713 (accessed
14 June 2012).

24. 'Eurozone May Drop Private Sector from ESM Bailout', Reuters, 25
November 2011.

25. European Council, *Revised Version of the Conclusions of the European
Council*, p. 19.

CHAPTER 6

1. For discussion of the unpredictability produced by non-linearity,
turning points and crises, see Charles F. Doran, 'Why Forecasts Fail:
The Limits and Potential of Forecasting in International Relations
and Economics', *International Studies Review* 1(2) (1999): 11–41;
Fred Chernoff, *The Power of International Theory: Reinforcing the
Link to Foreign Policy-Making through Scientific Enquiry*, London:
Routledge,2005, pp. 143–52.

2. See e.g. 'Balls to Warn of Economic "Hurricane"', *Financial Times*,
27 August 2010. The Finnish daily *Helsingin Sanomat* reported on 9
August 2011 a quasi-poetic statement by the Finnish prime minister
Jyrki Katainen, using the same metaphor.

3. See e.g. Heikki Patomäki, 'What Next? An Explanation of the 2008–9
Slump and Two Scenarios of the Shape of Things to Come', *Globalizations* 7(1) (2010): 67–84.

4. Heikki Patomäki, 'Realist Ontology for Futures Studies', *Journal of
Critical Realism* 5(1) (2006): 1–31.

5. Karl Marx, *The Eighteenth Brumaire of Louis Bonaparte*, in *The Collected Works of Karl Marx and Friedrich Engels*, ed. Eric Hobsbawm et al., various translators, Vol. 11: *Marx and Engels: 1851–53*, London: Lawrence & Wishart, 1979 (1852), pp. 99–197; 103.

6. The dramatic increase in the frequency of short-term price fluctuations does not in itself necessarily mean an increase in the risk of genuine financial crises (the cause of crises is not volatility, but rather self-fulfilling economic prophecies and self-reinforcing bubbles, accumulation of debt, and weakening of the financial base). Often the direction of influence is the other way round: that is, crises bring an increase in volatility. Independently of which way the causal relation principally works, much credible evidence has been presented in the literature to support the claim that the price fluctuations caused by financialization have increased significantly on stock markets, currency markets, commodities markets, and so on. Depending on the markets, one can say that leaps to a higher level of uncertainty and volatility occurred during the 1970s, 1980s, 1990s, and in some cases only during the 2000s (there have also been occasional and partial counter-trends, which further complicates the picture). The increases in the amount of simultaneous price fluctuations at the same time as financial crises have gradually become more widespread and more serious. Nonetheless, many neoclassical economists have tried to prove that despite possible increases in price volatility, prices generally follow the basic economic indicators; and that although 'overshoot' can sometimes occur on financial markets, balance over the long term is maintained (even the long term cannot be known, and is thus simply assumed). See e.g. Rudi Dornbusch, 'Expectations and Exchange Rate Dynamics', *Journal of Political Economy* 84(6) (1976): 1161–76; 1163. Data on price changes, therefore, do not force anyone to accept or reject any more substantive hypotheses; interpretation of data and other evidence is invariably guided by presumptions and theories. For this reason, it is essential to assess the conceptual credibility and realism of the theories and background assumptions one employs. On evidence relating to price fluctuations, see e.g. Malcom Edey and Ketil Hviding, *An Assessment of Financial Reform in OECD Countries*, OECD Economics Department Working Papers 154, OCDE/GD (95) (1995): 69; Barry Eichengreen and Hui Tong, 'Stock Market Volatility and Monetary Policy: What the Historical Record Shows', University of California, Berkeley, 2003, http://elsa.berkeley.edu/~eichengr/research/sydneywithhui9sep26-03.pdf (accessed 17 June 2012); United Nations Conference on Trade and Development, *Price Formation in Financialized Commodity Markets: The Role of*

Information, New York and Geneva: United Nations, 2011, www. unctad.org/en/docs/gds2011_en.pdf (accessed 17 June 2012).

7. George Soros, *The New Paradigm for Financial Markets: The Credit Crisis of 2008 and What It Means*, New York: Public Affairs, 2008. In chapter 4 Soros discusses why the neoclassical economic theories of financial market balance are wrong. He also shows how reflexive information on self-creating bubbles – which in the end are self-defeating – has helped him to make large profits as an investor.

8. A Pareto-optimal situation is one in which nobody's circumstances can be improved any further without causing a worsening of someone else's circumstances. At first glance the definition can seem technical and neutral, but it is ideological. The concept of Pareto-optimality rules out, for example, redistribution of income if it worsens the position of any single actor in terms of his or her subjective preferences. (An alternative model of optimality, the Kaldor–Hicks model, allows for the possibility of hypothetical compensation, so that under this model the overall situation can be improved even when this could worsen some party's position.) Pareto-optimality and its variations are based on the goal of maximizing the sum of private goods measured in terms of monetarized subjective preferences; on this view, nothing that is just, common or public can be good in itself (only a strong version of the liberal no-harm principle is deemed acceptable). Neither do the various conceptions of Pareto-optimality have anything to do with input–output efficiency, for example. They are definitions of efficiency that only take account of timeless market allocations – as opposed to real-world dynamics of production and growth – and the interests of the well-off owners and managers of private property.

9. The dominant conception of justice in neoclassical economics is only one of ten basic models of justice (different theories and ideologies of justice combine different models). The basic model of distribution in neoclassical economics is scalar distribution: what each receives is determined by his or her contribution to the process, and not by for example contracts, rights, needs or considerations related to some conception of fairness. The purpose of the 'general theory of equilibrium' is to demonstrate that perfectly competitive markets can, at least when one grants some imaginary conditions, ensure both Pareto-optimal equilibrium (see n. 8) and a just scalar distribution of income. But neoclassical economists are generally reluctant to speak of justice, preferring instead the idea that the prices of factors of production (including workers' wages) accord with their marginal productivity. This, however, is much the same thing as the conception of

justice based on the maxim 'To each according to his contribution'. As such, according to orthodox neoclassical theory 'perfectly competitive' markets are able to guarantee that each does indeed receive his due. The intuitive plausibility of this assumption stems from the theory of justice that neoclassical theorists have tacitly adopted (without necessarily being consciously aware of it themselves, since their metatheory involves a principled agnosticism about questions of value; they believe themselves to be merely delineating the technical outcomes of various options, without any heed to value-related considerations). An abstract model of 'perfect competition' is then used in practical rhetoric to justify the inequalities in the capitalist real-world market economy. The standard introduction to the general theory of equilibrium is Kenneth Arrow and Frank Hahn, *General Competitive Analysis*, Amsterdam: North Holland, 1971. On basic models of justice and various theories and ideologies of justice, see Heikki Patomäki, 'Global Justice: A Democratic Perspective', *Globalizations* 3(2) (2006): 99–120.

10. Philip E. Tetlock, 'Theory-Driven Reasoning about Plausible Pasts and Probable Futures in World Politics: Are We Prisoners of Our Preconceptions?', *American Journal of Political Science* 43(2) (1999): 335–66.

11. On the 1970s' neoclassical theories in which European Central Bank monetary policy is rooted, see e.g. Robert E. Lucas, 'Expectations and the Neutrality of Money', *Journal of Economic Theory* 4(2) (1972): 103–24; Robert Barro, 'Are Government Bonds Net Wealth?', *Journal of Political Economy* 82(6) (1974): 1095–117; T. Sargent and N. Wallace, '"Rational" Expectations, the Optimal Monetary Instrument and the Optimal Money Supply Rule', *Journal of Political Economy* 83(2) (1975): 231–54.

12. An orthodox neoclassical version of the theory is presented by William Nordhaus, 'The Political Business Cycle', *Review of Economic Studies* 42(2) (1975): 169–90. Efforts have been made to statistically test the theory in recent decades. On a general level the results have been negative, but some examples and weak, sporadic or partial correlations between the effects of impending elections on some countries' budgets have been found (the central hypothesis of the theory can be understood and operationalized in many ways, which effects whether any kind of statistical connection can be seen in any situation). In sum, a plausible conclusion is that the relatively rare election budget episodes depend on institutional arrangements, on the political state of play in the country in question in the run-up to the elections, and on the ethical-political choices of those involved (it is in the nature

of action that one could always act otherwise). It is internationally transmitted business cycles that have the greater effect on unemployment, which is reflected also in electoral behaviour and in the chances of electoral success for the various parties. Trust in ahistorical and abstract political business cycles and in their explanatory power are directly linked to how strongly committed the researcher in question is to the orthodox neoclassical world-view (cf. note 9). See e.g. Ann Mari May, 'The Political Business Cycle: An Institutional Critique and Reconstruction', *Journal of Economic Issues* 21(2) (1987): 713–22; Marc A. Kayser, 'Partisan Waves: International Business Cycles and Electoral Choice', *American Journal of Political Science* 53(4) (2009): 950–70.

13. In the academic literature, agnosticism concerning economic developments is combined with legitimation-theoretical criticisms by e.g. Josep R. Llobera, 'The Role of the State and Nation in Europe', in S. García (ed.), *European Identity and the Search for Legitimacy*, London: Pinter, 1993, pp. 64–80; Claus Offe, 'The European Model of "Social" Capitalism: Can It Survive European Integration?', *Journal of Political Philosophy* 11(4) (2003): 437–69; Teivo Teivainen, 'The Independence of the European Central Bank: Implications for Democratic Governance', in P. Minkkinen and H. Patomäki (eds), *The Politics of Economic and Monetary Union*, Dordrecht: Kluwer, 1997, pp. 55–75.

14. See e.g. Philip Arestis and Malcolm Sawyer, 'Macroeconomic Policies of the Economic Monetary Union: Theoretical Underpinnings and Challenges', *Levy Economics Institute Working Paper* 385 (2003), www.levyinstitute.org/pubs/wp385.pdf (accessed 18 June 2012); Randall L. Wray, 'Is Euroland the Next Argentina?', Center for Full Employment and Price Stability, University of Missouri–Kansas City, *Working Paper* No. 23 (2003), www.cfeps.org/pubs/wp-pdf/WP23-Wray.pdf (accessed 18 June 2012); Philip Wyman, Brian Burkitt and Mark Baimbridge, 'Post-Keynesianism and a Neo-Liberal EMU: The Case for Economic Independence', *Contemporary Politics* 11(4) (2005): 259–70; Rosaria Rita Canale and Oreste Napolitano, 'The Recessive Attitude of EMU Policies: Reflections on the Italian Experience, 1998–2008', *MPRA Paper* No. 20207 (2009), http://mpra.ub.uni-muenchen.de/20207 (accessed 18 June 2012).

15. Andrea Boltho, 'What's Wrong with Europe?', *New Left Review* 22(3) (2003): 5–26; George Irvin, 'Europe vs. USA: Whose Economy Wins?', *New Federalist*, 16 January 2007, www.thenewfederalist.eu/Europe-vs-USA-Whose-Economy-Wins (accessed 18 June 2012).

16. On the global and especially OECD-area recessionary economic

trends of the past several decades, see Heikki Patomäki, *The Political Economy of Global Security: War, Future Crises and Changes in Global Governance*, London: Routledge, 2008, ch. 5.

17. See e.g. Alan W. Cafruny and Magnus J. Ryner, *Europe at Bay: In the Shadow of US Hegemony*, Boulder CO: Lynne Rienner, 2007.

18. For an interview with Habermas on the European crisis, see 'A Philosopher's Mission to Save the EU', *Der Spiegel Online International*, 25 November 2011, www.spiegel.de/international/europe/0,1518,799237,00.html (accessed 18 June 2012).

19. Globally networked and flexible consumer capitalism, commoditization, increased inequality and the fear of alienation easily give rise to morally regressive movements and/or counter-efforts to create a new sense of communal belonging by imagining a new community. People whose lifeworld is subjectivistic to begin with can easily become nihilistic in the midst of affluence if they find themselves on the receiving end of constantly changing but purposeless upheavals by overwhelming powers of production and consumption. See Kathryn Dean, *Capitalism and Citizenship*, London: Routledge, 2003, pp. 36–7. A cynical subjectivist can at best see something sensible only in (ironic) attempts to deviate from the shackles of modern, disciplinary normality. He or she may therefore come to identify with everything that is a rejection of normality, including derangement, terrorism and violence for its own sake; see Pauline Marie Rosenau, *Postmodernism and the Social Sciences: Insights, Inroads, and Intrusions*, Princeton NJ: Princeton University Press, 1992, pp. 138–44. For others, a moralism anchored in austere nationalism or religion can in similar situations come to seem like the only acceptable option, and the routes out of a suffocating situation to these sorts of escapes verging on desperation can be surprisingly short. What is paradoxical about the postmodern hermeneutics of suspicion, however, is that it has no counter-arguments against absolute truth or absolute virtue. Also from a sociological perspective, suspicion, pluralism and fundamentalism are usually closely linked. According to Anthony Giddens, 'The defence of tradition only tends to take on the shrill tone it assumes today in the context of detraditionalization, globalization and diasporic cultural interchanges The point about fundamentalism is not its defence of tradition as such, but the manner of its defence in relation to a world of interrogation and dialogue ... Refusing the discursive engagements which a world of cosmopolitan communication tends to enforce, fundamentalism is protecting a *principle* as much as a set of particular doctrines.' Anthony Giddens, *Beyond Left and Right: The Future of Radical Politics*, Cambridge: Polity Press,

1994, p. 85, emphasis in the original. See also e.g. Malise Ruthven, *Fundamentalism: A Very Short Introduction*, Oxford: Oxford University Press, 2007. Ideas, including fundamentalist ones, are also always a reaction to certain historical situations. If the prevailing social relations are widely held to be unjust, oppressive or even violent, they have a tendency to provoke criticism that can easily be bent into us-against-them antagonisms with the aid of fundamentalist doctrines. For example, real and imagined competition for jobs between immigrants and native citizens can fuel nationalism, and can also engender radical dogmas about 'the fates of nations', which are easily amalgamated with various forms of religious fundamentalism. The decline of the welfare state contributes to unemployment and the fear of alienation, and increases the risk of absolutist antagonisms.

20. Loïs Wacquant, *Punishing the Poor: The Neoliberal Government of Social Insecurity*, Durham NC: Duke University Press, 2009.

21. This is essentially a result of (self-centred) skewed cognitive processing and the pathological learning to which it leads. Through false generalizations, this process can lead to the construction of structures of meaning that make future learning more difficult. Pathological learning hardens the political will of individuals or organizations, and thereby tends to lead to the creation of stark oppositions. This typically entails an increased propensity to resort to violence in order to punish others, or to make them comply with the pathological learners' own dictates. Creation of enemies and the resort to security can also be used to obtain or generate approval. When strategically framed in the right way, enemies and securitization serve to legitimate the sorts of compulsion that can be explained away as protection from external threats. On the dynamics of neoliberalism, the formation of enemies, and propensities for violence, see Patomäki, *The Political Economy of Global Security*, pp. 147–55.

22. See e.g. Joanna Apap and Sergio Carrera, 'Maintaining Security within Borders: Toward a Permanent State of Emergency in the EU?', *Alternatives* 29(4) (2004): 399–416; Thomas Diez 'Constructing Threat, Constructing Political Order: On the Legitimisation of an Economic Community in Western Europe', *Journal of International Relations and Development* 2(1) (1999): 29–49; Volker Heins, 'Orientalising America? Continental Intellectuals and the Search for Europe's Identity', *Millennium: Journal of International Studies* 34(2) (2005): 433–48.

23. These four options are adapted to the neoliberal ideology and prevailing world economic context from Kalecki's alternative proposal, presented already in the 1940s, for increasing aggregate demand.

Michał Kalecki, 'Political Aspects of Full Employment', *Political Quarterly* 14(4) (1943): 322–31.

24. See notes 19–21.

25. Johan Galtung, *The European Community: A Superpower in the Making*, London: George Allen & Unwin, 1973, pp. 18–32.

26. See 'Crisis as Capitalist Opportunity', an interview with Ursula Huws, *The New Left Project*, 7 December 2011, www.newleftproject. org/index.php/site/article_comments/crisis_as_capitalist_opportunity (accessed 18 June 2012).

27. However, the way the questions in the Eurobarometer are framed may have a major effect on the answers received. The question 'Taking everything into account, would you say that (OUR COUNTRY) has on balance benefited or not from being a member of the EU?' cannot necessarily be interpreted as meaning that '(OUR COUNTRY)'s membership of the European Union is … (1) a good thing'. Eurobarometer 75 (Standard) *Public Opinion in the European Union Spring 2011*, Questions A10c and A11C, p. 82, Brussels: European Commission, 2011, http://ec.europa.eu/public_opinion/archives/eb/eb75/eb75_publ_en.pdf (accessed 19 June 2012). On the significance of framing and the multiple possible interpretations of European 'public opinion', see Heikki Patomäki, 'EMU and the Legitimation Problems of the European Union', in Minkkinen and Patomäki (eds), *The Politics of Economic and Monetary Union*, esp. pp. 165–73.

28. Reader's Digest, 'Confidence in Institutions, Results for: European Union', 2012, www.rdtrustedbrands.com/tables/Confidence%2520in%2520institutions.category.European%2520Union.shtml (accessed 7 July 2012).

29. Paul Krugman, 'Depression and Democracy', *New York Times*, 11 December 2011, www.nytimes.com/2011/12/12/opinion/krugman-depression-and-democracy.html (accessed 18 June 2012). Krugman refers to the recession and unemployment produced by the neoliberal programmes of savings and cuts, and to how these have increased or are increasing the popularity of nationalistic and xenophobic parties, for example in Finland and Hungary. This trend will drag state politics in even more authoritarian directions. Krugman does not discuss the possibility of EU-European or global democracy, however.

30. I draw here on several sources and on my own analyses, but a particularly helpful source in summarizing the essential points is Wyman, Burkitt and Baimbridge, 'Post-Keynesianism and a Neo-Liberal EMU', p. 263 Table 1.

31. As far back as 1977, the MacDougall Report proposed that the European community budget, corresponding in size to between 5 and 7 per cent of

the community area's GDP, would be enough for an active development-balancing regional policy, and also for responding to downturns in business cycles. 7 per cent of the EU's GDP in 2010 figures is approximately 850 billion euros. For discussion, see Alberto Majocchi, 'Financing the EU Budget with a Surtax on National Income Taxes', Centre for Studies on Federalism, 2011, www.csfederalismo.it/images/stories/discussion_papers/01_a.majocchi.pdf (accessed 18 June 2012).

32. For the most dynamic interpretations, see Thomas Meyer with Lewis Hinchman, *The Theory of Social Democracy*, Cambridge: Polity Press, 2007, esp. 89–92; Heikki Patomäki, 'Neoliberalism and the Global Financial Crisis', *New Political Science* 31(4) (2009): esp. 438–40; Heikki Patomäki, 'Democracy Promotion: Neoliberal vs. Social Democratic *Telos*', in C. Hobson and M. Kurki (eds), *The Conceptual Politics of Democracy Promotion*, London: Routledge, 2011, pp. 85–99, esp. 92–5

33. *A Secure Europe in a Better World: The European Security Strategy*, approved by the European Council, Brussels, 12 December 2003, www.consilium.europa.eu/uedocs/cmsUpload/78367.pdf (accessed 18 June 2012).

34. Johan Deprez and John Harvey (eds), *Foundations of International Economics: Post-Keynesian Perspectives*, London: Routledge, 1999.

35. Jürgen Habermas, 'Discourse Ethics: Notes on a Program of Philosophical Justification', in J. Habermas, *Moral Consciousness and Communicative Action*, trans. Christian Lenhardt and Shierry Weber Nicholsen, Cambridge MA: MIT Press, 1990 (1983), pp. 43–115; 93.

36. Jürgen Habermas, 'Toward a Cosmopolitan Europe', *Journal of Democracy* 14(4) (2003): 86–100.

37. On the theory and practice of pluralistic cosmopolitan dialogue, see Heikki Patomäki, 'From East to West: Emergent Global Philosophies – Beginnings of the End of the Western Dominance?', *Theory, Culture & Society* 19(3) (2002): 89–111; and David Held and Heikki Patomäki, 'Problems of Global Democracy: A Dialogue', *Theory, Culture & Society* 23(5) (2006): 115–33.

38. Johan Galtung goes so far as to claim that it has become offensive to call the United States a democracy. Johan Galtung, 'To Call the US a Democracy Is an Insult to the Word', *TRANSCEND/Human Wrongs Watch*, 2011, www.other-news.info/2011/12/%E2%80%9Cto-call-the-usa-a-democracy-is-an-insult-to-the-word%E2%80%9D (accessed 18 June 2012). For a systematic and detailed investigation, see e.g. Sheldon S. Wolin, *Democracy Incorporated: Managed Democracy and the Specter of Inverted Totalitarianism*, Princeton NJ: Princeton University Press, 2008.

39. Henri Poincaré, *The Foundations of Science: Science and Hypothesis, The Value of Science, Science and Method*, trans. George Halsted. Lancaster PA: Science Press, 1946 (1913), p. 129.

CHAPTER 7

1. See e.g. 'Analysis: Planning for Greek Debt Default Gathering Pace?', Reuters, 21 September 2011.

2. According to some developmental psychologists, it is characteristic of early childhood that the child selects some immediately available and tangible outcome and then judges and acts in light of that. Additionally, judgements and actions also waver inconsistently from one situation to whatever is most immediately at hand. Integral to cognitive and moral development is learning to leave behind this fixation on oneself and on the immediate present; that is, the developing child learns to see things from a more diverse range of perspectives, in accordance with consistent general rules and principles, and within the context of a broader space–time framework. See John C. Gibbs, *Moral Development and Reality: Beyond the Theories of Kohlberg and Hoffman*, Thousand Oaks CA: Sage, 2010, pp. 17–36.

3. Karl Marx, *The Eighteenth Brumaire of Louis Bonaparte*, in *The Collected Works of Karl Marx and Friedrich Engels*, ed. Eric Hobsbawm et al., various translators, Volume 11: *Marx and Engels: 1851–53*, London: Lawrence & Wishart, 1979 (1852) pp. 99–197; 103. Many online translations of the full text of *The Eighteenth Brumaire of Louis Bonaparte* are available, e.g. from the Marxists Internet Archive: www.marxists.org/archive/marx/works/1852/18th-brumaire/ch01.htm (accessed 20 June 2012).

4. The First World War had no real victors. Of the countries that took part in the Paris Peace Conference in 1919, the only countries that could reasonably be described as victors were the United States and Japan. The war also contributed to revolution in Russia and to the creation of many new nation-states throughout Europe, so that it is perhaps natural to say that the Bolsheviks and some nationalist movements also 'won' World War I. The Bolsheviks and several of these new movements were not at the Peace Conference.

5. On the causes of the First World War, see Heikki Patomäki, *The Political Economy of Global Security: War, Future Crises and Changes in Global Governance*, London: Routledge, 2008, esp. ch. 4.

6. See e.g. N. Choucri and R.C. North, *Nations in Conflict: National Growth and International Violence*, San Francisco: W.H. Freeman, 1975, p. 102.

7. See Patomäki, *The Political Economy of Global Security*, esp. pp. 65–7.

8. For a detailed examination of the history of Germany's debt problems at this time, see Timothy W. Guinnane, 'Financial *Vergangenheitsbewältigung*: The 1953 London Debt Agreement', *Center Discussion Paper* No. 880, 2004, Economic Growth Center, Yale University, pp. 4–17, www.econ.yale.edu/growth_pdf/cdp880.pdf (accessed 20 June 2012).

9. 'Nowotny Links Austerity with Rise of Nazism', *Wall Street Journal*, 19 June 2012, http://blogs.wsj.com/eurocrisis/2012/06/19/nowotny-links-austerity-with-rise-of-nazism (accessed 20 June 2012).

10. John Maynard Keynes, *The Economic Consequences of the Peace*, New York: Harcourt, Brace & Howe, 1920, http://openlibrary.org/books/OL7081304M/The_economic_consequences_of_the_Peace (accessed 20 June 2012).

11. He put this very forcefully: 'If the European Civil War is to end with France and Italy abusing their momentary victorious power to destroy Germany and Austria–Hungary now prostrate, they invite their own destruction also, being so deeply and inextricably intertwined with their victims by hidden psychic and economic bonds' (ibid., p. 5).

12. An excellent study of Keynes's role in practical politics and of his views on international relations is Donald Maxwell, *John Maynard Keynes and International Relations: Economic Paths to War and Peace*, Oxford: Oxford University Press, 2006, esp. 54–139.

13. Keynes, *The Economic Consequences of the Peace*, pp. 41, 39, 54–5, 56.

14. Many historians have been more interested in the border disputes and speculation about German fragmentation than the economic outcomes of peace. However, Étienne Mantoux did respond directly to Keynes, writing during the Second World War and published in 1946: *The Carthaginian Peace: The Economic Consequences of Mr Keynes*, Oxford: Oxford University Press.

15. Keynes argued clearly and unequivocally at several points that this would be to the benefit of all parties, including the United States. See e.g. his 1921 paper 'War Debts and the United States', republished in J.M. Keynes, *Essays in Persuasion*, New York: W.W. Norton, 1963, pp. 52–73.

16. Hansjörg Klausinger, 'Gustav Stolper, *Der Deutsche Volkswirt*, and the Controversy on Economic Policy at the End of the Weimar Republic', *History of Political Economy* 33(2) (2001): 241–67; Roger B. Myerson, 'Political Economics and the Weimar Disaster', *Journal of Institutional and Theoretical Economics* 160(2) (2004): 187–209; 189.

17. See Myerson, 'Political Economics and the Weimar Disaster'.

18. The exact cause of the fire has never been determined, and it is possible, though perhaps unlikely, that the Nazis started it themselves.

19. Nazi economic policy, which included cessation of debt payments, detachment from the gold standard, deficit budgets, land reforms, social reforms, job creation programmes, dissolution of trade unions, massive infrastructural investments, gradually intensifying military rearmament, and bilateral trade agreements, was successful at least in the sense that it restored strong growth to industrial production. By 1938, German industrial output was, depending on the sector, between 20 and 100 per cent above 1928 levels. Employment also increased. Indeed, full employment of sorts was the norm in Nazi Germany throughout the 1930s, although 'full' is highly qualified: it did not include women, who were encouraged to stay at home, or Jews and other oppressed groups, many of whom were not allowed to work. The four-year plan drawn up by Herman Goering in 1937 prepared Germany for war, and for a war economy. By the following year, military spending already accounted for 30 per cent of GDP. According to Kalecki, large-scale armament projects 'are inseparable from the expansion of the armed forces and the preparation of plans for a war of conquest. They also induce competitive rearmament of other countries.' Michał Kalecki, 'Political Aspects of Full Employment', *Political Quarterly* 14(4) (1943): 322–31; 126.

20. Guinnane, 'Financial *Vergangenheitsbewältigung*', pp. 13–38.

21. For a history of the debt problems of sovereign states in the nineteenth and twentieth centuries, see Kunibert Raffer, *Debt Management for Development: Protection of the Poor and the Millennium Development Goals*, Cheltenham: Edward Elgar, 2010, chs 1 and 2.

22. The classic text of the debt relief movement is Susan George, *The Debt Boomerang: How Third World Debt Harms Us All*, London: Pluto Press, 1992.

23. The legal principle of 'odious debt' was first proposed by Russian jurist Alexander Nahum Sack in the 1920s, in the context of the Mexican debt crisis. It was introduced to contemporary debate by Patricia Adams, *Odious Debts: Loose Lending, Corruption and the Third World's Environmental Legacy*, London: Earthscan, 1992.

24. See Kuniber Raffer, 'Solving Sovereign Debt Overhang by Internationalising Chapter 9 Procedures', *Austrian Institute for International Affairs Working Paper* 35 (2001), revised version available at http://sovins.files.wordpress.com/2009/05/oiipjp.pdf (accessed 20 June 2012).

25. See Barry Herman, José Ocampo and Shari Spiegel (eds), *Overcoming Developing Country Debt Crisis*, Oxford: Oxford University Press,

NOTES

NOTES 239

2010; Robert W. Kolb (ed.), *Sovereign Debt: From Safety to Default*, Hoboken NJ: Wiley, 2011.

26. Debt servicing alone is not enough if the lenders are able to maximize their benefits in the form of accrued interest. Decreasing the size of the loan may be sensible either for reducing the risk to the lender, or for putting the debt situation on a more sustainable basis. This perspective is also narrow, however, since deflationary and some other means of repaying debt are usually detrimental to growth of GDP. On the many normative and technical problems with the concept of GDP, see Joseph E. Stiglitz, Amartya Sen and Jean-Paul Fitoussi, *Mismeasuring Our Lives: Why GDP Doesn't Add Up*, New York: New Press, 2010.

27. United Nations Conference on Trade and Development, *The Least Developed Countries Report 2000: Aid, Private Capital Flows and External Debt*, New York: United Nations, 2000, ch. 4; quotation from p. 110; www.unctad.org/en/docs/ldc2000_en.pdf (accessed 20 June 2012).

28. On the differences between gross national product and gross domestic product and the reasons for them, see Stiglitz et al., *Mismeasuring Our Lives*, pp. 28–31; for criticisms of the effects of structural adjustment on companies, income distribution and development, see The Structural Adjustment Participatory Review International Network, *Structural Adjustment: The Policy Roots of Economic Crisis, Poverty and Inequality*, London: Zed Books, 2004.

29. See e.g. Susan George, *Another World is Possible if...*, London: Verso, 2004, esp. 193–6; Jan Joost Teunissen and Age Akkerman (eds), *HIPC Debt Relief: Myths and Reality*, The Hague: Forum on Debt and Development, 2004, www.fondad.org/uploaded/HIPC%20Debt%20Relief/Fondad-HIPC-Contents-Authors.pdf (accessed 20 June 2012); United Nations Conference on Trade and Development, *The Least Developed Countries Report 2010: Towards A New International Development Architecture For LDCs*, New York: United Nations, 2010, esp. 6–9, 27, www.unctad.org/en/docs/ldc2010_en.pdf (accessed 20 June 2012).

30. Joseph E. Stiglitz, 'Don't Let America Bankrupt International Bankruptcy Reform', *Project Syndicate*, 9 April 2002, www.project-syndicate.org/commentary/stiglitz13/English (accessed 20 June 2012).

31. Ibid.

32. Raffer, 'Solving Sovereign Debt Overhang', p. 25.

33. See Stiglitz, 'Don't Let America Bankrupt International Bankruptcy Reform'.

34. On the role of the dissolution of the Glass–Steagall Act in the 2008–

09 financial crisis, see Jack Rasmus, *Epic Recession: Prelude to Global Depression*, London: Pluto Press, 2010, pp. 207, 255–64, 310–12. A good presentation of the Dodd–Frank Act can be found in Wikipedia, http://en.wikipedia.org/wiki/Dodd-Frank_Wall_Street_Reform_and_Consumer_Protection_Act (accessed 20 June 2012).

35. A debate between Ross Levine and Joseph E. Stiglitz on financial innovations is available at www.economist.com/debate/days/view/471 (accessed 20 June 2012). Levine, a believer in free-market doctrine, emphasizes the high-risk financing of new technologies, but Stiglitz draws on historical and empirical examples to argue that this kind of financing is irrelevant to most kinds of financial innovations.

36. With the appropriate modifications, the arguments I have made in favour of a currency transaction tax also apply to all other financial taxes; see Heikki Patomäki, *Democratising Globalisation: The Leverage of the Tobin Tax*, London: Zed Books, 2001, ch. 4.

37. See Maureen Ramsay, 'A Modest Proposal: The Case for a Maximum Wage', *Contemporary Politics* 11(4) (2005): 201–15.

38. See Ronen Palan, Richard Murphy and Christian Chavagneux, *Tax Havens: How Globalization Really Works*, Ithaca NY: Cornell University Press, 2010.

39. For example, the draft treaty of the global currency transaction tax contains a provision that would make it possible to shut down tax paradises as economically non-viable. Article 3 (4): 'The Council, on a motion of the Democratic Assembly, established under art 19 shall set a tax of 25% on any capital outflows or inflows to and from non-cooperative tax havens, which threaten, in any possible way, the prospects of success of this Treaty. Failure to do so in six months, on the request of the Democratic Assembly, will result in the Democratic Assembly having the full capacity to act on this matter autonomously.' Heikki Patomäki and Lieven A. Denys, 'Draft Treaty of Global Currency Transactions Tax', *NIGD Discussion Paper* 1/2002 (2002), Helsinki and Nottingham, available in six languages at www.nigd.org/ctt; also published in Bart de Schutter and Johan Pas (eds), *About Globalisation: Views on the Trajectory of Mondialisation*, Brussels: VUB Press, 2003, pp. 185–203.

40. The 'global money parade' is a network of investors, commercial financial institutions and shadow banks that continually creates new financial instruments and speculation techniques. It handles between US$10 and US$20 trillion worth of open, relatively liquid investments annually. See Rasmus, *Epic Recession*, pp. 316–17.

41. These suggestions are among the actions proposed by Rasmus, *Epic Recession*, ch. 9.

42. Keynes himself supported productive public works and investments
in order to create employment, and in certain conditions these can
be financed with debt (which eventual profits on the investments
can be used to pay off), but more usually recommended keeping
budgets balanced, and sometimes even in the black in order to stall
inflation. See Bradley W. Bateman, 'Keynes and Keynesianism', in R.
Backhouse and B.W. Bateman (eds), *The Cambridge Companion to
Keynes*, Cambridge: Cambridge University Press, 2006, pp. 271–90.

43. The so-called principle of functional finance was developed in the
conditions of a relatively closed war economy and self-reliant financial
system by Abba P. Lerner, 'Functional Finance and the Federal Debt'
(1943), in A.P. Lerner *Selected Economic Writings of Abba P. Lerner*,
New York: New York University Press, 1983, pp. 297–310. Functional
Finance prescribes 'the adjustment of total spending (by everybody
in the economy, including the government) in order to eliminate both
unemployment and inflation, using government spending when total
spending is too low and taxation when total spending is too high;
second, the adjustment of public holdings of money and of government bonds, by government borrowing or debt repayment, in order
to achieve the rate of interest which results in the most desirable level
of investment; and, third, the printing, hoarding, or destruction of
money as needed for carrying out the first two parts of the program'
(ibid., p. 300).

44. Keynes presented various versions of this from 1941 to 1943, and
they can be found in his *Collected Works*. J.M. Keynes, *The Collected
Writings of John Maynard Keynes*, Volume XXV: *Activities 1940–44*,
London: Macmillan, 1980. See also George Monbiot, 'Clearing Up
This Mess', 18 November 2008, www.monbiot.com/2008/11/18/clear-
ing-up-this-mess (accessed 20 June 2012).

45. Raffer, 'Solving Sovereign Debt Overhang', p. 37.

46. See Ajit Singh, '"Asian Capitalism" and the Financial Crisis', in J.
Michie and J.G. Smith (eds), *Global Instability: The Political Economy of World Economic Governance*, London: Routledge, 1999, pp.
9–36.

CHAPTER 8

1. Wade Jacoby and Sophie Meunier, 'Europe and Globalization', in
M. Egan, N. Nugent and W. Paterson (eds), *Research Agendas in
European Union Studies: Stalking the Elephant*, Basingstoke: Pal-
grave Macmillan, 2010, p. 361.

2. Globalization in this sense is not a thing, an actor or a mechanism
that explains much else apart from the possibility that social relations

can be maintained with increasing ease and intensity across time and space. Many theorists of globalization have mistakenly used globalization to 'explain' various concrete phenomena, without having specified the relevant structures, forces and mechanisms. See Justin Rosenberg, *The Follies of Globalisation Theory*, London: Verso, 2001.

3. See e.g. John M. Hobson and Leonard Seabrooke, *Everyday Politics of the World Economy*, Cambridge: Cambridge University Press, 2007.

4. Theodore Levitt, 'The Globalization of Markets', *Harvard Business Review*, May–June 1983: 92–102, www.vuw.ac.nz/~caplabtb/m302w07/levitt.pdf (accessed 26 June 2012).

5. Before coming to power Thatcher frequently spoke of how societies based on 'free enterprise' are the morally superior choice; see e.g. her speech launching 'Free Enterprise Week' on 1 July 1975, www.margaretthatcher.org/document/102728 (accessed 26 June 2012). After becoming prime minister, however, Thatcher began to justify her political choices on the lack of alternatives. A collection of Thatcher's speeches and public statements from the 1940s onwards can be found at www.margaretthatcher.org/speeches/default.asp (accessed 26 June 2012). Alternatives, and the lack of them, are mentioned in many of the speeches.

6. On the term 'neoliberalism' and the reasons for its controversy, see Heikki Patomäki, 'Neoliberalism and the Global Financial Crisis', *New Political Science* 31(4) (2009): esp. 432–6.

7. The ten points are more of a reconstruction of the policies that have been and still are being imposed throughout the world from Washington, rather than being a declaration of the IMF's, the World Bank's or the White House's own programme. See John Williamson, 'What Washington Means by Policy Reform', in John Williamson (ed.), *Latin American Readjustment: How Much has Happened*, Washington DC: Institute for International Economics, 1990, ch. 2, www.iie.com/publications/papers/paper.cfm?researchid=486 (accessed 26 June 2012).

8. Ignacio Ramonet, 'Désarmer les marchés', *Le Monde diplomatique* December 1997, www.monde-diplomatique.fr/1997/12/ramonet/9665 (accessed 26 June 2012).

9. On the foundation of Attac, see the interview with Bernard Cassen 'On the ATTACK', *New Left Review* 19(1) (2003): 41–60, http://newleftreview.org/II/19/bernard-cassen-on-the-attack (accessed 26 June 2012). On the rise of the global taxation movement, see Heikki Patomäki, 'Global Tax Initiatives: The Movement for the Currency

Transaction Tax', 2007, available from the website of the United Nations Research Institute for Social Development, www.unrisd.org.

10. James Tobin, *The New Economics One Decade Older*, Eliot Janeway Lectures in Honour of Joseph Schumpeter, Princeton NJ: Princeton University Press, 1974, pp. 88–92; James Tobin, 'A Proposal for International Monetary Reform', *Eastern Economic Journal* 4(3–4) (1978): 153–9.

11. John Maynard Keynes, *The General Theory of Employment, Interest and Money*, London: Macmillan, 1961 (1936), pp. 159–60.

12. The interdependency perspective is evident in many of Keynes's writings and proposals regarding international affairs and the envisioned new economic global order. Nonetheless, in his 1936 *General Theory* Keynes seems to be examining economy in abstraction from the wider world. In the last two chapters, however, he does explicate how his theory connects to international cooperation and questions of war and peace. See also Donald Markwell, *John Maynard Keynes and International Relations: Economic Paths to War and Peace*, Oxford: Oxford University Press, 2006, esp. pp. 182–90.

13. On the conflict between national democracy and the spread of the effects of transnational power relations and decisions, see various works by David Held, for example D. Held, *Cosmopolitanism: Ideals and Realities*, Cambridge: Polity Press, 2010; David Held and Heikki Patomäki, 'Problems of Global Democracy: A Dialogue', *Theory, Culture & Society* 23(5) (2006), pp. 115–33.

14. James Tobin, 'An Old Keynesian Counterattacks', *Eastern Economic Journal* 18(4) (1992): 387–400.

15. See Markwell, *John Maynard Keynes and International Relations*, esp. pp. 241–2.

16. Tobin, 'A Proposal for International Monetary Reform', p. 154.

17. Ibid., p. 159.

18. Ibid., p. 154.

19. Ibid., p. 158. Areas that the European Commission's proposed tax will not cover include markets in currency spot agreements; the EC justifies this omission on the grounds that the greatest possible fluidity and liquidity of currency markets promote trade and investment. The omission is also based on the ideological ground that a currency transaction tax would violate the principle of the free movement of capital. At a minimum, the Commission's proposal would presuppose some version of orthodox neoclassical economic theory. For example, according to Rudiger Dornbusch's hypothesis on exchange rate overshooting, although markets can either exceed or fall below the long-term equilibrium point, they have a tendency, at least in some

sense, to more or less oscillate around the point (even when they approach it they may never attain it, since new interferences enter the system all the time). But in models like this, the existence of an equilibrium point is simply assumed, and the whole ideational structure is completely hypothetical. On the other hand, in so far as the neoclassical equilibrium model included the idea that it could sometimes be rational for investors to push prices away from the equilibrium point, they can also justify occasional public interventions in the exchange rate. Tobin went further than this, and argued that even when 'rational expectations' are by and large met, markets can push movements in any of a number of paths that lead away from the unique equilibrium path, irrespective of any sort of equilibrating logic and even without any limits. In Tobin's view, it would be best for public authorities to state their view on where the equilibrium lies, and then to try to influence its attainment. Rudiger Dornbusch, 'Expectations and Exchange Rate Dynamics', *Journal of Political Economy* 84(6) (1976): 1161–76; Tobin, 'A Proposal for International Monetary Reform', p. 158.

20. I have discussed the goals of currency transaction tax on several occasions: see e.g. Heikki Patomäki, 'The Tobin Tax and Global Civil Society Organisations: The Aftermath of the 2008–9 Financial Crisis', *Ritsumeikan Annual Review of International Studies* 8(1) (2009): esp. 2–5, www.ritsumei.ac.jp/acd/cg/ir/college/bulletin/e-vol.8/01_Hekki.pdf (accessed 26 June 2012).

21. Kalecki's early models, based on linear equations, show that the capitalist market economy oscillates on stable, ascending and descending wavelengths. Kalecki soon began using non-linear equations to make his models more general and to avoid the need to refer to external shocks. The Keynesian multiplier was not invented by Keynes, but he contributed to its development in his *General Theory* (1936). According to an estimate Kalecki made in 1937, the two theories are similar apart from the determination of the level of investment, on which the theories are 'radically different'. But Keynes theorized the role of money and financing far more clearly than did Kalecki, who did, however, also draw attention to power relations, company structure and the degree of monopolization in markets (rather than the neoclassical premiss of 'perfectly competitive' markets, Kalecki started from the assumption of oligopolistic markets). Both Keynes's and Kalecki's theories suffer from being ahistorical: they have inherited from neoclassical economic theory a conception of time as being abstracted from real historical time. See Michał Kalecki, 'A Macrodynamic Theory of Business Cycles', *Econometrica* 3(3) (1935): 327–44;

M. Kalecki, 'A Theory of the Business Cycle', *Review of Economic Studies* 4(2) (1937): 77–97; M. Kalecki, *Theory of Economic Dynamics: An Essay on Cyclical and Long-Run Changes in Capitalist Economy*, New York: Augustus M. Kelley, 1969; Keynes, *General Theory*, pp. 113–31.

22. Keynes, *General Theory*, p. 120.

23. Ibid., ch. 23; see also Markwell, *John Maynard Keynes and International Relations*, 182–90; Paul Davidson, 'Global Employment and Open Economy Macroeconomics', in J. Deprez and J.T. Harvey (eds), *Foundations of International Economics: Post-Keynesian Perspectives*, London: Routledge, 1999, pp. 9–34. In the same collection, see also Johan Deprez, 'Aggregate Supply and Demand in an Open Economy Framework', pp. 93–115.

24. It is outside the scope of this book to explore the economic theory and legitimation problems of the radically expanded free-market doctrine of the World Trade Organization; but see Heikki Patomäki and Teivo Teivainen, *A Possible World: Democratic Transformation of Social Institutions*, London: Zed Books, 2004, ch. 3, 'The World Trade Organization', pp. 70–93.

25. On the one-sidedness and lack of transparency of the Bretton Woods institutions and attempts to democratize them, see ibid., ch. 2, 'The Bretton Woods Institutions', pp. 41–69.

26. Stephen Gill and David Law, 'Global Hegemony and the Structural Power of Capital', in Stephen Gill (ed.), *Gramsci, Historical Materialism and International Relations*, Cambridge: Cambridge University Press, 1993, pp. 93–126.

27. Gernot Köhler, 'What Is Global Keynesianism?', working paper, 1999, http://wsarch.ucr.edu/archive/papers/kohler/kohler2.htm (accessed 26 June 2012).

28. The chair of the Commission was former chancellor of the Federal Republic of Germany, Willy Brandt. Independent Commission on International Development Issues, *North–South: A Programme for Survival. Report of the Independent Commission on International Development Issues under the Chairmanship of Willy Brandt*, London: Pan Books, 1980. A summary of the report is available at www. stwr.org/special-features/the-brandt-report.html (accessed 26 June 2012).

29. See e.g. W.R. Mead, 'American Economic Policy in the Antemillenial Era', *World Policy Journal* 6(3) (1989): 385–468.

30. Independent Commission, *North–South*, p. 47.

31. Ibid., p. 67.

32. These challenges are discussed by the Independent Commission,

North–South, ch. 11, pp. 172–86.

33. Independent Commission, *North–South*, ch. 13, pp. 201–20.

34. The European Monetary System was a system of fixed but variable exchange rates between several EU member states. It operated from 1979 until 1999, when it was replaced by the European Monetary Union.

35. Special Drawing Rights are supplementary foreign exchange reserve assets, the value of which is set by the IMF. SDRs were established by the Fund in 1969, and can be exchanged for money by IMF member countries. In practice, however, they have so far been used mostly for bookkeeping purposes. By 2011 over 200 billion SDRs were in existence, with values set at the weighted average of the exchange rates of the US dollar, the euro, the yen and the British pound. In early 2012, for example, the value of 1 SDR was 1.20 euros. Prior to 1981, the SDR was a mandatory bond of sorts, of which the central banks of IMF member states each held a specific amount. Since then the requirement to maintain SDRs has been relaxed, and the unit has consequently become (increasingly) less important. A central consideration in the discussion of and struggle over the future of the SDR is the extent to which the role of the US dollar could be taken on by a common global currency. Many commentators and researchers, and since the 2008–09 global crisis China and several other states, have argued for a significantly expanded role for SDRs. For a typically sceptical but exceptionally insightful perspective on the debate, see Ronald McKinnon, 'Reconsidering SDRs', *Harvard International Review*, 6 July 2009, http://hir.harvard.edu/frontiers-of-conflict/re-considering-sdrs (accessed 26 June 2012).

36. Report of the Independent Commission, *North–South*, pp. 212–20.

37. See Echardt Hein and Achim Truger, 'Finance-Dominated Capitalism in Crisis: The Case for a Global Keynesian New Deal', *Working Paper* 06/2010, 2010, Institute for International Political Economy, Berlin School of Economics and Law, Berlin, p. 14, http://mpra.ub.uni-muenchen.de/21175 (accessed 26 June 2012).

38. Ibid., pp. 14–21, for sketches of many of the ideas outlined in Chapter 7 and this chapter of the present book.

39. For some of the most recent proposals, see Davidson, 'Global Employment and Open Economy Macroeconomics', pp. 26–31; Randall L. Wray, 'The Development and Reform of the Modern International Monetary System', in Deprez and Harvey (eds), *Foundations of International Economics*, pp. 171–99.

40. For this reason, maintenance of aggregate demand would not by itself be enough. Other considerations that would also have to be taken into

account include technological development, the country's position in
the international division of labour, and the distribution of increased
labour productivity in the world economy. See Mario Cimoli and
Gabriel Porcile, 'Global Growth and International Cooperation: A
Structuralist Perspective', *Cambridge Journal of Economics* 35(2)
(2011): 383–400.

41. See e.g. James K. Galbraith and Hyunsub Kum, 'Inequality and Economic Growth: A Global View Based on Measures of Pay', *CESifo
Economic Studies* 49(4) (2003): 527–56; James K. Galbraith 'Global
Inequality and Global Macroeconomics', *Journal of Policy Modeling*
29(4) (2007): 587–607.

42. The combined effect of increased domestic demand in India, China
and other surplus countries is not very great on the world economic
scale, but it is positive. Internationally coordinated economic policies
are also needed. For various scenarios relating to increased global
aggregate demand, see Francis Cripps, Alex Izurieta and Ajit Singh,
'Global Imbalances, Under-consumption and Over-borrowing: The
State of the World Economy and Future Policies', *Development and
Change* 42(1) (2011): 228–61.

43. When arms markets are registered they can also be taxed; both regulation and taxation reduce arms market activity. A comprehensive
arms market register could also be part of an early warning system
and would facilitate prevention of violent conflicts. The United Nations' Register of Conventional Arms (UNROCA) came into operation at the end of 1991, after the UN General Assembly Resolution
on General and Complete Disarmament: Transparency in Armaments (A/RES/46/36) was passed with 150 votes in favour and none
against. UNROCA only applies to seven categories of arms that are
deemed the most lethal; later in the decade then-UN secretary general
Boutros Boutros-Ghali repeatedly proposed amending UNROCA to
also cover other arms categories, and to aid in reducing direct trade
in arms. Small arms and other trade in arms between states could
at least be added to the arms register, even if it were not possible to
make them subject to taxation.

44. Technical Group on Innovative Financing Mechanisms, *Action
Against Hunger and Poverty: Report of the Technical Group on Innovative Financing Mechanisms*, September 2004, pp. 36–41, www.
diplomatie.gouv.fr/en/IMG/pdf/rapportdugroupequadripartite.pdf
(accessed 26 June 2012).

45. See Patomäki and Teivainen, *A Possible World*, ch. 10, 'Global Tax
Organizations', pp. 163–82; Shannon Brincat, 'A 'Global Greenhouse
Gas Tax': Background Issues for the Draft Treaty Workshop', Centre

for Excellence in Global Governance Research, University of Helsinki, 2011, unpublished draft (available on request from the present author).

46. For a brief retrospective, see James Tobin, 'A Currency Transactions Tax, Why and How?', *Open Economies Review* 7(1) (1996): 493–9; on the main overall goal of the proposal, see p. 493; http://cowles. econ.yale.edu/P/cp/p09a/p0939.pdf (accessed 26 June 2012).

47. James Tobin, 'What kind of Socially Responsible Economy Do We Want?', a presentation by videolink to the Council of Europe fiftieth anniversary conference in 1999. Tobin's presentation is summarized in *Market-Oriented Society, Democracy, Citizenship and Solidarity: an Area of Confrontation? Conference Proceedings, 31 May–1 June 1999*, Council of Europe Parliamentary Assembly, Strasbourg: Council of Europe Publishing, pp. 42–5; 43, http://assembly.coe. int/Conferences/2008Strasbourg/Doc/Conf99_NGO_E.pdf (accessed 26 June 2012); also published in James Tobin, *World Finance and Economic Stability: Selected Essays of James Tobin*, Cheltenham: Edward Elgar, 2003, ch. 29.

48. The essence of emancipation is in the transition from unwanted, unnecessary and oppressive sources of causal determination to wanted or needed and empowering or more flourishing sources of causal determination. In conditions where asymmetric power relations are in force, emancipation means on the one hand the increase of actors' abilities and possibilities, and on the other the reduction or removal of relations of domination – that is to say, democratization and turning power into common capacity for action, individually or collectively. See Roy Bhaskar, *Dialectic: The Pulse of Freedom*, London: Verso, 1993.

49. For example, my proposal for a currency transaction tax combines the traditional state-centric principle of democracy, indirect representative democracy (through national parliamentary representation), and the principle of participatory democracy (through national civil societies). Heikki Patomäki, *Democratising Globalisation: The Leverage of the Tobin Tax*, London: Zed Books, 2001, ch. 7, pp. 193–216.

50. For more detailed discussion of this point, see Heikki Patomäki, 'Rethinking Global Parliament: Beyond the Indeterminacy of International Law', *Widener Law Review* 13(2) (2007): 373–91.

51. The question was posed by Kant, but the answer I give to it adapts modern social theories. See Immanuel Kant, 'On the Proverb: That May be True in Theory, But is of No Practical Use', in *Perpetual Peace and Other Essays*, trans. Ted Humphrey, Indianapolis: Hackett, 1983 (1793), pp. 61–92; 61–2.

52. On the history and philosophical structure of cosmopolitanism and its relation to the evolution of scientific thought, see Heikki Patomäki 'Cosmological Sources of Critical Cosmopolitanism', *Review of International Studies* 36 (2010), Supplement S1: 181–200.

53. See Heikki Patomäki and Manfred B. Steger, 'Social Imaginaries and Big History: Towards a New Planetary Consciousness?', *Futures* 42(10) (2010): 1056–63.

54. Karl Jaspers, *The Origin and Goal of History*, trans. Michael Bullock, London: Routledge & Kegan Paul, 1953 (1949), pp. 117–27.

55. On the concept of social imaginaries, see Patomäki and Steger, 'Social Imaginaries and Big History'.

56. This is not a general theory of truth – 'truth' is also a metaphor for the correspondence between claims and the world – but above all an ontological theory of the construction of the historical social world. The principle was proposed by philosopher Giambattista Vico in the 1700s.

57. The modern national social imaginary includes:
    (i) visual prototypes (e.g. the United States' Uncle Sam, the Russian bear);
    (ii) prototypical stories, figures and practices (e.g. American exceptionalism, the Fourth of July and the Founding Fathers in the USA; French *laicité*, the secularist tradition prohibiting religious involvement in government affairs, and vice versa; the *Kalevala* national epic and the Winter War film *Tuntematon sotilas* [*The Unknown Soldier*] in Finland;
    (iii) metaphors, such as the nation-as-family, the fatherland;
    (iv) conceptual merging: typically, the state-as-person metaphor is blended with the idea of the nation with a particular 'character' that is determined through stories and images;
    (v) many types of framing: for example, the question 'Are you prepared to die for your country?' gets it meaning partly from the nation-as-family metaphor, which is not the case if the same question is framed as a question of universal morality ('Are you ready to kill innocent people on the orders of the political leadership of your country?').

58. See Patomäki, 'Cosmological Sources', pp. 189–90.

59. Denis Cosgrove, 'Contested Global Visions: One-World, Whole-Earth, and the Apollo Space Photographs', *Annals of the Association of American Geographers* 84(2) (1994): 270–94.

60. Nancy Ellen Abrams and Joel R. Primack, *The New Universe and the Human Future: How a Shared Cosmology Could Transform the World*, New Haven CT: Yale University Press, 2011, pp. xv, 120.

61. H.G. Wells, *The New and Revised Outline of History, Being a Plain History of Life and Mankind*, Garden City NY: Garden City Publishing, 1931, Section 40.1, 'The Possible Unification of Men's Wills in Political Matters', p. 1158.

62. Wells, *The New and Revised Outline of History*, p. 1124.

63. David Christian, *Maps of Time: An Introduction to Big History*, Berkeley CA: University of California Press, 2005, pp. 478–9.

64. Warren W. Wagar, *A Short History of the Future*, Chicago: University of Chicago Press, 1999.

65. I have tried to develop Wagar's prototype in a more value-pluralistic way so as to take better account of the principles of global democratic Keynesianism, in Heikki Patomäki, 'Towards Global Political Parties', *Ethics & Global Politics* 4(2) (2011), www.ethicsandglobalpolitics.net/index.php/egp/article/view/7334 (accessed 26 June 2012).

66. The term was coined by Joseph A. Camilleri and Jim Falk, *Worlds in Transition: Evolving Governance Across a Stressed Planet*, Cheltenham: Edward Elgar, 2009, pp. 535–8.

Bibliography

Abrams, N.E., and J.R. Primack (2011) *The New Universe and the Human Future: How a Shared Cosmology Could Transform the World*, New Haven CT: Yale University Press.

Adams, P. (1992) *Odious Debts: Loose Lending, Corruption and the Third World's Environmental Legacy*, London: Earthscan.

Altavilla, C. (2004) 'Do EMU Members Share the Same Business Cycle?', *Journal of Common Market Studies* 42(5): 869–96.

Apap, J., and S. Carrera (2004) 'Maintaining Security within Borders: Toward a Permanent State of Emergency in the EU?', *Alternatives* 29(4): 399–416.

Archer, M.S. (1995) *Realist Social Theory: The Morphogenetic Approach*, Cambridge: Cambridge University Press.

Arestis, P., and M. Sawyer (2003) 'Macroeconomic Policies of the Economic Monetary Union: Theoretical Underpinnings and Challenges', *Levy Economics Institute Working Paper* 385, www.levyinstitute.org/pubs/wp385.pdf (accessed 18 June 2012).

Arrow, K., and F. Hahn (1971) *General Competitive Analysis*, Amsterdam: North Holland.

Atwell, W.S. (2005) 'Another Look at Silver Imports into China, ca. 1635–1644', *Journal of World History* 16(4): 467–89.

Auerback, M. (2011) 'Europe's Non-Solution: The"Bazooka" Turned on Itself', *Real-World Economics Review* 58: 69–76, www.paecon.net/PAEReview/issue58/Auerback58.pdf (accessed 12 June 2012).

Backhouse, R.E. (2006) 'The Keynesian Revolution', in R.E. Backhouse and B.W. Bateman (eds), *The Cambridge Companion to Keynes*, Cambridge: Cambridge University Press, pp. 19–38.

Baker, D. (2002) 'The Run-up in Home Prices: Is It Real or Is It Another Bubble?', Washington DC: CEPR (Centre for Economic and Policy Research) Briefing Paper, www.cepr.net/documents/publications/housing_2002_08.pdf (accessed 8 June 2012).

Bank of Ireland (2011) 'Ireland's Gross Debt Ratio Set to Rise Further According to Bank of Ireland's Monthly Bulletin', 6 May, www.bankofireland.com/fs/doc/press-releases/may-bulletin-2011.pdf (accessed 12 June 2012).

Barclays Bank (2012) 'Ecb Smp: Marking To Market', *Barclays Capital Interest Rates Research*, Europe, 6 January, www.teinteresa.es/dinero/Informe-Barclays-Capital-compra-BCE_TINFIL20120109_0007.pdf (accessed 12 June 2012).

Barro, R. (1974) 'Are Government Bonds Net Wealth?' *Journal of Political Economy* 82(6): 1095–117.

Bateman, B.W. (2006) 'Keynes and Keynesianism', in R. Backhouse and B. W. Bateman (eds), *The Cambridge Companion to Keynes*, Cambridge: Cambridge University Press, pp. 271–90.

Benhabib, S. (1996) *Critique, Norm and Utopia: A Study of the Foundations of Critical Theory*, New York: Columbia University Press.

Bhaskar, R. (1993) *Dialectic: The Pulse of Freedom*, London: Verso.

Boltho. A. (2003) 'What's Wrong with Europe?', *New Left Review* 22(3): 5–26.

Brincat, S. (2011) 'A "Global Greenhouse Gas Tax": Background Issues for the Draft Treaty Workshop', Centre for Excellence in Global Governance Research, University of Helsinki, unpublished draft (available on request from the present author).

Cafruny, A.W., and M.J. Ryner (2007) *Europe at Bay: In the Shadow of US Hegemony*, Boulder CO: Lynne Rienner.

Camilleri, J.A., and J. Falk (2009) *Worlds in Transition: Evolving Governance Across a Stressed Planet*, Cheltenham: Edward Elgar.

Canale, R.R., and O. Napolitano (2009) 'The Recessive Attitude of EMU Policies: Reflections on the Italian Experience, 1998–2008', MPRA Paper No. 20207, http://mpra.ub.uni-muenchen.de/20207 (accessed 18 June 2012).

Cassen, B. (2003) 'On the ATTACK: Interview with Ignacio Ramonet', *New Left Review* 19(1): 41–60, http://newleftreview.org/II/19/bernard-cassen-on-the-attack (accessed 26 June 2012).

Cassidy, J. (2008) 'He Foresaw the End of an Era', *New York Review of Books* 55(16), 23 October, www.nybooks.com/articles/21934 (accessed 8 June 2012).Centre for Research on Multinational Corporations (2011) 'Newsletter – EU Financial Reforms', part of the project Towards a Global Finance System at the Service of Sustainable Development, July 3–4, http://somo.nl/dossiers-en/sectors/financial/eu-financial-reforms/newsletters (accessed 12 July 2012).

Cerny, P.G. (1997) 'Paradoxes of the Competition State: The Dynamics of Political Globalization', *Government and Opposition* 32(2): 251–74.

Chernoff, F. (2005) *The Power of International Theory: Reinforcing the Link to Foreign Policy-Making through Scientific Enquiry*, London: Routledge.

Choucri, N., and R.C. North (1975) *Nations in Conflict: National Growth and International Violence*, San Francisco: W.H. Freeman.

Christian, D. (2005) *Maps of Time: An Introduction to Big History*, Berkeley: University of California Press.

Christian, J.W., R. Shapiro and J.-P. Whalen (2006–07) 'Naked Short Selling: How Exposed Are Investors?', *Houston Law Review* 43(4): 1033–90.

CIA World Factbook, 'United States', www.cia.gov/library/publications/the-world-factbook/geos/us.html (accessed 8 June 2012).

Cimoli, M., and G. Porcile (2011) 'Global Growth and International Cooperation: A Structuralist Perspective', *Cambridge Journal of Economics* 35(2): 383–400.

Committee for the Study of Economic and Monetary Union (1989) *Report on Economic and Monetary Union in the European Community*, Luxembourg: Office for Official Publications in the European Communities.

Cosgrove, D. (1994) 'Contested Global Visions: One-World, Whole-Earth, and the Apollo Space Photographs', *Annals of the Association of American Geographers* 84(2): 270–94.

Cowling, K., S.P. Dunn, and P.R. Tomlinson (2011) 'Global Imbalances and Modern Capitalism: A Structural Approach to Understanding the Present Economic Crisis', *Journal of Post Keynesian Economics* 33(4): 575–96.

Cripps, F., A. Izurieta and A. Singh (2011) 'Global Imbalances, Under-consumption and Over-borrowing: The State of the World Economy and Future Policies', *Development and Change* 42(1): 228–61.

Davidson, P. (1999) 'Global Employment and Open Economy Macroeconomics', in J. Deprez and J.T. Harvey (eds), *Foundations of International Economics: Post-Keynesian Perspectives*, London: Routledge, pp. 9–34.

de Grauwe, P. (2003) 'The Enlarged Eurozone: Can it Survive?', Wassenaar, the Netherlands: Netherlands Institute for Advanced Study in the Humanities and Social Sciences, www.nias.knaw.nl/Content/NIAS/Publicaties/Jelle%20Zijlstra/JelleZijlstraLecture2.pdf (accessed 12 June 2012).

Dean, K. (2003) *Capitalism and Citizenship*, London: Routledge.

Deprez, J. (1999) 'Aggregate Supply and Demand in an Open Economy Framework', in J. Deprez and J.T. Harvey (eds), *Foundations of International Economics: Post-Keynesian Perspectives*, London: Routledge, pp. 93–115.

Deprez, J., and J. Harvey (eds) (1999) *Foundations of International Economics: Post-Keynesian Perspectives*, London: Routledge.

Deprez, J., and L.R. Wray (1999) 'Monetary Theory of Production', in P.A.

O'Hara (ed.), *Routledge Encyclopedia of Political Economy*, Vol. II, London: Routledge, pp. 759–61,

Diez, T. (1999) 'Constructing Threat, Constructing Political Order: On the Legitimisation of an Economic Community in Western Europe', *Journal of International Relations and Development* 2(1): 29–49.

Doran, C.F. (1999) 'Why Forecasts Fail: The Limits and Potential of Forecasting in International Relations and Economics', *International Studies Review* 1(2): 11–41.

Dornbusch, R. (1976) 'Expectations and Exchange Rate Dynamics', *Journal of Political Economy* 84(6): 1161–76.

The Economist (2005) 'The Corporate Savings Glut', 7 July, www.economist.com/node/4154491?story_id=4154491 (accessed 8 June 2012).

Edey, M., and K. Hviding (1995) *An Assessment of Financial Reform in OECD Countries*, *OECD Economics Department Working Papers* 154, OCDE/GD (95) 69.

Eichengreen, B., and H. Tong (2003) 'Stock Market Volatility and Monetary Policy: What the Historical Record Shows', University of California, Berkeley, http://elsa.berkeley.edu/~eichengr/research/sydneywithhui9sep26–03.pdf (accessed 17 June 2012).

Elster, J. (1978) *Logic and Society: Contradictions and Possible Worlds*, Chichester: John Wiley.

Engels, F. (1998 [1895]) 'Supplement to Capital, Volume Three', in Karl Marx, *The Collected Works of Karl Marx and Friedrich Engels*, ed. Eric Hobsbawm et al., various translators, Volume 37: *Capital: A Critique of Political Economy, Vol. 3*, London: Lawrence & Wishart, pp. 873–97; 895.

Erskine, T. (ed.) (2003) *Can Institutions Have Responsibilities? Collective Moral Agency and International Relations*, Basingstoke: Palgrave Macmillan.

European Commission (2011) *Eurobarometer 75 (Standard): Public Opinion in the European Union Spring 2011*, Brussels: European Commission, http://ec.europa.eu/public_opinion/archives/eb/eb75/eb75_publ_en.pdf (accessed 19 June 2012).

European Commission (2011) *Executive Summary of the Impact Assessment, accompanying the document Proposal for a Council Directive on a Common System of Financial Transaction Tax, and amending Directive 2008/7/EC*, p. 2, http://ec.europa.eu/taxation_customs/index_en.htm.

European Council (2003) *A Secure Europe in a Better World: The European Security Strategy, Approved by the European Council*, Brussels, 12 December 2003, www.consilium.europa.eu/uedocs/cmsUpload/78367.pdf (accessed 18 June 2012).

European Council (2011) *Commission Staff Working Paper Executive Summary of the Impact Assessment Accompanying the document Proposal for a Council Directive on a common system of financial transaction tax and amending Directive 2008/7/EC*, Brussels, 28.9.2011 SEC(2011) 1103 final, http://ec.europa.eu/taxation_customs/index_en.htm.

European Council (2011) *Green Paper on the Feasibility of Introducing Stability Bonds*, Brussels, 23 November, COM (2011) 818 final, http://ec.europa.eu/europe2020/pdf/green_paper_en.pdf (accessed 14 June 2012).

European Council (2011) *Proposal for a Council Directive on a Common System of Financial Transaction Tax and Amending Directive 2008/7/EC*, Brussels, 28 September 2011 COM(2011) 594 final, http://ec.europa.eu/taxation_customs/index_en.htm.

European Council (2011) *Proposal for a Regulation of the European Parliament and of The Council on Common Provisions for Monitoring and Assessing Draft Budgetary Plans and Ensuring the Correction of Excessive Deficit of the Member States in the Euro Area*, Brussels, 23.11.2011, COM (2011) 821 final, 2011/0386 (COD), http://ec.europa.eu/commission_2010–2014/president/news/documents/pdf/regulation_1_en.pdf (accessed 14 June 2012).

European Council (2011) *Revised Version of the Conclusions of the European Council*, 24 and 25 March, EUCO 10/1/11 REV 1, Appendix II, p. 21, www.consilium.europa.eu/uedocs/cms_data/docs/pressdata/en/ec/120296.pdf (accessed 14 June 2012).

European Council (2011), *Revised Version of the Conclusions of the European Council*, CO EUR 4 CONCL 2, p.12, http://consilium.europa.eu/uedocs/cms_data/docs/pressdata/en/ec/131388.pdf (accessed 3 July 2012).

European Council (2012) *Conclusions of the European Council* (28/29 June), CO EUR 4 CONCL 2, p. 12, http://consilium.europa.eu/uedocs/cms_data/docs/pressdata/en/ec/131388.pdf (accessed 3 July 2012).

European Council (2012) *Treaty Establishing the European Stability Mechanism* [between the euro area member states], T/ESM 2012/en 1, www.european-council.europa.eu/media/582311/05–tesm2.en12.pdf (accessed 14 June 2012).

Eurostat (2009) *External and Intra-European Union Trade: Data 2002–07*, European Commission, Brussels, http://epp.eurostat.ec.europa.eu/cache/ITY_OFFPUB/KS-CV-08–001/EN/KS-CV-08–001–EN.PDF (accessed 12 June 2012).

Evans-Pritchard, A. (2011) 'Professor Mundell, Euro, and 'Pessimal Currency Areas'', *Telegraph*, 25 August, available from the *Telegraph* website (accessed 12 June 2012).

Feldstein, M. (1992) 'Europe's Monetary Union: The Case Against EMU', *The Economist*, 13 June, p. 26, available from www.nber.org/feldstein/economistmf.pdf (accessed 12 June 2012).

Financial Times (2010) 'Balls to Warn of Economic "Hurricane"', 27 August.

Flassbeck, H. (2011) 'The Euro – a Story of Misunderstanding', *Intereconomics*

4: 180–87, www.ceps.eu/system/files/article/2011/07/Forum.pdf (accessed 12 June 2012).

Frankel, J.A., and A.K. Rose (2001) 'The Endogeneity of the Optimum Currency Area Criteria', *Economic Journal* 108(449): 1009–25.

Friedman, M. (1956 [1953]) 'The Case for Flexible Exchange Rates', in *Essays in Positive Economics*, Chicago: University of Chicago Press. pp. 157–203.

Galbraith, James K. (2007) 'Global Inequality and Global Macroeconomics', *Journal of Policy Modeling* 29(4): 587–607.

Galbraith, James K., and H. Kum (2003) 'Inequality and Economic Growth: A Global View Based on Measures of Pay', *CESifo Economic Studies* 49(4): 527–56.

Galbraith, John K. (1987) *A History of Economics: The Past as the Present*, London: Hamish Hamilton.

Galtung, J. (1973) *The European Community: A Superpower in the Making*, London: George Allen & Unwin.

Galtung, J. (2011) 'To Call the US a Democracy is an Insult to the Word', *TRANSCEND/Human Wrongs Watch*, www.other-news.info/2011/12/%E2%80%9Cto-call-the-usa-a-democracy-is-an-insult-to-the-word%E2%80%9D (accessed 18 June 2012).

Geopolitique (1996) 'Un Entêtemant Suicidaire. Entretien Exclusif avec Milton Friedman', *Geopolitique* 53 (Spring): 58–66.

George, S. (1992) *The Debt Boomerang: How Third World Debt Harms Us All*, London: Pluto Press.

George, S. (2004) *Another World Is Possible If...*, London: Verso.

Gibbs, J. C. (2010) *Moral Development and Reality: Beyond the Theories of Kohlberg and Hoffman.*, Thousand Oaks CA: Sage.

Giddens, A. (1994) *Beyond Left and Right: The Future of Radical Politics*, Cambridge: Polity Press.

Gill, S. (2008) [2003] *Power and Resistance in the New World Order*, 2nd edn, London: Palgrave MacMillan.

Gill, S., and D. Law (1993) 'Global Hegemony and the Structural Power of Capital', in Stephen Gill (ed.), *Gramsci, Historical Materialism and International Relations*, Cambridge: Cambridge University Press, pp. 93–124.

Goodhardt, C.A.E. (1998) 'The Two Concepts of Money: Implications for the Analysis of Optimal Currency Areas', *European Journal of Political Economy* 14(3): 407–32.

Grierson, P. (1978) 'The Origins of Money', *Research in Economic Anthropology* 1: 1–35, www.anthrofoology.com/post/4550568332/philip-grierson-the-origins-of-money (accessed 12 June 2012).

Group of 20 (G20) (2009) 'Leaders' Statement: The Pittsburgh Summit', 24–25 September, http://ec.europa.eu/commission_2010–2014/president/pdf/statement_20090826_en_2.pdf (accessed 8 June 2012).

Guardian (2000) 'The New Endangered Species: Small Currencies Vanishing as Big Bucks Take Over', 14 January, www.guardian.co.uk/business/2000/jan/14/9 (accessed 12 June 2012).

Guardian (2008) 'Brussels Proposes £170bn Spending Plan', 27 November, www.guardian.co.uk/business/2008/nov/27/europe-union-spending-recession-tax-recovery (accessed 29 June 2012).

Guardian (2011) 'China Uneasy over US Troop Deal in Australia', 16 November 2011, www.guardian.co.uk/world/2011/nov/16/china-us-troops-australia (accessed 5 June 2012).

Guinnane, T.W. (2004) 'Financial Vergangenheitsbewältigung: The 1953 London Debt Agreement', *Center Discussion Paper* No. 880, Economic Growth Center, Yale University, pp. 4–17, www.econ.yale.edu/growth_pdf/cdp880.pdf (accessed 20 June 2012).

Habermas, J. (1990) [1983] 'Discourse Ethics: Notes on a Program of Philosophical Justification', in *Moral Consciousness and Communicative Action*, trans. Christian Lenhardt and Shierry Weber Nicholsen, Cambridge MA: MIT Press, pp. 43–115.

Habermas, J. (2003) 'Toward a Cosmopolitan Europe', *Journal of Democracy* 14(4): 86–100.

Hein, E., and A. Truger (2010) 'Finance-Dominated Capitalism in Crisis: The Case for a Global Keynesian New Deal', *Working Paper* 06/2010, Institute for International Political Economy, Berlin School of Economics and Law, Berlin, p. 14, http://mpra.ub.uni-muenchen.de/21175 (accessed 26 June 2012).

Heins, V. (2005) 'Orientalising America? Continental Intellectuals and the Search for Europe's Identity', *Millennium: Journal of International Studies* 34(2): 433–48.

Held, D. (2010) *Cosmopolitanism: Ideals and Realities*, Cambridge: Polity Press.

Held, D., and H. Patomäki (2006) 'Problems of Global Democracy: A Dialogue', *Theory, Culture & Society* 23(5): 115–33.

Helsingin Sanomat (Finland) (International Edition) (2011) 'Investor Responsibility Divides Euro Countries', 25 May, www.hs.fi/english/article/Investor+responsibility+divides+euro+countries+1135266291713 (accessed 14 June 2012).

Herman, B., J. Ocampo and S. Spiegel (eds) (2010) *Overcoming Developing Country Debt Crisis*, Oxford: Oxford University Press.

Hobson, J.M., and L. Seabrooke (2007) *Everyday Politics of the World Economy*, Cambridge: Cambridge University Press.

Howells, P. (1999) 'Velocity and the Money Multiplier', in P.A O'Hara (ed.), *Routledge Encyclopedia of Political Economy*, Vol. II, London: Routledge, pp. 1226–8.

Hutchinson, F., M. Mellor and W. Olsen (2002) *The Politics of Money*, London: Pluto Press.

Independent Commission on International Development Issues (1980) *North–South: A Programme for Survival. Report of the Independent Commission on International Development Issues under the Chairmanship of Willy Brandt*, London: Pan Books. A summary of the report is available at www.stwr.org/special-features/the-brandt-report.html (accessed 26 June 2012).

Ingham, G. (2004) *The Nature of Money*, Cambridge: Polity Press.

International Monetary Fund (2007) *World Economic Outlook*, October, Washington DC: IMF.

Irvin, G. (2007) 'Europe vs. USA: Whose Economy Wins?', *New Federalist*, 16 January, www.thenewfederalist.eu/Europe-vs-USA-Whose-Economy-Wins (accessed 18 June 2012).

Jaspers, K. (1953 [1949]) *The Origin and Goal of History*, trans. Michael Bullock, London: Routledge & Kegan Paul, pp. 117–27.

Johnson, A. (2001) *Key Issues in Analysing Domestic Debt Sustainability*, London: Debt Relief International Ltd, www.dri.org.uk/pdfs/EngPub5_DomDebt.pdf (accessed 12 June 2012).

Kaldor, N. (1972) 'The Irrelevance of Equilibrium Economics', *Economic Journal* 82(328): 1237–55.

Kalecki, M. (1935) 'A Macrodynamic Theory of Business Cycles', *Econometrica* 3(3): 327–44.

Kalecki, M. (1937) 'A Theory of the Business Cycle', *Review of Economic Studies* 4(2): 77–97.

Kalecki, M. (1943) 'Political Aspects of Full Employment', *Political Quarterly* 14(4): 322–31.

Kalecki, M. (1969) *Theory of Economic Dynamics: An Essay on Cyclical and Long-Run Changes in Capitalist Economy*, New York: Augustus M. Kelley.

Kant, I. (1983 [1793]) 'On the Proverb: That May be True in Theory, But Is of No Practical Use', in *Perpetual Peace and Other Essays*, trans. T. Humphrey, Indianapolis: Hackett, pp. 61–92.

Kaufmann, S. (2011), *Sell Your Islands, You Bankrupt Greeks: 20 Popular Fallacies Concerning the Debt Crisis*, published by the Rosa Luxemburg Foundation, www.rosalux.de/fileadmin/rls_uploads/pdfs/sonst_publikationen/Broschur_Pleite-Griechen_eng.pdf (accessed 5 June 2012).

Kayser, M.A. (2009) 'Partisan Waves: International Business Cycles and Electoral Choice', *American Journal of Political Science* 53(4): 950–70.

Keen, S. (2001) *Debunking Economics: The Naked Emperor of the Social Sciences*, London: Zed Books.

Keynes, J.M. (1920) *The Economic Consequences of the Peace*, New York: Har-

court, Brace & Howe, http://openlibrary.org/books/OL7081304M/The_eco-
nomic_consequences_of_the_Peace (accessed 20 June 2012).

Keynes, J.M. (1961 [1936]) *General Theory of Employment, Interest and Money*,
London: Macmillan.

Keynes, J.M. (1963 [1921]) 'War Debts and the United States', in *Essays in
Persuasion*, New York: W.W. Norton, pp. 52–73.

Keynes, J.M. (1980) *The Collected Writings of John Maynard Keynes*, Volume
XXV: *Activities 1940–44*, London: Macmillan.

Kindleberger, C.P., and R.Z. Aliber (2011) *Manias, Panics, and Crashes: A History of Financial Crises*, 6th edn, Basingstoke: Palgrave Macmillan.

Klausinger, H. (2001) 'Gustav Stolper, Der Deutsche Volkswirt, and the Controversy on Economic Policy at the End of the Weimar Republic', *History
of Political Economy* 33(2): 241–67.

Köhler, G. (1999) 'What Is Global Keynesianism?', working paper, http://
wsarch.ucr.edu/archive/papers/kohler/kohler2.htm (accessed 26 June
2012).

Kolb, R.W. (ed.) (2011) *Sovereign Debt: From Safety to Default*, Hoboken NJ:
Wiley.

Kolko, G. (2006) Weapons of Mass Financial Destruction', *Le Monde diplomatique*, October, pp. 1–3.

Krugman, P. (2005) 'Greenspan and the Bubble', *New York Times*, 29 August,
www.nytimes.com/2005/08/29/opinion/29krugman.html?_r=1 (accessed
8 June 2012).

Krugman, P. (2009) 'The Paradox of Thrift', *New York Times*, 3 February,
http://krugman.blogs.nytimes.com/2009/02/03/paradox-of-thrift (accessed
6 June 2012).

Krugman, P. (2011) 'Depression and Democracy', *New York Times*, 11 December,
www.nytimes.com/2011/12/12/opinion/krugman-depression-and-democracy.
html (accessed 18 June 2012).

Lakoff, G., and M. Johnson (1999) *Philosophy in the Flesh: The Embodied Mind
and Its Challenge to Western Thought*, New York: Basic Books.

Lakoff, G., and M. Johnson (2003 [1980]) *Metaphors We Live By*, Chicago:
University of Chicago Press.

Lavoie, M. (2009) *Introduction to Post-Keynesian Economics*, Basingstoke:
Palgrave Macmillan.

Lerner, A.P. (1983 [1943]) 'Functional Finance and the Federal Debt', in *Selected
Economic Writings of Abba P. Lerner*, New York: New York University
Press, pp. 297–310.

Levine, R., and J.E. Stiglitz (2010) '*Economist* Debates: Financial Innovation',
www.economist.com/debate/days/view/471 (accessed 20 June 2012).

Levitt, T. (1983) 'The Globalization of Markets', *Harvard Business Review*,

May–June, pp. 92–102, www.vuw.ac.nz/~caplabtb/m302w07/levitt.pdf (accessed 26 June 2012).

Lim, M., and H.E. Khor (2011) 'From Marx to Morgan Stanley: Inequality and Financial Crisis', *Development and Change* 42(1): 209–27.

Lipsey, R., and K. Lancaster (1956–57) 'The General Theory of Second Best', *Review of Economic Studies* 24(1): 11–32.

Llobera, J.R. (1993) 'The Role of the State and Nation in Europe', in S. García (ed.), *European Identity and the Search for Legitimacy*, London: Pinter, pp. 64–80.

Lucas, R.E. (1972) 'Expectations and the Neutrality of Money', *Journal of Economic Theory* 4(2): 103–24.

Luckert, S., and S. Bachrach (2009) *State of Deception: The Power of Nazi Propaganda*, New York: W.W. Norton.

Majocchi, A. (2011) 'Financing the EU Budget with a Surtax on National Income Taxes', Centre for Studies on Federalism, www.csfederalismo. it/images/stories/discussion_papers/01_a.majocchi.pdf (accessed 18 June 2012).

Mandeville, B. (1924 [1714]) *The Fable of the Bees, Or, Private Vices, Publick Benefits*, First Volume, commentary F.B. Kaye, Oxford: Oxford University Press.

Mantoux, É. (1946) *The Carthaginian Peace: The Economic Consequences of Mr Keynes*, Oxford: Oxford University Press.

Marcussen, M. (1997) 'The Role of "Ideas" in Dutch, Danish and Swedish Economic Policy in the 1980s and the Beginning of the 1990s', in P. Minkkinen and H. Patomäki (eds), *The Politics of Economic and Monetary Union*, Dordrecht: Kluwer, pp. 76–101.

Marx, K. (1973 [1939]) *Grundrisse: Foundations of the Critique of Political Economy (Rough Draft)*, trans. M. Nicolaus, London: Penguin/New Left Review.

Marx, K. (1979 [1852]) *The Eighteenth Brumaire of Louis Bonaparte*, in *The Collected Works of Karl Marx and Friedrich Engels*, ed. E. Hobsbawm et al., various translators, Volume 11: *Marx and Engels: 1851–53*, London: Lawrence & Wishart, pp. 99–197.

Marx, K. (1990 [1867]) *Capital: A Critique of Political Economy*, Volume 1, intr. Ernest Mandel, trans. Ben Fowkes, London: Penguin.

Maxwell, D. (2006) *John Maynard Keynes and International Relations: Economic Paths to War and Peace*, Oxford: Oxford University Press.

May, A.M. (1987) 'The Political Business Cycle: An Institutional Critique and Reconstruction', *Journal of Economic Issues* 21(2): 713–22.

McCloskey, D. (1986) *The Rhetoric of Economics*, Brighton: Harvester Wheatsheaf.

McKinnon, R. (2009) 'Reconsidering SDRs', *Harvard International Review*,

6 July, http://hir.harvard.edu/frontiers-of-conflict/reconsidering-sdrs (accessed 26 June 2012).

Mead, W.R. (1989) 'American Economic Policy in the Antemillenial Era', *World Policy Journal* 6(3): 385–468.

Meyer, T., with L. Hinchman (2007) *The Theory of Social Democracy*, Cambridge: Polity Press.

Minkkinen, P., and H. Patomäki (eds) (1997) *The Politics of Economic and Monetary Union*, Dordrecht: Kluwer.

Minsky, H. (1985) 'The Financial Instability Hypothesis: A Restatement', in Philip Arestis and Thanos Skouras (eds), *Post-Keynesian Economic Theory: A Challenge to Neoclassical Economics*, Brighton: Wheatsheaf, pp. 24–55.

Minsky. H. (2008 [1986]) *Stabilizing an Unstable Economy*, New York: McGraw-Hill.

Monbiot, G. (2008) 'Clearing Up This Mess', 18 November, www.monbiot.com/2008/11/18/clearing-up-this-mess (accessed 20 June 2012).

Mundell, R.A (1961) 'A Theory of Optimum Currency Areas', *American Economic Review* 51(4): 657–65.

Myerson, R.B. (2004) 'Political Economics and the Weimar Disaster', *Journal of Institutional and Theoretical Economics* 160(2): 187–209.

New Left Project (2011) 'Crisis as Capitalist Opportunity: Interview with Ursula Huws, 7 December, www.newleftproject.org/index.php/site/article_comments/crisis_as_capitalist_opportunity (accessed 18 June 2012).

New York Times (2008) 'Dr. Doom', 17 August, p. MM26.

New York Times (2011) 'A Marine Base for Australia Irritates China', 17 November, p. A1.

New York Times (2011) 'Bank Chief Hints Help for Europe Is Possible', 2 December, p. B1.

New York Times (2012) 'A Greek Exit? Europe May Be Ready', 18 May, p. B1.

Nordhaus, W. (1975) 'The Political Business Cycle', *Review of Economic Studies* 42(2): 169–90.

Nystrom, P.H. (1928) *Economics of Fashion*, New York: Ronald Press.

O'Hara, P.A. (1999) *Encyclopedia of Political Economy*, Volume 2: *L–Z*, Routledge: London.

O'Hara, P.A. (2006) *Growth and Development in the Global Political Economy: Social Structures of Accumulation and Modes of Regulation*, London: Routledge.

Offe, C. (2003) 'The European Model of "Social" Capitalism: Can It Survive European Integration?', *Journal of Political Philosophy* 11(4): 437–69.

Organisation for Economic Cooperation and Development (2007) *Economic Outlook* No. 82, December, preliminary edn, www.oecd.org/dataoecd/60/0/39727868.pdf (accessed 8 June 2012).

Palan, R., R. Murphy and C. Chavagneux (2010) *Tax Havens: How Global-ization Really Works*, Ithaca NY: Cornell University Press.

Palley, T.I. (2008) 'Financialization: What It Is and Why It Matters', *IMK Working Paper* 4/2008, Hans Böckler Stiftung, www.boeckler.de/pdf/p_imk_wp_04_2008.pdf (accessed 8 June 2012).

Patomäki, H. (2001) 'Appendix 1: Monetarism and the Denial of Reality', in H. Patomäki, *Democratising Globalisation: The Leverage of the Tobin Tax*, London: Zed Books, pp. 223–31.

Patomäki, H. (2001) *Democratising Globalisation: The Leverage of the Tobin Tax*, London: Zed Books.

Patomäki, H. (2002) *After International Relations: Critical Realism and the (Re)Construction of World Politics*, London: Routledge.

Patomäki, H. (2002) 'From East to West: Emergent Global Philosophies – Beginnings of the End of the Western Dominance?', *Theory, Culture & Society* 19(3): 89–111.

Patomäki, H. (2005) 'The Long Downward Wave of the World Economy and the Future of Global Conflict', *Globalizations* 2(1): 61–78.

Patomäki, H. (2006) 'Global Justice: A Democratic Perspective', *Globalizations* 3(2): 99–120.

Patomäki, H. (2006) 'Realist Ontology for Futures Studies', *Journal of Critical Realism* 5(1): 1–31.

Patomäki, H. (2007) 'Global Tax Initiatives: The Movement for the Currency Transaction Tax', available from the website of the United Nations Research Institute for Social Development, www.unrisd.org.

Patomäki, H. (2008) *The Political Economy of Global Security: War, Future Crises and Changes in Global Governance*, London: Routledge.

Patomäki, H. (2009) 'Neoliberalism and the Global Financial Crisis', *New Political Science* 31(4): 431–42.

Patomäki, H. (2009) 'The Tobin Tax and Global Civil Society Organisations: The Aftermath of the 2008–9 Financial Crisis', *Ritsumeikan Annual Review of International Studies* 8(1), www.ritsumei.ac.jp/acd/cg/ir/college/bul-letin/e-vol.8/01_Hekki.pdf (accessed 26 June 2012).

Patomäki, H. (2010) 'Cosmological Sources of Critical Cosmopolitanism', *Review of International Studies* 36, Supplement S1: 181–200.

Patomäki, H. (2010) 'What Next? An Explanation of the 2008–9 Slump and Two Scenarios of the Shape of Things to Come', *Globalizations* 7(1): 67–84.

Patomäki, H. (2011) 'Democracy Promotion: Neoliberal vs. Social Democratic Telos', in C. Hobson and M. Kurki (eds), *The Conceptual Politics of Democracy Promotion*, London: Routledge, pp. 85–99.

Patomäki, H. (2011) 'Towards Global Political Parties', *Ethics & Global Politics* 4(2), www.ethicsandglobalpolitics.net/index.php/egp/article/view/7334 (accessed 26 June 2012).

Patomäki, H. (2007) 'Rethinking Global Parliament: Beyond the Indeterminacy of International Law', *Widener Law Review* 13(2): 373–91.

Patomäki, H., and L.A. Denys (2002) 'Draft Treaty of Global Currency Transactions Tax', Network Institute for Global Democratisation Discussion Paper, 1/2002, Helsinki and Nottingham, available in six languages at www.nigd.org/ctt. Also published in B. de Schutter and J. Pas (eds), *About Globalisation: Views on the Trajectory of Mondialisation*, Brussels: VUB Press, pp. 185–203.

Patomäki, H., and M.B. Steger (2010) 'Social Imaginaries and Big History: Towards a New Planetary Consciousness?', *Futures* 42(10): 1056–63.

Patomäki, H., and T. Teivainen (2004) *A Possible World: Democratic Transformation of Social Institutions*, London: Zed Books.

Pettifor, A. (2006) *The Coming First World Debt Crisis*, Basingstoke: Palgrave MacMillan.

Pierson, P. (2004) *Politics in Time: History, Institutions, and Social Analysis*, Princeton NJ: Princeton University Press.

Poincaré, H. (1946 [1913]) *The Foundations of Science: Science and Hypothesis, the Value of Science, Science and Method*, trans. George Halsted, Lancaster PA: Science Press.

Raffer, K. (2010) *Debt Management for Development: Protection of the Poor and the Millennium Development Goals*, Cheltenham: Edward Elgar.

Raffer, K. (2001) 'Solving Sovereign Debt Overhang by Internationalising Chapter 9 Procedures', *Austrian Institute for International Affairs Working Paper* 35, rev. version, http://sovins.files.wordpress.com/2009/05/oiipjp.pdf (accessed 20 June 2012).

Raffer, K., and H.W. Singer (2001) *The Economic North–South Divide: Six Decades of Unequal Development*, Cheltenham: Edward Elgar.

Ramonet, I. (1997) 'Désarmer les marchés', *Le Monde diplomatique*, December, www.monde-diplomatique.fr/1997/12/RAMONET/9665 (accessed 26 June 2012).

Ramsay, M. (2005) 'A Modest Proposal: The Case for a Maximum Wage', *Contemporary Politics* 11(4): 201–15.

Rasmus, J. (2010) *Epic Recession: Prelude to Global Depression*, London: Pluto Press.

Reader's Digest (2012) 'Confidence in Institutions, Results for: European Union', www.rdtrustedbrands.com/tables/Confidence%2520in%2520instit utions.category.European%2520Union.shtml (accessed 7 July 2012).

Reuters (2011) 'Analysis: Planning for Greek debt default gathering pace?', 21 September.

Reuters (2011) 'ESM Cloud Partly Lifts', 24 June.

Reuters (2011) 'Eurozone May Drop Private Sector from ESM Bailout', 25 November.

Reuters (2011) 'G20 Fails to Endorse Financial Transaction Tax', 4 November.

Robinson, J. (1956) *The Accumulation of Capital*, London: Macmillan.

Rosenau, P.M. (1992) *Postmodernism and the Social Sciences: Insights, Inroads, and Intrusions*, Princeton NJ: Princeton University Press.

Rosenberg, J. (2001) *The Follies of Globalisation Theory*, London: Verso.

Roubini, N. (2008) 'The Coming Financial Pandemic', *Foreign Policy* 165, March–April.

RTÉ News (Ireland) (2011) 'Greek Economy Slumps 6.9% to Second Quarter', 12 August, www.rte.ie/news/2011/0812/greece-business.html (accessed 12 June 2012).

Ruthven, M. (2007) *Fundamentalism: A Very Short Introduction*, Oxford: Oxford University Press.

Sargent, T., and N. Wallace (1975) '"Rational" Expectations, the Optimal Monetary Instrument and the Optimal Money Supply Rule', *Journal of Political Economy* 83(2): 231–54.

Sauramo, P. (2011) 'Saako EMUssa nuijia naapureita?' ['Is Beggar-Your-Neighbour Allowed within the EMU?'], *Talous & yhteiskunta* [Economy & Society] 3: 70–76. Available (Finnish only) at www.labour.fi/TjaYpdf/ty32011.pdf (accessed 12 June 2012).

Sawyer, M. (1985) 'Towards a Post-Kaleckian Macroeconomics', in Philip Arestis and Thanos Skouras (eds), *Post-Keynesian Economic Theory: A Challenge to Neoclassical Economics*, Brighton: Wheatsheaf.

Sinclair, T. (2008) *The New Masters of Capital: American Bond Rating Agencies and the Politics of Creditworthiness*, Ithaca NY: Cornell University Press.

Singh, A. (1999) '"Asian Capitalism" and the Financial Crisis', in J. Michie and J.G. Smith (eds), *Global Instability: The Political Economy of World Economic Governance*, London: Routledge, pp. 9–36.

Soros, G. (2008) *The Crash of 2008 and What it Means: The New Paradigm for Financial Markets*, New York: Public Affairs.

Soros, G. (2008) 'The Crisis and What to Do about It', *New York Review of Books* 55(19), 4 December, www.nybooks.com/articles/22113.

Soros, G. (2008) *The New Paradigm for Financial Markets: The Credit Crisis of 2008 and What It Means*, New York: Public Affairs.

Der Spiegel Online International (2011) 'A Philosopher's Mission to Save the EU', 25 November, www.spiegel.de/international/europe/0,1518,799237,00.html (accessed 18 June 2012).

Standard & Poor's (2012) 'S&P/Case-Shiller Home Price Indices', www.standardandpoors.com/indices/ (accessed 8 June 2012).

Steindl, J. (1952) *Maturity and Stagnation in American Capitalism*, New York: Monthly Review Press.

Stiglitz, J.E. (2002) 'Don't Let America Bankrupt International Bankruptcy

Reform', *Project Syndicate*, 9 April, www.project-syndicate.org/commentary/stiglitz13/English (accessed 20 June 2012).

Stiglitz, J.E., A. Sen and J.-P. Fitoussi (2010) *Mismeasuring Our Lives: Why GDP Doesn't Add Up*, New York: New Press.

Stiglitz, J.E., and A. Weiss (1981) 'Credit Rationing in Markets with Imperfect Information', *American Economic Review* 71(3): 393–410.

Structural Adjustment Participatory Review International Network (2004) *Structural Adjustment: The Policy Roots of Economic Crisis, Poverty and Inequality*, London: Zed Books.

Sutton, J. (1991) *Sunk Costs and Market Structure: Price Competition, Advertising, and the Evolution of Concentration*, Cambridge MA: MIT Press.

Taleb, N. (2007) *The Black Swan: The Impact of the Highly Improbable*, London: Penguin.

Taylor, C. (2011) *A Macroeconomic Regime for the 21st Century: Towards a New Economic Order*, London: Routledge.

Technical Group on Innovative Financing Mechanisms (2004) *Action Against Hunger and Poverty: Report of the Technical Group on Innovative Financing Mechanisms*, September, pp. 36–41, www.diplomatie.gouv.fr/en/IMG/pdf/rapportdugroupequadripartite.pdf (accessed 26 June 2012).

Teivainen, T. (1997) 'The Independence of the European Central Bank: Implications for Democratic Governance', in P. Minkkinen and H. Patomäki (eds), *The Politics of Economic and Monetary Union*, Dordrecht: Kluwer, pp. 55–75.

Telegraph (2009) 'Bonus Culture to Blame for Banking Crisis, Say MPs', 15 August.

Tetlock, P.E. (1999) 'Theory-Driven Reasoning about Plausible Pasts and Probable Futures in World Politics: Are We Prisoners of Our Preconceptions?', *American Journal of Political Science* 43(2): 335–66.

Teunissen, J.J., and A. Akkerman (eds) (2004) *HIPC Debt Relief: Myths and Reality*, The Hague: Forum on Debt and Development, www.fondad.org/uploaded/HIPC%20Debt%20Relief/Fondad-HIPC-Contents-Authors.pdf (accessed 20 June 2012).

Thatcher, M. (1975) 'Speech Launching Free Enterprise Week', 1 July, www.margaretthatcher.org/document/102728 (accessed 26 June 2012).

Tobin, J. (1974) *The New Economics One Decade Older: The Eliot Janeway Lectures in Honour of Joseph Schumpeter*, Princeton NJ: Princeton University Press.

Tobin, J. (1978) 'A Proposal for International Monetary Reform', *Eastern Economic Journal* 4(3–4): 153–9.

Tobin, J. (1992) 'An Old Keynesian Counterattacks', *Eastern Economic Journal* 18(4): 387–400.

Tobin, J. (1996) 'A Currency Transactions Tax, Why and How?', *Open*

Economies Review 7(1): 493–99, http://cowles.econ.yale.edu/P/cp/p09a/p09g9.pdf (accessed 26 June 2012).

Tobin, J. (1999) 'What Kind of Socially Responsible Economy Do We Want?', http://assembly.coe.int/Conferences/2008Strasbourg/Doc/Conf99_NGO_E.pdf (accessed 26 June 2012). Also published in *World Finance and Economic Stability: Selected Essays of James Tobin*, Cheltenham: Edward Elgar, ch. 29.

United Nations Conference on Trade and Development (2000) *The Least Developed Countries Report 2000: Aid, Private Capital Flows and External Debt*, New York: United Nations, www.unctad.org/en/docs/ldc2000_en.pdf (accessed 20 June 2012).

United Nations Conference on Trade and Development (2010) *The Least Developed Countries Report 2010: Towards A New International Development Architecture For LDCs*, New York: United Nations, www.unctad.org/en/docs/ldc2010_en.pdf (accessed 20 June 2012).

United Nations Conference on Trade and Development (2011) *Price Formation in Financialized Commodity Markets: The Role of Information*, New York and Geneva: United Nations, www.unctad.org/en/docs/gds20111_en.pdf (accessed 17 June 2012).

van Treeck, T. (2009) 'The Macroeconomics of "Financialisation", and the Deeper Origins of the World Economic Crisis', *IMK Working Paper*, 9/2009, www.boeckler.de/pdf/p_imk_wp_9_2009.pdf (accessed 8 June 2012).

van Treeck, T. (2009) 'The Political Economy Debate on "Financialization" – A Macroeconomic Perspective', *Review of International Political Economy* 16(5): 907–44.

Varian, H.R. (1992) *Microeconomic Analysis*, 3rd edn, New York: W.W. Norton.

Veblen, T. (1923 [1904]) *The Theory of Business Enterprise*, New York: Scribner.

Veblen, T. (2002) [1899], *The Theory of the Leisure Class*, intr. A. Wolfe, annotated by J. Danlyn, New York: The Modern Library.

Wacquant, L. (2009) *Punishing the Poor: The Neoliberal Government of Social Insecurity*, Durham NC: Duke University Press.

Wagar, W.W. (1999) *A Short History of the Future*, Chicago: University of Chicago Press.

Wall Street Journal (2012) 'Nowotny Links Austerity With Rise of Nazism', 19 June, http://blogs.wsj.com/eurocrisis/2012/06/19/nowotny-links-austerity-with-rise-of-nazism (accessed 20 June 2012).

Wells, H.G. (1931) *The New and Revised Outline of History, Being a Plain History of Life and Mankind*, Garden City NY: Garden City Publishing.

Wikipedia (2012) 'The Dodd–Frank Act', http://en.wikipedia.org/wiki/Dodd-

Frank_Wall_Street_Reform_and_Consumer_Protection_Act (accessed 20 June 2012).

Williamson, J. (1990) 'What Washington Means by Policy Reform', in John Williamson (ed.), *Latin American Readjustment: How Much has Happened*, Washington DC: Institute for International Economics, www.iie.com/publications/papers/paper.cfm?researchid=486 (accessed 26 June 2012).

Wisman, J.D., and B. Baker (forthcoming) 'Increasing Inequality, Inadequate Demand, Status Insecurity, Ideology and the Financial Crisis of 2008', American University Working Paper 1-12-11, www.american.edu/cas/economics/pdf/upload/2011-1.pdf (accessed 8 June 2012).

Wolin. S.S. (2008) *Democracy Incorporated: Managed Democracy and the Specter of Inverted Totalitarianism*, Princeton NJ: Princeton University Press.

Wray, R.L. (1999) 'The Development and Reform of the Modern International Monetary System', in J. Deprez and J. Harvey (eds), *Foundations of International Economics: Post-Keynesian Perspectives*, London: Routledge, pp. 171–99.

Wray, R.L. (2003) 'Is Euroland the Next Argentina?', Center for Full Employment and Price Stability, *University of Missouri–Kansas City, Working Paper* No. 23, www.cfeps.org/pubs/wp-pdf/WP23-Wray.pdf (accessed 18 June 2012).

Wyman, P., B. Burkitt and M. Baimbridge (2005) 'Post-Keynesianism and a Neo-Liberal EMU: The Case for Economic Independence', *Contemporary Politics* 11(4): 259–70.

Index